Called. Christian. Caregiver

The Joy of the Lord gives me strength.

By Kimberly Cordoves

The will of God is never exactly what you expect it to be. It may seem to be much worse, but in the end it's going to be a lot better and a lot bigger.

- Elisabeth Elliot

ISBN: 978-1-7342559-0-4

This book is dedicated:

To three wonderful women of our Rice family who were taken from us by a CURRENTLY fatal disease: My mom, Nancy Carol Toms and her two cousins, Beverly and Jolene.

For two women who demonstrated an amazing Christian love for my parents. **Jean Haggy**, who spent hours talking to mom. For **Sandra Reed**, who cared for my dad not simply as an employee, but as a dear friend.

For my family members who are or have been caregivers.

On behalf of Pastor Bill, I also dedicate this to his caregiver, his amazing wife **Nancy Jean**.

Finally, for Omar, a stranger at a gas station who stopped to help a stranger when he fell. Dios te Bendiga, Omar!

I would like to express special thanks and appreciation to:

Pastor Bill Balson, who beautifully shares how the best way to care for, anyone in need, which is to share the Gospel of Christ, and care for the eternal state of their soul.

And

My husband, Pastor Tony Cordoves, who partnered with me to care for dad and helps us see that while suffering is inevitable in this fallen world, our Hope is in Christ.

Thank you for my troop of editors: Tony, Mary Roberts, Pastor Bill, Pastor James Crawford. God bless you!

Table of Contents

Introduction: The Joy of the Lord gives me strength.

1 Thessalonians 5:16-18 (ESV)
Rejoice always, pray without ceasing, give thanks in
all circumstances; for this is the will of God in
Christ Jesus for you.

I think back to the moment as I watched the man get out of his car and fall to the ground, hitting his head and lying motionless at the gas station pump, I was reminded why I felt I needed to write a book on Christian Caregiving. To share my experience as a caregiver to encourage others who are going through their own caregiving experience.

On my way home from work on April 12th, 2016, I drove into a McDonald's gas station to feed my desire for a large caramel iced coffee (and maybe a chocolate dip cone). I needed a caffeine "pick me up" on my way home. At the pickup window, while being handed my ice cream cone (sadly, they were out of ice coffee) I looked up towards the pumps and saw an older gentleman getting out of his truck. Sliding out of his seat, he appeared to lose balance. He made a grab for his truck door but this motion caused him to twist and he fell backward, hitting his head on the ground. I sat in my car momentarily dumbfounded thinking that he would get up. If that had been me, that fall wouldn't have been that bad - I would have been more worried about my damaged pride than my body. However, he just lay there with his arms and legs spread, not moving.

I grabbed the ice cream cone they were handing me and yelled at the lady in the window to call 911 and then sped over to where the man was lying on the ground. No one had noticed in the busy gas station, despite it being 4:45 pm and "going home" time, I put my car in park, blocking an area around where the man was lying and jumped out of my car. In retrospect, leaving my car running, door open, purse sitting on the front passenger seat, was probably not the wise. However, I was in "rescue mode". I knelt beside the gentleman and said "Sir, are you okay? Can you hear me?"

He was conscious and opened his eyes and looked at me when he heard my voice. He acknowledged that he could hear me. Just the action of me skidding to a stop by him and trying to get his attention drew the attention of a few other gas station patrons and people began to come over and see what was happening. I am particularly grateful to a group of gentlemen who brought a first aid kit, particularly a man named Omar, who stripped off his shirt and used it to cushion the gentlemen's head from the hard asphalt. This also led to us discovering he was bleeding from hitting his head as he fell.

Over approximately the next 35 minutes I tried to keep him calm while waiting for the ambulance. The gentleman was so confused that I had a hard time understanding his name, only getting his last name after multiple requests. Every time I tried to get him to tell me who I could call for help, he would tear up and become emotional. It took 20 minutes before he would tell me the name of someone to call to let know of his accident. Omar continued to help, even calling 911 and dialing the number for his wife when I finally got her name and number from the injured man. While his head was bleeding, it dried up fairly quickly with the use of Omar's shirt, and he was trying to sit up and protesting that he didn't want us to call emergency services.

The entire time this was happening I kept thinking about all I had gone through with my dad Brian (step-dad) during periods in his illness when the pain he experienced had led him to alcohol abuse and overuse of prescription pain medication. The gentleman was probably intoxicated, based on the smell, and he was confused; not knowing why he was on the ground and where he was or what had happened. He kept focusing on me, and sometimes Omar, stroking our faces, trying to hug me, and repeating that he needed help to get out of his situation. He kept stroking my face and saying, "you're nice, thank you so much, you're a sweet girl". I just kept remembering my intoxicated dad doing the same thing as I waited for the ambulance to come to the house because he had fallen and lay bleeding on our floor. All I could think of was - where is this guy's daughter or wife? Where are the people who care for this man? Why is he behind the wheel of a vehicle if he is intoxicated or if there is something else wrong, such as dementia? Why is he so confused? The fall didn't seem bad enough to have caused that much confusion.

All of these questions kept going through my head as this stranger clung to me, and I kept thanking the Lord for allowing me to be there at that moment. At the same time, I felt like I was reliving the trauma from my dad's illness.

At the end of the day I realize that this experience was a prompting. As Christians we don't believe in coincidence; we know that God has a purpose and a plan for our lives.

I had been meaning to tell the story about my parent's illness and being a caregiver for a while but have been dragging my feet. I knew this would be emotionally challenging. This experience made me realize that I needed to tell this story sooner rather than later. If other people besides me are going, or have gone through, similar situations, then I need to let them know they are not alone. Also, some are not caregivers but might know a caregiver and needs to understand what it's like to be a caregiver.

I wrote this book with a desire to help the caregiving community. My faith is central to my being and this story, because I know I couldn't have gotten through these circumstances without God. Without having a Savior who forgives and who supports and gives peace I wouldn't have made it through mom and dad's illnesses. I also want to tell a little bit about my parent's story, which was inspirational. If telling my experience in some way encourages or supports other caregivers or gives a little insight to those people who know a caregiver, then I will have accomplished what I set out to do. If there are situations that I experienced that help other caregivers, then that is the icing on the cake and the ultimate goal.

I must confess something before we begin the book. I inherited one of those personalities that like to be the center of attention and life of the party. You know the person who's always telling a joke and trying to fill awkward moments with chatter. Before writing I wanted to delve into my need and reason to talk about my caregiving experience. I wanted to make sure that the reason I was writing this wasn't to draw attention to myself or to say, "look what I've done, look at me", but to instead show what God has done in and through my life. The point of this book isn't to exaggerate the experience or to make light of a serious topic, and especially not to try to make myself look like an amazing human. Instead, I intend to show how God can use you if you give Him a chance when it comes to caregiving and serving those in need. This story isn't merely my own, it belongs to my mom and dad and to all those who influenced their life as well. To quote a Big Daddy Weave song, "to tell my story is to tell of Him". I hope that God's power is revealed in my life and this situation.

Thank you in advance for sharing this experience with me. Just a little warning - I'm not an expert on anything other than knowing what I went through. I'm not a nurse or doctor, not truly clinically trained. All I can relate is my own experience and what I've learned over the years. I'm not a minister, so this is not a book on the theology of caregiving. However, I can't not include the Word of God because faith is what keeps me going and it's gotten me through every situation.

Also, if you are a harried caregiver, and you need to get to the "meat" of this book right away, because you need facts, not stories, please look towards the end, the Chapter entitled "Extras". There, I have compiled all of the "Lessons Learned" that I highlight in the book. Also located there are various checklists. Chapter 16 is primarily about financial considerations and can be viewed as one big lesson learned.

Parts of this story may seem bleak, funny, hard, and I hope uplifting. While I wrote I ran the gamut of emotions, which only makes sense because that is what I experienced being a caregiver. I wanted to be true to the reality of caregiving. What I hope see, as you read, is that through it all, the joy of the Lord was my strength. One day, before I started writing this, I woke up singing this song. A song my mother sang to me. Lines from the song are:

> *The joy of the Lord is my strength*
> *He fills my mouth with laughter, ha ha ha ha ha*
> *He gives me living water, and I thirst no more*
> *He heals the broken-hearted, and they cry no more*
> *The joy of the Lord is my strength*

No matter what happens in this life, no amount of suffering or trials can take you away from the joy that comes from being in a relationship with God. May the Joy of the Lord be your strength, also.

Chapter 1 – The Melee Begins: Background

Psalm 25:4-5 (ESV)
Make me to know your ways, O Lord; teach me your
paths. Lead me in your truth and teach me, for you
are the God of my salvation; for you I wait all the
day long.

It's amazing how sometimes God gives you 20/20 hindsight. It's a gift. How many times do we look at what has happened in our life and wonder "Why did that happen? How did I get here?" When it comes to being a caregiver I can look back and see how God led me along that path.

When I was young, I couldn't imagine being anything except a veterinarian. My mom told me that when I was about five years old her Siamese cat had kittens in the garage. She says I watched the entire birth process with the kittens coming out all covered in goo and, while other kids would have said *that's gross*, she said I looked at the newborn kittens and said, "mommy how beautiful!" She said she knew then that I would do something in science or medicine.

Fast-forward to college, and I was studying zoology with plans of going to vet school. However, things didn't work out the way I planned. I didn't apply myself very well my freshman year, my sophomore year I got very ill, in junior year I just wandered around trying to figure out what I was going do now that my dream of going into vet school was crushed. I finally dropped out of school with 100 credit hours of zoology, with no idea what I was to do with my life.

After spending a little time in retail, one of my college buddies talked me into applying for a job at the nursing home where he worked. I applied for the position of recreational therapist working with Alzheimer's patients. It didn't pay well, but it allowed me to work in the medical field – or at least the medical industry. I spent the next 13 months getting to know Alzheimer's from a caregiver's perspective. Staffing was specialized in the Alzheimer's unit, so I was called upon to do other duties than would normally have been given to a recreational or nonclinical staff member. I was able to help with feeding, bathing, and clothing as well as my regular duties to try to keep the Alzheimer's patients as engaged mentally as possible considering the stage of their illness. I worked closely with doctors, nurses, nurse aides, and other therapists such as speech therapists. It was here that I learned about difficulties in swallowing and speech, how to transfer patients from chair to bed or pick them up off the floor without injuring yourself. I learned about the importance of nutrition for patients with chronic illness, and how all types of caregivers work together for the good of the patient.

What made the biggest impression on me while working in the nursing home was the way the patients were treated both by family members and staff. In the 13 months that I worked in the nursing home, there were patients on the Alzheimer's unit who never received visitors. I would talk to the staff about this and ask them – are these patients all alone? So often they would tell me that these patients had children or grandchildren, brothers or sisters, or even a spouse who lived within a short drive but who didn't or rarely came for a visit. This saddened me. I couldn't understand how you could let someone you love to go through this alone.

Occasionally one of the family members would show up unexpectedly. One of the duties of my job as a recreational therapist was to talk to the family members and tell them how their loved one was doing from an "illness development" stage. While I couldn't discuss medical diagnosis, I could say what it was that the patient did daily as I spent more time with many of these patients than any other staff member. So often after explaining the feeding process, the hygiene process, what we were doing to help keep their minds sharp and help them focus, I would hear the same story over and over from the family. They would look at me and say, "we don't come very often because it's just too painful for us to see our loved one this way". I would look at this family member and try to keep my face neutral but, in my mind,, I would think "if it's hard for you how do you think they feel?" I wasn't trying to be callous or judgmental (but, honestly, I probably was). After observing the patients day in and day out my sympathy lies with them and not with the family member. While these patients weren't the people they used to be, they still had so much value.

Lesson Learned: I quickly learned that when I was working with Alzheimer's patients, to them I was mother, sister, daughter, friend, care team member - you name it that's, what I could be on any given day. Many of them could not remember me specifically from day-to-day but it seemed as if they came to recognize my face and my presence, so I became familiar even if they didn't know who I was.

It might have been that I was just somebody, anybody, who would sit and speak to them or spend time listening to them. None of these patients were family members of mine so the extreme emotional pain that comes with watching somebody that you love suffer, I didn't feel for these patients (of course, I felt sadness and compassion). However, the previous year I had spent the summer with my paternal grandmother who, at the time, was suffering from undiagnosed pancreatic cancer. We knew she was sick but we didn't yet know from what she was suffering. Every day my cousin and I would go and check on her to make sure that she had eaten, that she had everything she needed, and that she was taking her medication. We would watch a TV show with her or just chat and spend time in her company. The reason I'm writing this is that I had seen what it was like to watch somebody you love suffer. What I didn't understand is how you could let your emotional suffering excuse you from doing what's right by your loved one? That being said I tried to be what I could for the patients in the Alzheimer's unit. In reality, I have God to thank for giving me compassion. I shouldn't give myself credit for feeling something, because it is very human to protect yourself.

2 Corinthians 1:3-4 (ESV)
God of All Comfort
Blessed be the God and Father of our Lord Jesus
Christ, the Father of mercies and God of all
comfort, who comforts us in all our affliction, so
that we may be able to comfort those who are in any
affliction, with the comfort with which we ourselves
are comforted by God.

The great thing about working in the Alzheimer's unit is that the nurses and medical assistants or nurse aides that worked in that unit were a breed all to their own. Patients couldn't remember their history very well so these caregivers became their memory. Some of the patients had been in the unit for years, and the nurses and aides had watched them slowly deteriorate. They remembered what the patients couldn't, and they served as the patient's memories. By speaking with the nurses and the aides in this area I was able to paint a picture of their lives before Alzheimer's for each of the patients. My job as the recreational therapist was to then try and revive or sustain those memories from their earlier life, engaging them in activities that they had previously enjoyed, or simply talk about past experiences. Some of the patients were amazing, and it was my pleasure to hear them speak of their childhood.

Lesson Learned: This book is mostly autobiographical with my caregiving experience, but I don't want to assume everyone who becomes a caregiver is caring for a family member. If you don't know the history of the person you are caring for, try and learn it. This will help you be a better caregiver. You can remind them of their youth, their career, their hobbies and what they enjoy. You can get books that cover their topics of interest or show them pictures or shows that will hold their attention.

One of the patients had only one arm. I asked how she had lost her arm and they told me that it was in a horse-riding accident when she was 19 or so. What was amazing about this one-armed woman was that she could play the piano like a concert pianist! Typical of Alzheimer's, her memories would come and go depending on the day or the hour so we never knew when she would recall her piano playing past. The unit had an older player piano that had reels of music but could also be played like a standard piano. The music reels were typical music from the 20s through the 50s because that was the era most of the patients had grown up in. I liked to put on songs such as "Sentimental Journey", or "Mack the Knife" and try to get the patients to sing or dance around with me. Sometimes this patient would start shaking her head in what appeared exasperation, stand up, and walk over to the piano. She would then proceed to take out the music reel that was playing and play herself. She played mostly classical music. Once I asked her family member who came to visit about her past. She said she had played before her accident and was able to transition to playing one-armed after the accident. They told me she had been feisty and stubborn and didn't let the accident prevent her from doing what she loved. Other times she couldn't even remember that she'd ever played the piano.

Lesson Learned: There are various stages in Alzheimer's and other dementia-related disorders. Sometimes you can interact as if there is nothing wrong, haveing lengthy, in-depth conversations. Other times you may see someone gazing off and not saying a word.

Speaking of dancing, one of the other gentleman patients had been quite the ladies' man in his younger years. He would always wag his eyebrows at cute girls when they would walk in. Whenever the music was playing, he would grab my hand and start swinging and twirling me around the whole time waggling his eyebrows at me. Whenever he appeared sad, I would put on an upbeat song, and try and entice him into a dance. He had a pressure sore on the bottom of his foot, so often he couldn't dance, instead he would sit in a chair and bounce, grinning and waggling those eyebrows at me.

Before I paint a sad picture of those in nursing homes, I think I should say that many there had loved ones who were very active in their lives. I don't want it to appear as if all of the Alzheimer's patients were neglected by their family at the facility in which I worked. There is one patient in particular whose daughter came every day. If we didn't see her, we knew she had to be sick or away, because she was so faithful to her mother. Her mother was sweet and kind and most the time didn't realize it was her daughter who was visiting but thought it was her sister. Her daughter would sit there holding her hands, painting her nails, brushing her hair or just loving on her not once appearing that this woman may not recognize her. Those like her were my role models in love and kindness, the people that I admired most.

I could tell all kinds of stories about working in the nursing home – such as when somebody handed me what looked like a cup of chocolate ice cream but was actually a cup of poop (I mean, it looked just like soft-serve, complete with the shape – but, the warmth gave it away), or talk about the effects of sundowner's syndrome.

Lesson Learned: Sundowners meant that we sometimes had to keep people from climbing the fence surrounding their outdoor space, or if we weren't fast enough, pull people off the fence because the sun was going down and that meant they needed to go home. This is something to be aware of, as you don't want to have to issue a Silver Alert because your care receiver is out looking for their home.

However, the reason I brought up working in the nursing home is that that's where I saw the institutional version of caregiving. This experience allowed me to learn so much but also showed me that if possible, being a home caregiver is a more ideal situation. That's not to say that this book shouldn't be, or couldn't be, useful to somebody who's loved one is in a nursing home; but I will focus more on home caregiving because that's what I did with my parents and that's what I experienced with my grandmothers as well. There are going to be situations where a nursing home is the best situation. Not everyone has the strength and health, the facility or the financial ability to be a home caregiver. Please, continue to be an active participant in your loved one's care, no matter where they are.

The reason for this chapter is to give you a little bit of the background that led me to feel somewhat experienced enough to create this book. I'm going to delve into a couple of experiences in caregiving that go deeper and are more personal than the 13 months I spent in a nursing home caring for Alzheimer patients. Primarily, who I write about caring for is my mom Nancy and my stepfather Brian (most the time I will simply refer to as dad). I also helped care for my paternal grandmother a few of the last months of her life and briefly "dropped in" when my mom was caring for my maternal grandmother in her last few months. I might mention my step father's mother who I recently lost, not because I was her caregiver, but because of the loss process. There will be a chapter later dealing with end of life and with death.

Returning to the concept of 20/20 hindsight. That girl who went to school to be a veterinarian, who dropped out with only 20 hours short of a bachelor's degree in zoology, can now see God's plan working. God's timing is perfect even if we don't understand it. If I had gone on to veterinanrian school, I would have been in my senior year of school and probably $100,000+ in debt when my mom became ill. I would not have had 13 months of experience working in a nursing home from which I could draw when it came to caregiving for my mother. I might have been so tied to a path that I would've made the wrong decision by not quitting my job and moving back home to my parents to help my dad care for my mom. On top of that I might not have moved jobs/careers from working in the nursing home into a computer career, which has allowed me to get a job anywhere I need to be; including back "home" in Oklahoma, where I never thought I would end up. I am not in a job that consumes me, such as veterinary medicine, but instead, I have a flexible career. **In other words, God freed up my passion from my career so that I could use my compassion to be a caregiver,** and still pay my bills. That's the 20/20 hindsight that I was talking about. God is always steps ahead of me, preparing my way, in paths that I never would've foreseen for myself.

Romans 8:28 ESV
And we know that for those who love God all things
work together for good, for those who are called
according to his purpose.

I hope that by starting with this introduction to my caregiving journey you'll see that the Lord has led me, equipped me, and He has given me a heart for other caregivers.

Throughout the book, I refer to caregiving in military terms. It occurred to me while I was writing that being a caregiver is a battle, sometimes against an enemy (the disease) you know will eventually win. (What a blessing to those who see their loved ones make a recovery and win the war!) The strategy is about persevering, not always about winning, and bout fighting with dignity, for dignity.

Know this, though. For those who are in Christ, death is not defeat. Christ defeated death on the cross at Calvary. He overcame it's terrible sting and rose again, victorious! Believers have that promise. The promise of life eternal in a new body in the Kingdom God creates for us. Able to rejoice for eternity with the Father, to walk among believers, including those we have loved and lost in this mortal world. Hold fast to this during the caregiving process. Remember, the battle here on earth might be lost, but Christ has ultimately defeated the enemy, and He has won us the victory with Him.

1 Corinthians 15:51-57 (ESV)
51 Behold! I tell you a mystery. We shall not all sleep, but we shall all be changed, 52 in a moment, in the twinkling of an eye, at the last trumpet. For the trumpet will sound, and the dead will be raised imperishable, and we shall be changed. 53 For this perishable body must put on the imperishable, and this mortal body must put on immortality. 54 When the perishable puts on the imperishable, and the mortal puts on immortality, then shall come to pass the saying that is written:
"Death is swallowed up in victory."
55 "O death, where is your victory?
O death, where is your sting?" 56 The sting of death is sin, and the power of sin is the law. 57 But thanks be to God, who gives us the victory through our Lord Jesus Christ.

Timeline

Throughout the book, I jump around between experiences caring for my mom and dad, as well as others. Here is a *rough* timeline. Please excuse the "jumping" as sometimes it seemed logical to go in chronological order, while other times it seemed logical to discuss similar situations or experiences that may have happened years apart.

Pre-book Timeline Activities

1. Maternal grandmother dies.
2. Spend a summer caring for paternal grandmother with my cousin prior to her death.

both mentioned in the book

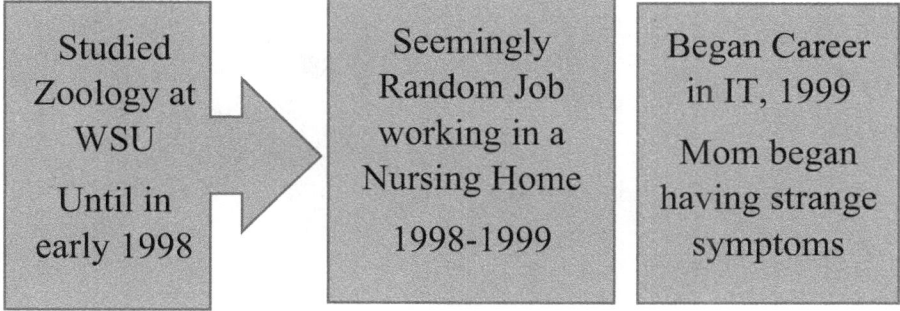

Studied Zoology at WSU

Until in early 1998

Seemingly Random Job working in a Nursing Home

1998-1999

Began Career in IT, 1999

Mom began having strange symptoms

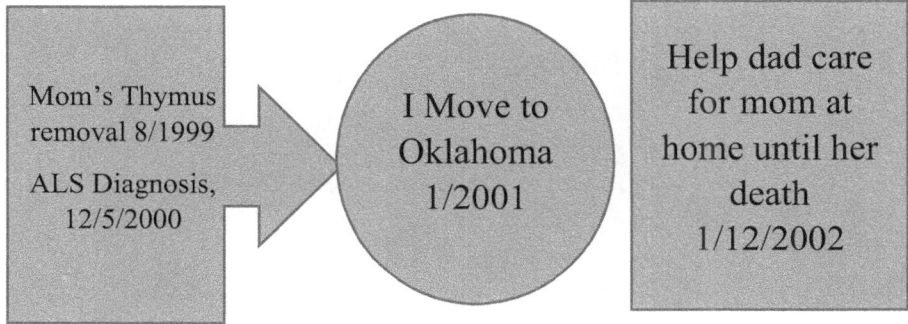

Mom's Thymus removal 8/1999

ALS Diagnosis, 12/5/2000

I Move to Oklahoma 1/2001

Help dad care for mom at home until her death 1/12/2002

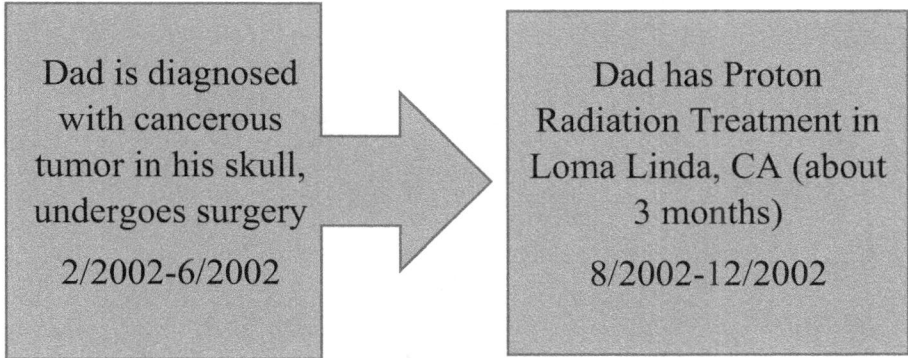

Dad is diagnosed with cancerous tumor in his skull, undergoes surgery

2/2002-6/2002

Dad has Proton Radiation Treatment in Loma Linda, CA (about 3 months)

8/2002-12/2002

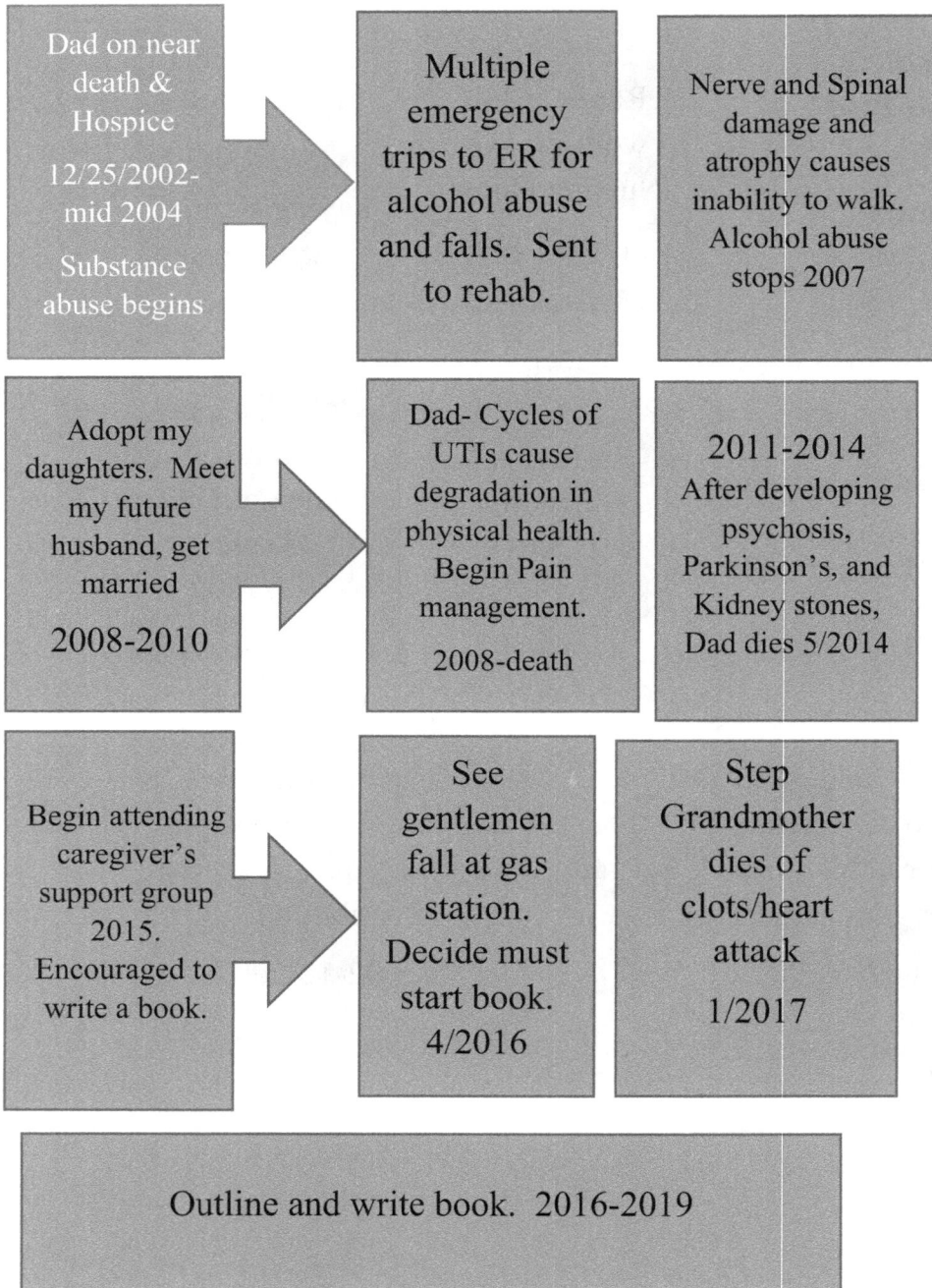

Dad on near death & Hospice

12/25/2002- mid 2004

Substance abuse begins

→

Multiple emergency trips to ER for alcohol abuse and falls. Sent to rehab.

Nerve and Spinal damage and atrophy causes inability to walk. Alcohol abuse stops 2007

Adopt my daughters. Meet my future husband, get married

2008-2010

→

Dad- Cycles of UTIs cause degradation in physical health. Begin Pain management.

2008-death

2011-2014 After developing psychosis, Parkinson's, and Kidney stones, Dad dies 5/2014

Begin attending caregiver's support group 2015. Encouraged to write a book.

→

See gentlemen fall at gas station. Decide must start book. 4/2016

Step Grandmother dies of clots/heart attack

1/2017

Outline and write book. 2016-2019

Chapter 2 - Legacy of Caregiving

A legacy is something of value that is left to members of your family. Often it denotes money or property. In this case, I want to speak about the legacy of being a caregiver.

Philippians 2:4 ESV
Let each of you look not only to his own interests,
but also to the interests of others.

Teaching your family to care for others, even at the expense of their own interests, is not a natural part of being human. The ability to be selfless is a gift bestowed by God. James 1:17 tells us that every good and perfect gift comes down from the unchangeable Father. Not some good and perfect gifts, but all. Therefore, the gift of caregiving is given to us by God. Even though you can't "give" this gift to a family member (it isn't hereditary), you can model and teach it. Titus Chapter 2 instructs men and women to do good for the sake of the Gospel and is specific to how we can show the Gospel in our behaviors, including instructing others.

Being a Christian does mean that God has given us specific instructions in the Bible which includes providing for our relatives, especially those who are members of our household. The Bible says that if we do not care for them, we are denying the faith.

1 Timothy 5:8 ESV
But if anyone does not provide for his relatives, and
especially for members of his household, he has
denied the faith and is worse than an unbeliever.

However, I hope my children don't have to be compelled to care for others, but are open to the Holy Spirit moving within them, and this generates a desire to care for their loved ones in need.

In the book of Ruth, Naomi and her husband and sons, who were Jewish, had been living in the foreign land of Moab because of a famine in their home of Bethlehem in Judah. She lost her husband and then within ten years she lost her two sons as well. She decided to move back to her hometown and decided to set her daughters-in-law, both of whom were Moabites, free from obligation to her.

One daughter in law agreed, but Ruth did not. Ruth decided to stay with her mother-in-law, to leave her birthland, and to go to Bethlehem. She told Naomi:

Ruth 1:16-18 (ESV)
16 But Ruth said, "Do not urge me to leave you or to return from following you. For where you go I will go, and where you lodge I will lodge. Your people shall be my people, and your God my God. 17 Where you die I will die, and there will I be buried. May the Lord do so to me and more also if anything but death parts me from you." 18 And when Naomi saw that she was determined to go with her, she said no more.

Ruth committed to going with and caring for Naomi. Why, I do not know. I suspect that God moved her heart and she was called to follow God, and that included caring for her mother-in-law.

You may know how this story turns out. Ruth moves to Bethlehem and meets a godly man, who happened to be related to Naomi. They get married and she becomes the great-grandmother of King David, who in turn is the familial line which Jesus is born into. A caregiver is honored by being an ancestor of the Christ. Her good deed led to historical honor.

I think it is beautiful how, near the end of the book of Ruth, Ruth and Boaz have a son, Obed. Naomi places Obed on her lap and becomes his nurse, his caregiver. This relationship isn't just beneficial to Obed and his parents, but also Naomi. The Bible tells us that "15 *He shall be to you a **restorer of life** and **a nourisher of your old age**, for your daughter-in-law who loves you, who is more to you than seven sons, has given birth to him.*" The one who was cared for (Naomi) becomes a caregiver (to Obed) which in turn restores her life and nourishers her in her old age. Caregiver, even while you are pouring out care, God is pouring in through your service, restoration and nourishment.

Galatians 6:9-10 ESV
And let us not grow weary of doing good, for in due
season we will reap, if we do not give up. So then,
as we have opportunity, let us do good to everyone,
and especially to those who are of the household of
faith.

Caregiving can be difficult. It is messy. You have to give up a lot. You give up time, your freedom, possibly opportunities. If you are not careful, you may spend a lot of time focusing on the sacrifices and forget the joys, the fulfillment. You forget the changes that God works in you through the experience of submitting to Him and caring for someone who needs you. The truth is, as a caregiver, you don't always want to be a caregiver. However, with the Lord as your strength, your joy, you will see the good from the sacrifice.

Matthew 11:29-30 ESV

"Take my yoke upon you, and learn from me, for I am gentle and lowly in heart, and you will find rest for your souls. For my yoke is easy, and my burden is light."

I want my children to see that the yoke of caregiving, which rests on us as part of the yoke of faith in Christ, is indeed easy. How? With Christ as your Lord, confidence in God the Father and His promises, and powered and strengthened from within by the Holy Spirit. I saw my grandmother care for her husband and her children and grandchildren, and I admired her for that. I watched my mother care for her dying parents and not once do I remember her complaining. She considered it a privilege, and she took that yoke upon her shoulders gladly. I watched my father lovingly and without hesitation, yoked to mom in their marriage covenant, shoulder the burden of caring for her when she became sick.

I have seen the changes in their lives because of what some would call heavy burdens placed upon them. More than that, I have seen the influence that these sacrifices have had on others. My parent's story has inspired others. Dad's co-workers couldn't believe that a man could take such amazing care of a dying wife. Doctors have commented on the level of care dad took of mom. As a matter of fact, when mom died in our home, the nursing home director commented on the condition of her body. He said he rarely saw someone in such clean and well cared condition upon death. This is a testament to the care of my father. It has inspired me. I want my children to see that doing the right thing, even when difficult, has repercussions that ripple out like a rock dropped into a smooth pond, radiating out from the center. And that center isn't the person, that center is Christ and what faith empowers a normal human to do – to super humanely place someone else's needs above their own.

My children have had to sacrifice for me to be a caregiver. They had to live in a house that didn't always smell wonderful. They didn't get to do all the activities, or go on all the vacations we might have if we didn't have a live-in grandpa who was also a patient. What they did learn, from a young age, was how to serve someone besides themselves. All three kids learned how to balance a tray of food while walking through a door, trying not to trip over cables and cords hooked up to medical devices. They learned how to crawl into a hospital bed and snuggle grandpa without too much wiggling, so as not to hurt him or pull out an IV.

Lesson Learned: Benefits your family may reap when you are a caregiver and they actively participate in the care of your loved one:

- *Patience – caregiving can take time and specific care that builds patience.*
- *Service – they can learn to think of others before themselves and to sacrifice.*
- *Wisdom – particularly if you are caring for someone who is elderly, you can receive such amazing wisdom by interacting with them and learning from them.*
- *Self-Sacrifice – giving up to give to someone else is a beautiful lesson to be learned in caregiving.*
- *Trust – the ability to put your faith in God to get you through every activity*
- *Bravery – facing illness, injury, and even death strengthens you and allows you to learn to look up to God for strength.*
- *Time – being a caregiver allows you to fully understand the meaning of time. Both when time flies, because you have so much to do and also when you lose the one you love and wonder where the time went. Also, when you are waiting for something you need to help, and it seems like it will never come. See Patience*

Love is expressed in many ways. We are commanded to love one another. Love is action set to our beliefs. If we believe we must be kind, be supportive, live out our faith, we will do this with loving deeds. I hope my children learn this throughout their life, and that it started at home, at the foot of my father's hospital bed.

John 13:34-35 ESV
A new commandment I give to you, that you love
one another: just as I have loved you, you also are
to love one another. By this all people will know
that you are my disciples, if you have love for one
another.

Let me be perfectly honest. I hope my children never have to take care of me the way I cared for my parents. I hope, like most parents, that life is easier for them than for me. However, what I hope for most is that God does whatever it takes, and uses whatever circumstance necessary, to bring them to Him, and to grow them into mature Christian people. If this means they have to wipe my bottom... welllllllll... Okay Lord, whatever it takes ~LOL! Seriously, I want them to see the reward for bearing another's burden ...not to the other person, but oneself.

Galatians 6:2 ESV
Bear one another's burdens, and so fulfill the law of
Christ.

I have gained so much from being a caregiver, and I don't want them to be deprived of the blessings that this brought me. Reconciliation with my parents. We weren't ever "at odds" in a prodigal daughter manner, but we had unresolved issues, as most people do. We were able, through God's grace, to work through these in the time we had together. The knowledge that I can react, in a godly manner, under pressure, even witnessing the vices of death, is a gift. I have been able to comfort others, not thanks to my own knowledge and strength, but because of the knowledge and strength given me from God, through these hardships. To have the smallest of a glimpse, to understand the tiniest of a fraction, what it was like to sacrifice for someone else, like our Savior sacrificed for us all, and to be humbled by His ultimate gift.

Mark 10:45 ESV
For even the Son of Man came not to be served but
to serve, and to give his life as a ransom for many.

Since the time of Jesus' ministry and in the early church, the need to take care of others has always been present, and always been something that was made a priority. Jesus healed the sick, showing compassion so great that he would even heal on the Sabbath, angering the legalistic Pharisees who did not understand who he was and under what authority he did miracles on the Lord's day. Jesus took the time to feed thousands more than once, showing compassion for the hungry.

In the young Christian church, a concern arose around the proper care of the widows. It was not pushed aside as a trivial matter but was handled in an organized manner, by men full of Spirit and of wisdom.

Acts 6:1-4 ESV
Now in these days when the disciples were
increasing in number, a complaint by the Hellenists
arose against the Hebrews because their widows
were being neglected in the daily distribution. And
the twelve summoned the full number of the
disciples and said, "It is not right that we should
give up preaching the word of God to serve tables.

Therefore, brothers, pick out from among you seven men of good repute, full of the Spirit and of wisdom, whom we will appoint to this duty. But we will devote ourselves to prayer and to the ministry of the word.

Members of the early church shared their lives, their burdens, their blessings, their resources. This has been modeled to us, that Christians are caregivers to their families and their church families, and these should be taught in our churches and our homes.

We should view all that we are given as the blessing it is, and with that blessing, poured out from a Good God, we should bless others. We do this when we become caregivers, and when we teach our offspring to also carry on this legacy of caregiving. Romans 15:1 states that the strong should do more than just please themselves (we don't subscribe to a Darwinian survival of the fittest belief), but to bear with the failings of the weak. We should do this to emulate the Christ-like character we strive to have as a Christian, we should do this out of a love for our neighbors. I believe we should do this to instill these Biblical values in our children, so that the legacy we pass on is more than gold and jewels (or stocks and bonds), but values centered in Biblical Truth.

We joke in our family about who will take care of mom and dad when we get old. Brianna, the youngest, who wants to be a zookeeper, has offered to let daddy hang out in the monkey cage, where she will feed him and visit him on occasion. Brit has promised me a place with her! "I'll take care of you mommy, don't worry" she sweetly tells me. It is a cute joke and we tease each other, but I love that my family is already thinking about providing care for my husband and me if we should ever need it!

I want to end this chapter with one last passage from the Bible. This scene is from John, Chapter 19. Here, Jesus has been crucified on the cross and is dying. At his feet are his mother Mary as well as Mary Magdalene and Mary (wife of Clopas) are there with him, as is the disciple that he loved, John. Jesus, while dying, made provisions for his mother. He provided for her a new son. Jesus had other siblings, but at this moment, he designated someone to be her caregiving, and the passage tells us that from that day on, John took up this task. What a beautiful demonstration of the love of a child for his mother and from one friend (John) to another (Jesus).

John 19: 25-27 (ESV)
25 but standing by the cross of Jesus were his mother and his mother's sister, Mary the wife of Clopas, and Mary Magdalene. 26 When Jesus saw his mother and the disciple whom he loved standing nearby, he said to his mother, "Woman, behold, your son!" 27 Then he said to the disciple, "Behold, your mother!" And from that hour the disciple took her to his own home.

The next chapter is written by Pastor Bill Balson. Pastor Bill was my pastor when I was in high school and he has a unique perspective that I felt was very important to share. Pastor Bill, for years, was the ultimate earthly caregiver, a Pastor.

The title Pastor is from the Latin word, *pastorem* or *pastor*, which means shepherd. The verb form of this word means to lead to a place set for grazing or to tend, guard and protect. Pastors are natural caregivers, particularly of our souls. They are to guide their congregation (flock) towards a deeper relationship with the Lord.

What happens when a Pastor, used to being the one people come to when there are issues and they need care, finds himself in need of tending? Pastor Bill went from being the one who people look to for help, to himself needing help. I asked him to share his perspective on what he felt was the most important thing to know when caring for others when the Caregiver becomes the *care receiver*.

Chapter 3 - The "Care Receiver"

by Pastor Bill Balson

Almost everyone will be some type of caregiver at some time in their life. It may be as a parent, sibling, friend, being the boss, or part of their job duties, (teacher, nurse, etc.). It may be caring for the sick, wounded, elderly, as a spouse or as a simple act of kindness. In the same manner, almost everyone, if we live long enough, will become a care receiver. At some time, we will need a little help. (illness, accident, while recovering, becoming elderly).

The caregiver needs to try to understand the situation and the mindset of the care receiver. There may be times when the care-receiver may not seem appreciative, cooperative or even pleasant towards the very one who is sacrificially caring for them. This can lead to the caregiver becoming discouraged, resentful, burned out or even bitter. The purpose of this chapter is to offer some insight into understanding the heart and mind of the care receiver and to suggest some ways in which the care receiver might be helped to have a better perspective, attitude, and life.

As with almost everything in life, the choices we make affect everything. Very often we have little or no control of what is happening to us or all around us. What we can control, however, is how we choose to perceive things and how we choose to respond.

I'd like to share my own experience of going from caregiver to care receiver. It was one of the most difficult things I have ever done, and I am certain that I still have a way to go.

For almost 40 years I was a pastor/minister of an evangelical church. This meant that by the very nature of my calling much of my life and duties were to care for others. I visited, prayed, brought financial help or, sometimes, just sat and listened to those in need. I also became the caregiver for both of my parents in the years before they died, managing their finances and medical care, which was a difficult reversal of roles. At times I felt like a caregiver as a husband and father. I was always there and trying to be the strong one for my wife and family. I very much enjoyed my position and duties, being the one who had the time and resources to minister and to help. It became part of my identity, my expression of love, my purpose and how I valued my own self-worth.

As well as being a caregiver I was always a person who was strong, mentally sharp, and often in charge. I stayed physically strong and healthy into my early sixties, competing in the Senior Olympics, winning numerous medals, backpacking in the mountains, a rock climber, tree climber, skier, scuba diver, skydiver, and much more. I only share this to give some idea of where I was before I seemed to fall so far and so quickly. In 2011 I finished 5th in the nation in my track and field event, after winning more than 20 medals at the state level. By 2016 I was unable to do almost anything that required strength. I needed a walker at times and was often unable to walk to the mailbox without getting out of breath. In 2011 I could lift over 500 lbs. on the leg press and in 2016 I had a blue handicap tag hanging from my mirror as my wife had to drive me most of the time. In 2011 I could preach from any passage of the Bible with no preparation. In 2016 I often found that I could not remember the names of my closest friends.

For me, the process of becoming a care receiver was a traumatic event. It was the most unwanted journey and the hardest thing that I had ever done in my life. I struggled with shame, low self-esteem, and guilt. At times I was not sure if I could survive the great sense of loss that I felt. But for my faith in God and the help of a very loving, godly and patient wife I would not have made it.

I had always refrained from smoking and drinking, had eaten healthy and had exercised regularly, so I assumed I would be healthy until my 90s. In January 2012 I fell ill. From there my health continued to spiral downhill for the next 5 years. It seemed I was diagnosed with a new disease or problem constantly. I was told that I had chronic Lyme, Bartonella, coronary artery disease, peripheral artery disease, Reynaud's disease, Crohn's disease, coronary artery spasm, skin cancer, double vision, high blood pressure, high cholesterol, sepsis from a wound, 5 stents, a double bypass, pleurisy, 3 TIAs, and a rare form of Muscular Dystrophy called Mitochondrial Myopathy and then heart failure.

After becoming ill in 2012 I was no longer able to do my job, so I resigned and had to move back to where I grew up. That meant losing my position of leadership and caregiver, no longer being a wage earner, losing our friends, our home; plus having to move far away from our 2 daughters and their families. It meant growing continually weaker, constantly seeing doctors and being labeled and treated as disabled.

I was no longer in charge of anything, no longer able to financially contribute to our family, no longer able to be a caregiver, no longer the strong one, no longer as sharp as I had been. I began to feel as though I had lost my purpose and my value, (as a husband, father, person, and Christian). The way that people looked at me and treated me sometimes made me want to scream or cry. At times I felt as though I had lost all of my dignity, worth, and self-respect; I felt useless and as if my life was over.

Although I did my best to remain faithful to Christ and to trust Him daily, it took some time for me to adjust and to gain a new perspective, to have a better attitude and get the victory that God wanted for me to have. As I cried out to God, stayed in His Word, trusted Him and gave myself completely to Him, He began to change my heart. By God's grace and with my wife's help I began to be lifted out of the hole that I had dug for myself.

During my lowest times, there were several verses and passages that God gave me to minister to me. As long as I was in the Word it seemed as though He would bring the right verse or passage that I needed for that day. Some of the books, (in addition to the Bible), that helped me were "My Utmost For His Highest", a daily devotional by Oswald Chambers, "Valley of Vision" (Puritan prayers); and "The 4:8 Principle" by Tommy Newbury.

If you are a caregiver and are dealing with a person who may, at times, seem unappreciative, despondent, frustrated, disrespectful or even angry, it may have something to do with the great sense of loss that they feel in their life. They usually don't want your pity, but some patience and understanding toward them could go a long way.

In all honesty, if a care receiver does not have faith in God, does not have the peace that only Christ can give, nor do they have the enabling power of the Holy Spirit to strengthen them, then I have no idea how they can be truly helped to overcome their sense of loss and the dread of their future. In Christ, I can do all things and without Him, I can do nothing. *(Php.4:13; Jn.15:5)* If it is part of the caregiver's intent to truly help, then part of that help should be a conscientious effort to look to the care receiver's spiritual wellbeing as well as their other needs. The caregiver may not be the best person to do this in all cases, just as a spouse is often not the best one to reach the other spouse. To do so may require the assistance of someone other than the caregiver, but the caregiver should strive to find a person or a way to strengthen the care receiver spiritually. Most importantly, if the caregiver is not leaning on God for their strength, then they will not be able to give or share what they do not have. It is somewhat like the airline steward says on the plane; "Put on your oxygen mask first, before trying to help another."

I'd like to share ten things that God taught me that helped me through this journey of Him transforming me. Perhaps they could be used to help the person that you are caring for if you can find the right person, the right opportunity and the right way to share them?

I.   *Leaning on the Lord*

To "lean on God" is to give our heart, our life, and our circumstances completely over to Him. It means to have faith, to trust Him to supply you with the grace and the ability to get you through whatever you're going through. *("But he said to me, "My grace is sufficient for you, for my power is made perfect in weakness." Therefore, I will boast all the more gladly of my weaknesses, so that the power of Christ may rest upon me. ", 2Cor.12:9 ESV)* What seems impossible to us is easily possible with God. *("With man this is impossible, but with God all things are possible.", Mat.19:26 ESV")* To have faith, or to trust God, means to believe that He is all that He claims to be (what the Bible teaches about Him), and also to believe that He will do all that He has promised to do. *("⁶And without faith it is impossible to please him, for whoever would draw near to God must believe that he exists and that he rewards those who seek him. ", Heb.11:1-6 ESV)* It is being convinced that He can and will supply all that we need. *("And my God will supply every need of yours according to his riches in glory in Christ Jesus.", Php.4:19 ESV)* It is believing and claiming all of the promises that He gives us in His Word as though they were spoken directly to us in person. (... *"by which he has granted to us his precious and very great promises, so that through them you may become partakers of the divine nature...",2Peter 1:4)* It is finding a strength beyond our own that will transform us, both inwardly and outwardly.

Faith is not just having an intellectual belief in our heads. It is having a trust in God that profoundly changes our entire being. It cannot help but manifest itself outwardly in things like a Godly joy, attitudes, and actions. *("¹⁷So also faith by itself, if it does not have works, is dead. ¹⁸But someone will say, "You have faith and I have works. Show me your faith apart from your works, and I will show you my faith by my works.", Jas,2:17,18 ESV)* Upon receiving Christ He also gives us His Holy Spirit Who resides within us and becomes the Source of our ability to do the things that are beyond our strength. He will give us things like joy, peace, comfort, hope and the strength to do whatever God commands us. *(Jn.16:12-15)* It is trusting in God that releases the power of God and brings the blessings of God through His Spirit. *(Jn.14:16,17; "I can do all things through him who strengthens me.", Php.4:13 ESV)*

II. Leaving

The Word of God encourages us that to move forward we have to stop looking backward. We have to leave the past in the past. (*...“But one thing I do: forgetting what lies behind and straining forward to what lies ahead,”, Php.3:13 ESV)* I would never be able to accept the new person I had become until I went through the grieving process for the death of the person that I had been. Experts say that there are 5 stages of grief and I saw myself going through them.

> **Denial**: At first, I believed that I would bounce back. I was sure of it and planned for it. I did not and would not accept that I had had a fundamental change, that a chapter in my life was over and that a new one had begun. This was difficult and took quite some time to overcome. I still battle with it on occasion. At one point, after having lost about 80% of my strength, I thought that I could still do a cartwheel on the beach. It had always been so easy for me even into my 60s. I went down hard and stayed down. Foolish me. I could only laugh.

> **Anger**: It is common for anyone experiencing loss to feel some anger at some time. It may be expressed at ourselves, an inanimate object or another person. When we realize that we have lost something that can never return the deep hurt

may evoke a myriad of emotions. One of the most common is feeling anger over our loss. We have to recognize that most change or loss is nobody's fault, that it is simply a part of life. As believers, we must change and grow continually from the moment we are saved until we enter into heaven. We have to keep adding to our "saving faith", *(2Pet.1:3-6)*. Anger will accomplish nothing and will mostly end up hurting us even more than we are already. *("Refrain from anger and forsake wrath! Fret not yourself; it tends only to evil.", Psa.37:8 ESV)* I found that I was most angry at myself because I felt as though I had failed everyone around me. We must allow the Holy Spirit to control us and not anger. *("Be angry and do not sin; do not let the sun go down on your anger...Eph.4:26 ESV)* It is also very common for people to feel angry toward God. The problem with anger is that it never changes, nor improves anything. It usually hurts oneself and people that we don't want to hurt. There is an old quote that is believed to have come from the AA "12 Step" movement; "Holding on to anger is like swallowing rat poison and waiting for the rat to die."

Bargaining: We may find ourselves trying to bargain with God or going through the process of trying to lay blame. If only I had; *the should have, would have, could have battle.* We may try to deal with God; "If you will, then I will...". Some things cannot be changed because God knows His plans for us, plans that are for our good. *(" 11 For I know the plans I have for you, declares the LORD, plans for good and not for evil, to give you a future and a hope. Jer.29:11 ESV).* When people try to strike a deal with God, (If you will...then I will), they usually find themselves disappointed when God does not do what they want. This will most often just lead to more disappointment and anger.

Depression: We begin to find ourselves dealing with sadness and/or struggling with regret. Instead of thanking

God for all that we once had we wallow in our self-pity because we don't have it any longer. That's called "stinkin thinkin" and it will destroy us. We will not get out of this mire until we focus on things above and allow God to lift us. *("Set your minds on things that are above, not on things that are on earth." Colossians 3:2 ESV)* Once God lifts us, everything will change. Depression sat on my shoulders at times like a debilitating boulder until I let God lift the weight and set me free. *(Matthew11:28)* I knew that most of my life had been filled with God's blessings and His abundant grace. I realized that I had no right to be sad or angry now just because He was leading me into a new place with a new purpose in my life. It seemed as though I was acting completely ungrateful for the many gifts that He had given me; that I was complaining like a spoiled child. In time I came to realize that I still had a purpose for my life and value, both in the eyes of God and the hearts of people.

Acceptance: We must eventually accept the things we cannot change. (The Serenity Prayer) I'm not suggesting that we should ever give up all hope and settle into our loss and pain. On the contrary, we must look to God and rise above our loss by His grace as we begin to see things through His eyes and trusting Him; Walking by faith and not by sight. *(2Cor.5:7)* Many a person has grown and accomplished great things by taking a new path and accepting that their life has entered a new chapter. They find that they are doing and succeeding in things that they never dreamed possible.

III. Looking

Looking forward Having faith in God will fill our hearts with hope. Without hope, a person will have nothing to live for and will not be able to find any joy in their immediate day. *(Blessed is he whose help is the God of Jacob, whose hope is in the LORD his God...", Psalms146:5 ESV)* Hope is waiting in the constant expectation that there is still some good thing that is yet to come. *(Romans8:25)* God says that hope for believers is eternal, that it will never cease *(1Corinthians 13:13; 15:19)* If a person cannot look forward with hope, they will simply surrender to the gloom of hopelessness and give up. On the other hand, as long as we have hope we have a reason to get up and go on, a reason to welcome each new day. With hope, life will always have some measure of mystery and adventure just ahead. Who knows what good thing God will bring tomorrow?

Looking for God   I and many others that I know begin each day with a similar prayer. We pray that God would reveal Himself to us in whatever way He chooses. In truth, we are searching to see the evidence of Him in creation, in answered prayer, in other people, in His acts of grace or a thousand other ways in which He makes Himself known. He has promised that He would never leave us alone. *("I will never leave you nor forsake you." Hebrews 13:5 ESV)* If we ask Him to reveal Himself we will not see God, but we will see the evidence of God as we walk by faith and not by sight. *(2 Corinthians 5:7)* He is like the wind. You can't see the wind, but you can see where it is moving by the things that it touches *(John 3:8)*. If we ask God to reveal Himself, and we look for Him, then His grace we will see Him in places that we might never have expected; In a friend's voice, or a beautiful sunrise, an act of kindness or perhaps just a smile. If we ask He will answer. *("Ask, and it will be given to you; seek, and you will find; knock, and it will be opened to you. For everyone who asks receives, and the one who seeks finds, and to the one who knocks it will be opened.", Mat.7:7-8 ESV)*

IV. Listening to God

Listening to God requires that we are intimate with Him and that we are walking with Christ. This would certainly mean that we have to have a heart that has first confessed and dealt with our sin. If we confess, He will always forgive. *(John.1:9)* It would also require that to hear Him we must be in His Word and prayer. The Psalmist says; (*"Be still and know that I am God." Ps.46:10 ESV*) If we are intimate with God He may speak to our heart in a myriad of different ways. I'm not saying that you will hear an audible voice, but the Spirit of God will lead you, give you the words to say something, warn you, comfort you, help you to make some choice or empower you to do some type of ministry or kindness. (*"But the fruit of the Spirit is love, joy, peace, patience, kindness, goodness, faithfulness, gentleness, self-control...." Gal.5:22-23*) If we are not listening to God, we will miss many of the joys and blessings that He has for us. Most of the blessings that are often missed are in the little things, where God is revealing His presence, showing His grace, answering our prayers or giving us some private little insight or encouragement. We must learn to see Him and hear Him throughout our day and in all of His creation. *(Rom.1:20)*

V. Learning

As believers, we must never stop learning. I am not referring simply to gaining head knowledge of the Bible. While that is important, there are many other things that God wants us to learn. Things like contentment, patience, humility, trust, love and many more. These are the things that God teaches us as He is conforming us to the image of His Son. *(Rom.8:29)* The first thing required is that we are teachable. If I decide that I don't need to learn, grow or change, then that will make me unable to be taught by God. We will rob ourselves of His riches and grace.

VI. Loving

The first and greatest command is that we love God and the second is that we love our neighbor. We are told that He wants us to love Him with all our heart, all of our soul, and all of our mind. *(Matthew 22:37-39)* He also tells us that if we love Him we will also love one another. *(John 13:34-35; 1John.4:19-21)*

Godly love is to love others in the power of the love that God supplies so that we love each other as Christ loves us. *(John.15:12)* A Christ-like love comes from God, imitates God and glorifies God. To love others as Christ did will mean that we stop focusing on our self and begin to consider all the people that God has placed around us. It means that we become, "others minded". *(...² complete my joy by being of the same mind, having the same love, being in full accord and of one mind. ³ Do nothing from selfish ambition or conceit, but in humility count others more significant than yourselves. ⁴ Let each of you look not only to his own interests, but also to the interests of others. ⁵ Have this mind among yourselves, which is yours in Christ Jesus...", Php.2:2-5 ESV)*

Many care receivers tend to think that they have become a captive prisoner. The truth is that they often have a great opportunity in the captive audience all around them. Over time God has allowed me to witness and encourage doctors, nurses, therapists and other care receivers who are going through the same struggles as I am. Just a word of kindness, a smile or a small gesture of love can be a great witness to those around us. They will say things like, "How can you have such a good attitude?", which will open doors for you to share your faith.

VII. Laughing

One of the most important things that we can do to help ourselves through a difficult time is to learn to laugh at ourselves and some of the things that life throws our way. Just as love covers a multitude of sins, *(1Pet.4:8)*, a good sense of humor will cover a multitude of embarrassing moments. God gave us a sense of humor because we need it. We see humor all through the Bible. *(Esther 6:6-12)* As a result of having the mini-strokes, I often found myself staggering like a drunk, losing my balance, forgetting the names of my closest friends or doing something clumsy. When I first got my scooter, then my powered wheelchair, I engaged my 8-year-old granddaughter in races. My handicap became a hoot. When I laughed at myself, I found that it was impossible to pity myself.

VIII. Laboring

It is imperative that we, as human beings, find something to do, and especially something to do that blesses others. I have known people who lived in nursing homes that did things such as making gifts or faithfully praying for ministries and people. I think of the famous Joni Erickson-Tada who became a quadriplegic and has had a ministry that has blessed thousands for the past 40 years. I knew a woman who was 103 years old and would, on her good days, take her wheelchair and visit other rooms in her nursing home to encourage and pray for others. I once sent a small card to a couple telling them that I loved them and was praying for them. Years later they wrote to me and told me that they had been on the verge of divorce and that my card had encouraged them to turn their lives to God and save their marriage. You just never know what a simple act of love might do.

IX. Living

To truly live is to live in this day that God has given us. To live in and lament the past will only destroy God's gifts and all of the potential joy that He has for us today. To live in the future, wondering, worrying, is like paying a high price for something that you will probably never get. Only God knows the future and the best thing to do is for us to trust God today for whatever the future might bring. *("Trust in the LORD with all your heart, and do not lean on your own understanding. In all your ways acknowledge him, and he will make straight your paths.", Prov.3:5-6 ESV)* If there any bad memories from yesterday we are to give them over to God and to only allow the good memories to bring joy into today. Rather than lamenting the good things we once had, we should thank God that we ever had those blessings and trust God that He will bring us more blessings in this world and in the world to come. *(Luke.18:30)*

X. Lasting

To last is to hold on, to not give up, to persist because we believe that we are here by God's design until He calls us home. Paul said, "To live is Christ and to die is gain." Then he said that it was more necessary for him to stay here for now. *(Philippians.1:21-23)* All of my life as a Christian I have prayed to God that I would finish life as a Christian as well as I had begun it. I have witnessed far too many people who give up on God when they are facing discouragement, disability or death. Blessed are those who will endure to the end, who will never stop hoping, never stop loving and never stop living for Christ.

My Caregiver

I had mentioned that my primary caregiver was my wonderful wife. Before I tell you about what kinds of things she has done, I must first tell you about what I had to do regarding her.

For any caregiver to be truly effective we must first trust them enough to give them some authority in our life. We must surrender some of our rights and control to them and trust them that they want our best. I realize not every caregiver is good-hearted, but it is true in the vast majority of cases. We must realize that they are making some sacrifices in their life to help in our life. It is alright to discuss things with them in which we might disagree, but we should never accuse them of evil, nor should we try to judge their hearts or motives. Honest, open communication will make life easier for everyone.

By giving my wife permission to care for me it helped to make her task much easier. She would often be much better at telling the doctors about my actual conditions or progress. She would often write down or remember things that the doctor said that I had forgotten. When she became firm with me about something (taking my medications, not overdoing something), I found that she was almost always right and only being firm because she loved me. She was usually more objective about things than I.

If she had not been there to call 911 or take me to the hospital when I was being stubborn, I would be dead.

If you have ever spent much time in a hospital you will notice that the patients who are nicer to the nurses seem to be treated more pleasantly and report that their stay in the hospital was much more pleasant. Being pleasant and thankful to the nurses allows them to feel more pleasant and makes their job easier. The same is true with any person that is caring for us.

One thing that I have learned over the years is that the person standing beside a loved one who is going through a difficult time usually suffers as much, if not more, than the one who is sick or disabled. My wife has had to endure a lot for my sake, though she has never complained, nor even thought that I was a burden to her. It was not simply that I trusted her, but that I trusted God who put her there for this time in my life, that her faith and faithfulness to God were a source of strength in my life.

She has had to keep track of and drive me to hundreds of appointments for my medical needs. She has had to keep records, manage my medicines, and watch out for negative symptoms. She has had to spend countless hours in uncomfortable waiting rooms while I was undergoing examinations, tests or surgery. There were times when I was in the hospital for weeks on end that she came up every day spending hours if only to sit by my side. She too has had to endure a role reversal by having to firmly remind me about what I cannot do or what I must do in things that I don't want to do. Although she was glad that she could help me she has taken no joy in my being disabled and having to be more subject to her. As I have said, without her I would probably be dead.

Caregiver and Care receiver

I believe wholeheartedly that it is all a part of God's design for us as human beings and as part of the family of God that we are all to love and care for one another when and if we are able. (*"… and may the Lord make you increase and abound in love for one another and for all, as we do for you…", 1Thes.3:12 ESV)* It is part of the Divine that was built into us when God created us in His image. As God allows, we all must be willing both to give and to receive, to have much or have little, to learn how to find contentment in whatever God brings in our life until He calls us home. *(Not that I am speaking of being in need, for I have learned in whatever situation I am to be content.", Philippians.4:11 ESV).*

Chapter 4 – The Combatants: Family Introduction

Exodus 20:12 (ESV)
12 "Honor your father and your mother, that your
days may be long in the land that the Lord your God
is giving you.

My family is to whom I've been a caregiver. They are the combatants that I stand shoulder to shoulder with, armed with love and the promises of God. Many people are caregivers for others who are non-relatives – it may be part of their job/career - but my calling was towards those that are closest to me. Throughout the book, I'll refer to mom and that'll be my biological mother, who raised me. I also have a stepmom, who I'll refer to probably by her nickname, or what she likes to be called, my "bonus mom". Most of the time when I refer to my dad, I'll be talking about my stepdad, who I primarily lived with from the time I was seven when my parents divorced. I'm still blessed to have my biological dad or OD (for "original dad") in my life. I don't want this book in any way to take away from his role, or in any way to decrease how much I love him and appreciate him. However, the dad that I was a caregiver for was my stepdad and I began calling him dad when I was 8, so dad he will be in this book.

I do have three brothers. Two brothers, I was raised with - an older brother and a younger brother. One brother I was not raised with, the baby, born to my OD and "bonus mom" my senior year in high school. The youngest didn't share the same parents this story is about. I will not mention my brothers much in this book because they were not members of either my mom or dad's caregiving team, but visitors. The second reason, which I will expand upon in a later chapter, is that illness can bring families together, or tear families apart. I hope that if your family is going through a situation where a loved one needs care, that unlike mine, you pull closer together.

As I write this I need to be in constant prayer and humble myself before the Lord, so that my focus is always on glorifying God and showing how that can be done as a Christian caregiver and showing how the Spirit moved in me as a Christian caregiver. I will try to be honest about my shortcomings in the caregiving arena because there are many of them. If I'm not honest about how I failed, then I can't give a true telling of my parent's story or my story and I will appear to be somebody that I'm not. Also, God is glorified when out of our weaknesses and flaws, He enables us to do something that on our own, we couldn't. I'm very flawed, as all people are, but fortunately, the Lord can work through my flaws.

My stepdad's family is very small - primarily his mom, brother, and a few cousins. My grandmother or 'GiGi', as we called her (signifying her role as great-grandmother to my children and nieces and nephews) lived in Southern California. My uncle lives in Austin. Both were very supportive of my care of dad; however, due to the distance, their support was more encouragement and less actual hands-on caregiving. My grandmother was in her 80s and she did her best to come to visit us once or twice a year, as long as she was able. We also went to visit her whenever possible (including an epic 22 hour each way car-trip to SoCal with dad, Rick and myself about 4 years into his illness). The last five years of dad's life, however, he was in no condition to travel as he could not sit up for more than a few minutes without severe back and leg pain. This meant that the burden of visiting fell to grandma. She called him nearly every day and was a constant joy and comfort and support to him for his entire sickness. When we wanted to take a vacation, she would come and stay with dad (and the nurse's aide), to care for him so we could have much-needed breaks.

Much of my mom's family lives within 20 minutes of us in the greater Oklahoma City area. My mom was the traveler in her family, the one who roamed, with my dad. However, unbeknownst to them, God had prepared them for these illnesses, and mom and dad had moved back to the Oklahoma City area, where mom was raised, just prior to her illness onset. (Another example of God's perfect Providence for His children). This allowed a handful of my mom's cousins and aunts to visit. They were joy and a blessing to me during, and since my mom's illness. My mom's family has a huge age range between her cousins. My mom was the oldest granddaughter so some of her first cousins are closer to my age than to hers. Before moving home when mom became sick, these cousins I only remembered vaguely from my childhood, but have gotten to know much better now as an adult. Ironically, mom and dad's illnesses and my subsequent move back to Oklahoma City are what allowed me to have a renewed relationship with family; and for that, I am incredibly thankful. Many of mom's cousins and a couple of her aunts and their families did their best, even from a distance, to support, love, and to encourage us - to let us know that they were there for us if not physically than emotionally. With this group of cousins, I have been blessed to form, through my mom and dad's illnesses, a bond that is more than blood - it's Christ in us, holding us together. I will expound on that later in the chapter on family.

Some of my OD's family lived close in Oklahoma as well. During my mom's illness, my aunts and uncles on my paternal side, particularly my OD's younger brother and his wife and their two daughters and OD's youngest sister, were helpful with my mom's care. One of my aunts worked near the hospital and would occasionally pick up prescriptions or supplies for us as needed. These two aunts also helped me whenever I needed somebody to talk to and once even when I was hurt -which I'll also talk about in a later chapter on taking care of yourself. Some might find it ironic that my mom, who had a terminal illness, received care from her ex-husband's family. I don't find it ironic at all, having lived through this type of situation. God places burdens on hearts, and compassion in them, in each situation. I have observed that compassion and love and caring for others is something that people either

- Submit to and rejoice as a gift from God or
- Don't naturally possess the gift but recognize that it is a characteristic that is good and work on building that characteristic even though it may not be natural for them. There also maybe those who
- Don't seem to have the burden to offer care and seem content to live out their life without caring for others. I also believe some may have
- Tunnel vision – they are focused on our own lives, possibly because of overwhelming issues, and lack the ability to see or have the bandwidth to help others.

I am unsure why people react differently to those we love having an illness, but I am learning, observing, and being told by other caregivers, that not everyone feels the same sense of responsibility or urgency. I came back to this section later and wanted to write other possibilities because I believe that caregivers struggle with the question of why some people take on the role and responsibility of giving care, while others don't. Many caregivers I spoke to feel that some people stand in their way of being a caregiver and hinder the process. Of course, as the chapter on conflict resolution (Chapter 11) states, it is often best not to question someone's motivations, as we can't see their heart, but to instead address the actions we can see. Therefore, these observations are just that, observations. I don't know why, but I have seen different behaviors.

- Some can display compassion but know that in this situation their actual physical help is not needed (but this doesn't negate the importance of encouragement) and
- We can't ignore the fact that for whatever reason, some simply do not support their loved ones who are ill/suffering/in need, nor those who are caring for them.

In the next couple of chapters, I'm going to explain how I found out about my mom and later dad's illness and a little bit more about the illnesses. Before delving back into these memories, I want to share the verse that sustained dad and me; not only through mom's illness but later through dad's as well. This was "dad's passage" that he would repeat over and over in meditation.

> *Philippians 4:6-7 "be anxious for nothing, but in everything by prayer and supplication with thanksgiving let your requests be made known to God. And the peace of God, which surpasses all comprehension, will guard your hearts and your minds in Christ Jesus."*

It is hard not to be anxious when you're going through end-of-life or terminal disease situations, even if it is as the caregiver. It's hard to understand what is not understandable -so many terminal diseases are simply incomprehensible. Sometimes it can be hard to understand how somebody that we know to be a good person will suffer horribly at the hands of disease. These verses have to be read to truly be understood.

Verse six talks about not being anxious. ***Don't be anxious?*** I'm watching people that I love die - sometimes slowly, horribly and painfully! Before you stop, look what it says next. It tells us to take everything to God in prayer and supplication. I think the term supplication is important to remember because that's with all humility. Sometimes we ask in such a way that we feel we are entitled, but all things are gifts from God. All things can be used for God's Plan and God's Will. For us to forget that, and to demand or to expect special treatment, shows our lack of humility, faith, and in our understanding of the way God has designed and planned. He doesn't say *don't ask* but we are reminded many times, in different places in the Bible that we can ask; but we should ultimately be seeking His Will and therefore our asks should always be superseded by wanting God's Will for our lives and others'. This includes wanting His will for this entire planet and all those who are in it. Since we as humans are so small in comparison to God it would be ridiculous to think that we could fully understand His Will; so sometimes we must simply accept. I think the word supplication in verse six is a way of reminding us to put ourselves in our rightful place so that when we do go to Him and make our asks; that we should remember to desire His will above all, including miraculous healing. (If you want a book that helps understand our place and God's place, I highly recommend The Holiness of God by R.C. Sproul).

I think when we can go to God in that manner, then verse seven is possible. Verse seven says that the peace of God is possible – not the peace of man nor peace as opposed to war, but a spiritual peace in our soul, no matter what happens. When we as Christians put our hope in God and not in a cure. and put our trust in God not in medicine, and submit our will to God not our own desires, then God's peace which is so much greater than anything that we can even imagine, will truly guard our heart and our minds in Christ Jesus. I knew this verse before my mom was sick, but I didn't really *know* this verse until mom got sick. I am thankful to my dad for reminding me of these two verses over and over throughout the 13 months of my mom's illness so that later when he became ill, I could remind myself to go to them when he was no longer able to remind me.

Chapter 5 - War Breaks Out: Mom's Illness

Galatians 6:2 (ESV)
2 Bear one another's burdens, and so fulfill the law
of Christ.

My mom's name was Nancy. She was the parent who was my constant while I was growing up. I believe that being a caregiver directly comes from watching my mother be a caregiver. She modeled compassionate caregiving to me.

Her father (my grandfather) died of smoking-related cancer when I was in junior high and we were living in Houston. For approximately 8 weeks she relocated to Yukon, Oklahoma (a suburb of Oklahoma City) and took care of her father the last weeks of his life. She, along with her sister, lovingly cared for him and his physical needs. This might sound like "no big deal" if you didn't know that grandpa was not an easy man, not as an adult with his grandchildren, not as a father when mom was growing up. She had told me stories of their tumultuous relationship. He had been of a generation where the head of the household was not questioned and his rule was law. (Years later, when discussing my grandfather with my cousin, I found out he had been in a Naval ship carrying soldiers that day during World War II in 1944 at Normandy on D-Day. He had witnessed the death of thousands of soldiers. He never spoke of it, but it was what I needed to feel compassion for a man who was always cold and scary to me).

Being a Christian, I believe the Bible is clear that the man is the spiritual head and leader of the household. In a Christian family, we are taught that the husband and father should always put God first in his life and the needs of his family above his own. A sacrificial leader.

I don't want to speak ill of my grandfather. He did provide for his family by working long hours. I also knew that he spoke harshly to at least my mother, as well as to his grandchildren - that I witnessed and also received, and I know that I feared him. So, to watch my mother lovingly, sacrificially, care for her father; a father that had been physically heavy-handed in his discipline as well as emotionally and verbally heavy-handed, was inspirational. Her caregiving was a true testament not to his ability to parent, but to my mom's ability to love and forgive through Christ.

A few years later, when her mom (my maternal grandmother) began suffering from pancreatic cancer, my mother, who was living in Kansas City, again moved home to care for a parent (again, alongside her sister). Mom took a caregiver role for both of her parents, even though she had to "move" to do this. In both situations, our family had to sacrifice for her to fulfill this role, especially my dad who 'held down the fort' when grandpa was dying and took care of a household alone when grandma was ill. Some might say that our sacrifice wasn't fair (others were living closer), but I think someone who would say that does not understand the role of Christian caregiving. My mom knew that caring for her parents was something that she *needed* to do to honor them, glorify God, and to show Christ in her life. Therefore, she did not feel like she had any choice in caring for her dying parents. When I say "didn't have any choice" I don't mean she viewed this as a grievous obligation; she joyfully and obediently offered her service with all love and saw this opportunity as an expression of who she was as a Christian daughter.

I am very thankful that I got to see my mom in this caregiver role at an age that it could make a big impression. My grandmother died when I was in college, so I was not able to be much assistance to grandma, my aunt, or my mom. I was only able to fly and visit for one weekend and give mom and my aunt a very brief "break" to run some errands and to work on estate tasks while I cared for my grandmother.

Lesson Learned: If you aren't the caregiver, but have an opportunity to help, be respite care. Give someone who is giving care a few hours, an overnight, a day or two, respite. You will be rewarded, they will be rewarded, the person you are caring for, will be rewarded.

I also did my best to entertain them, doing hair and face make-overs, telling silly stories from college, and just trying to lighten the mood. I have some beautiful pictures from this time that I cherish.

Lesson Learned: Take pictures. A lot of them. You will cherish them later, and be able to laugh and cry through the memories.

When grandpa was sick, dad brought us kids up every weekend for six weekends in a row to visit mom. That was an eight-hour trip from Houston to Oklahoma City; made Thursday nights and returning Sunday night - frequently getting in at 2am after battling traffic. This meant that all three of us kids missed six Fridays in a row of school, which was an academic strain, and in my case meant getting kicked off the volleyball team because I wasn't making it to practice and games. This meant dad working 40+ hours in four days so that he could do his job, but also support his wife, as this was long before the days of cell phones and telecommuting.

I never truly understood when grandpa was dying that those trips were so that my mom had support at nights, someone to listen to her, pray for her, support her, hold her, LOVE HER, as she was lovingly caring for her dad. Years later, when I finally met Tony, who would become my husband, I realized what being supported as a caregiver felt like. I finally understood why my dad was willing to be a single dad for weeks, driving 16-hour round trips, for the opportunity to spend less than 48 hours with his wife. He was doing it to let her know how much he loved and supported her in her service.

The onset of Mom's Illness

Mom's diagnosis came about a year after she began showing signs when she was in her early 50s. I remember the first time she mentioned her symptoms to me. At that time, she and dad had moved to Oklahoma to be closer to her family. Dad had taken a less stressful job so that he could work from home. In his mind, he was "semi-retired". The men in dad's family were not typically long-lived, so he was afraid that with him dragging mom all over the country, and most recently the world; he would pass away and leave her alone, a long way from any family or help. So, after spending a year living in Moscow, Russia for work, dad moved them to the Mustang/Yukon area, to be close to mom's family.

They had found a church home, **Canadian Valley Baptist Church**, and typical of my parents dived right into church life. Mom and dad together decided to lead a young adult Sunday school class, and mom was very active with other children ministries. My parents, both *church caregivers* in their own rights, had noticed that many churches lacked groups for young singles. Being the parents of young singles whom they noticed were having difficulty finding church homes themselves, decided they could help fill this gap at CVBC. For mom, who loved to sing, the best part of this church was that she could sing in the choir.

Dad had befriended the pastor, Kevin Kellogg, and they had become confidants. Dad always went out of his way to get to know the pastors of our churches, feeling that they were an underserved member, being the Shepherd who had to tend so many. While not a deacon or elder in an official capacity, he frequently served that type of role.

The Christmas cantata was the first indicator of mom's illness. She loved to sing but had not been anywhere in recent years where she could join the choir (having moved 4 times in 5 years). I remember receiving a call, mid-December. I wasn't going to get to go home for Christmas, and we were both really upset about that. She was calling me to tell me about their new house, their new church, the guy she had "earmarked" to introduce me to in church, and of course, the cantata. She was complaining because since moving back to Oklahoma, her allergies had gotten really bad. This meant she couldn't sing like she was used to. She told me that she couldn't hit any higher notes, her bronchioles must be inflamed, and she was upset about her allergy symptoms.

In January, when we talked, she was upset at her performance and had decided to not be in the choir anymore until she could get her symptoms under control. This giving up was unusual for my mom, who loved to sing; but I didn't pay too much attention at the time.

I was living in the Seattle area, working as a contractor for a company that did tech support for Microsoft employees, and my parents and I spoke anywhere from every three days to 2 weeks. They were never the type of parents who needed to speak to their kids every day. By March of that year, I noticed my mom's voice changing. I think that not speaking every day made the change more noticeable to me (much like noticing when kids have a growth spurt, the parents don't notice because they see them every day, but others can see the difference). Her voice was deeper, huskier, and monotone. Much of the inflection I was used to my vocally dramatic mom speaking with, was gone from her voice. When I spoke to dad on the phone, I asked him about it.

Dad told me that he had been bugging mom to stop telling the doctor what was wrong with her and get the doctor to send her to a specialist. He said that she would go to the doctor, state that she had allergies, and demand a steroid treatment or an inhaler, and then walk out, complaining that she wasn't getting any better. This had been going on for months.

In May I found out that my landlord was going to sell the condo I was living in, and that my roommate and I needed to move. I didn't have a car, as the commute had killed the transmission in the car I had gotten from my other parents. I was riding public transportation and carpooling to work every day. There was no way I was going to be able to move all of my stuff without help, and I had only a couple of weeks to find a place to stay closer to my new job working for Boeing as a tech-support contractor. I needed help, and Mom came to the rescue!

Mom flew out for Memorial Day weekend, which is around the time of my birthday. She was not happy about having to help her grown daughter move. She had also been traveling with dad (an airshow in either Moscow or England) and was ready just to be home. Being a supportive mom, she still hopped a plane to see me and lend a hand. I got off work early and took a bus to meet her at Red Robin in a nearby mall. She had landed, rented a large car with lots of trunk space, and headed to our meeting place for lunch. I had found a daylight basement apartment near my new job, and she was going to take me there to meet the owners of the home and see if they would rent the apartment to me.

When we sat down to eat, as soon as I could see her and hear her talk, I immediately had a sinking feeling. Her voice was worse, and I noticed that she was constantly trying to clear her throat. It had been a year and a half since I had left my job as a Recreational Therapist at a nearby nursing home, but I had been taught some speech pathology observation skills by the Speech Therapist there, including how to notice issues when someone couldn't swallow (Dysphagia).

Lesson learned: Many people diagnosed with terminal illnesses develop difficulty swallowing. They may need specifically sized or textured food, thickened liquids, special cups, straws (or no straws), and constant observation to prevent aspiration (when food or liquid goes down your trachea instead of your esophagus) which can lead to infection and choking. Learning to recognize signs of difficulty swallowing and taking measures to help with food consistency and fluid density, can save the life of someone in your care.

Without trying to be too obvious, I watched mom talk and swallow as she sat across from me in Red Robin, and I noticed that her tongue seemed to just sit in her mouth, with very little movement. She was constantly and unconsciously clearing her throat, especially when she ate or drank. Her speech was slurred slightly, but I could understand all of her words. I asked her to do a few things, like move her tongue around and purposely over enunciate a few words, just to see if she could move her tongue if she was concentrating on the movement. At that time, she appeared to still be able to, but it took effort.

After lunch, we met my future landlords, a nice couple who lived with their young daughter and niece, and we went back to my old place to pack. I had reserved a moving truck and mom wanted to make the first trip that day, as she only had the weekend. We packed up the truck, and drove to the new house and unloaded. It was a long afternoon, but we were able to get all the major items into the moving truck. All that was left at the old apartment were a few small items that would fit into the back of her rental car. We started setting up the new one-bedroom basement apartment and collapsed exhaustedly that evening to rest.

That night, while mom was in the shower, I called dad on mom's cellphone. I had been trying to pretend the entire day like I wasn't terrified of mom's symptoms, but as soon as she was out of hearing, I was very honest with dad. I told him that I was worried that her issues were neurological, and I had a bad feeling about her symptoms. I begged him to make an appointment with the doctor immediately, and to go with mom so that he would tell the doctor her complete list of symptoms and stop letting her belittle the problems. I think I made him nervous because my "take charge, always in control" dad was also concerned, listened, and promised me he would do it. Mom spent the rest of the weekend helping me set up, including her first-ever trip to IKEA to find a shelving unit for my "kitchen" (a two-burner hot plate and toaster oven) and helped me purchase a freezer and a mini-frig. She flew home on Monday, and the waiting game began.

True to his word, dad took mom to the doctor that week. When the doctor heard of all the symptoms mom was having, not just the ones mom wanted to tell her, weeks and months of referrals, testing, and specialist visits began. At that time the symptoms, besides the ones I mentioned earlier, also included a very slight gate change (change in her walk) where she appeared to be favoring her right foot. She hadn't even noticed she was doing it.

Lesson Learned: Making note of symptoms and when they appear can be valuable when visiting multiple doctors over long periods. In this day, electronic heath records (EHRs) help document and transmit records, but keeping a small notebook with symptoms, doctors' names, diagnosis, medications, medical history, etc. can speed up the process of filling out paperwork and also help make sure you don't inadvertently "miss something" that might be vital to treatment and care.

When someone has or is suspected of having Amyotrophic Lateral Sclerosis (ALS), also known as Lou Gehrig's disease, doctors didn't seem to like to bring this diagnosis up at first (at least that was my impression at the time). After all, there are very few treatments or drugs for ALS, no cure, and the prognosis for ALS is death. At the time of her symptoms in 2000/2001, we were told that frequently ALS was diagnosed by ruling out other diseases that have similar symptoms. Mom was tested for Multiple Sclerosis and muscular dystrophy. She was examined to make sure she hadn't had a stroke and various blood tests were performed as well.

Finally, they diagnosed her with Myasthenia Gravis (MG), a neurological disorder where a person's immune system, particularly T-cells created by the Thymus gland, attack the nerves. They decided on a course of treatment which they hoped would slow the progression of the disease. They wanted to try dialysis where they removed her blood, filtered out the T cells, then put her blood back in, to see if that would slow the disease. This was a two-week, daily treatment, and she was told this would take a lot out of her. Mom was ready to try, as her voice was getting worse.

After two weeks of dialysis, my dad called me. He said that usually by performing dialysis there is a nearly immediate improvement if the treatment is going to work. He said that unfortunately, it didn't appear to work. The next step was to have her Thymus gland removed, stopping the maturation of T-helper cells. This was a drastic surgery since the gland was located under the sternum (breast bone). T-cells play a part in our body's immune system and help fight infection. They told mom that if she did this drastic step, her immune system would not be very strong, and she would be susceptible to other illness, however, it could save her life. Mom accepted that risk, considering the alternative was to die from MG.

I flew to Oklahoma for the surgery, as it was major surgery with serious potential complications. They were going to have to split open her breastbone/rib cage, similar to open-heart surgery. Since MG affected one's ability to breathe, they were very concerned about her ability to resume breathing after the surgery (because she intubated) and told us that instead of removing breathing tube soon after the surgery, they planned to leave it in longer, to guarantee she would recover and be able to breathe on her own. In the waiting room dad and I had lots of company and support from mom's aunts, uncles, and cousins who lived in the area while we waited for her to come out of surgery.

Seeing my mom post-surgery with all of the tubes going in and out of her body, including drains with bags of blood in them, made the seriousness of this illness very real for me. My mom frequently got ill while I was growing up and even had to have knee surgery when I was in elementary school, but this was the first time that I saw her in such a way that brought home her true vulnerability and mortality. I remember walking out of the ICU room she was in and back to the waiting room and bursting into tears, falling into the arms of one of my great aunts.

Lesson Learned: If you have family members, particularly young children, who are unused to seeing people post-surgery, complete with catheters, monitors, IVs, intubated, you might consider prepping them before they visit. I do NOT recommend "protecting them" from this sight, only equipping them with knowledge so that the shock is decreased. Also, accompanying them and being able to explain the equipment might also decrease the "scare factor".

This surgery began a weeklong vigil for dad and I. We didn't leave her side unless we were "forced" to for x-rays or for shift changes. I'm not sure that the ICU staff was expecting us to set up camp in her room, but after what happened the first day, they weren't about to tell us to leave.

Speaking of that "incident" (details to follow), I am not going to mention the name of the hospital where this occurred, because I don't feel that this represents the capability of that hospital. What occurred, I believe, was a fluke experience. The reason I'm mentioning this is that:

Lesson Learned: I strongly advocate caregivers continuing to fulfill the caregiver role, even if the person they are caring for is in a hospital or nursing home setting. Nursing staff in a hospital cannot replace the one-on-one quality care that you as a caregiver can provide because they have too many other responsibilities and patients to care for.

Here is the experience that led to the above lesson learned. On the day of mom's surgery, following the surgery while she was still on a breathing apparatus, the hospital lost power - including backup generator power. How does that happen one might ask? It seems that while repairs were underway on the primary power, several power lines, including the main power and the line to the generator, were cut.

Compounding this issue was that the nurse who was tending mom when this happened was a contract nurse unfamiliar with this building, having only worked in this area once before. What this meant was when all the power went out in the ICU, just about everybody panicked including the contract nurse. She tried to plug in mom's equipment, including the breathing device, into the backup power, but it didn't start working and she panicked even more.

In this particular unit, nurses had only two patients each, and thankfully most of the patients were not on life support systems that helped them breathe, so not as critical as my mom. This meant that a different nurse was able to cover the other patient our nurse was responsible for because she was trying to get my mom's respirator working. Mom was awake when this happened so she could see me, dad, and the nurse panicking and scrambling around.

The second I realized that the power in the backup plug wasn't working I started chanting over and over to the nurse "bag her, bag her, bag her". (Bag her – means hook up a manual "bag" to the intubation tube in her chest, which can then be pumped to supply oxygen to her lungs via the tube – thank you medical drama shows). My mom's eyes were getting big as she was beginning to feel distressed because she wasn't just trying to breathe on her own, she was trying to breathe on her own with a huge tube in her airway. I was realizing that the machine was not going to come back online anytime soon.

The nurse kept focused on trying to plug the respiratory device into the oxygen dispenser in the wall, because she wanted to get a steady stream of oxygen into my mom, even if the device wasn't pumping, at least oxygenation would be happening. I had recently attended a first responder and CPR class, so I went over to the manual air pump (the bag) grabbed it, unhooked the repiratory tube from the machine, hooked up the bag and began to "bag" my mom.

Meanwhile, dad was yelling "how can I get power, how can I get power?" to the nurse who was in charge (she had run in when she saw that mom was in trouble) while the contract nurse working on mom was still trying to get oxygen to flow through the wall dispenser. The new nurse told dad that the battery backup outlet, which was the secondary backup for electricity, was in the ceiling. She pointed up at a bright orange outlet. I have never seen my dad climb so fast. He had to climb on top of a hospital serving table with the plug in his hand, me trying to balance the tray and bag mom at the same time, so he could plug mom into the brightly colored outlet for the battery backup. The whole time that this was going on I had been looking my mom in the eyes trying to stay calm and saying "breathe", as I pumped with the bag into her lungs, "breath".

It worked! The machine began to hum, the new nurse hooked her back up and her chest began to move up and down with the machine! I think this entire scenario played out in a minute or two but it seemed like an eternity for the four of us involved, including mom, who was helpless to help us.

Lesson Learned: Accidents happen. That doesn't make them less scary or life-threatening. If you have someone you love or are caring for in ICU or critical care, I highly suggest you have someone with them. I have heard enough "alarms" going off in hospitals for long stretches of time, to not fully trust the responsiveness, even of the best hospitals.

Needless to say, the hospital never once tried to make us move out of the ICU for the rest of her seven or eight-day stay - probably out of fear that we were going to sue them. The other thing they did was give us who I believe was their best nurse for at least one shift every day. I remember when she came in after this incident. She took one look at all the tubes running in all different directions after our mad scramble from the power outage and said, "this won't do". She spent 30 to 45 minutes crawling around, organizing cables and labeling them, then taping them together in logical groupings; just to make sure if anything ever happened, we would know exactly what cable went which device. The rest of our stay was great and after three days they removed the breathing tube from mom's trachea, and we were all so relieved that she could breathe on her own.

Lesson Learned: Familiarize yourself with the equipment and monitors in the room. Make sure that the area is kept tidy. This means cables, cords, tables, sheets, blankets, etc. We have found twisted catheter lines that the staff didn't catch, and prevented discomfort at the very least (or infection at the worst) by straightening it.. Knowing what is beeping, and how critical that device, is can help you to call for help or wait until the next staff member comes in to stop the beeping.

Unfortunately removing mom's thymus was not the solution we had hoped for. Her condition continued to deteriorate and soon after she was diagnosed with the actual disease.

Diagnosis

I'll never forget the day that I got the call from dad with her diagnosis. December 5, 2000. I was at home (Newcastle, Wa) and dad called me when he was alone and away from mom. I could tell that he had been crying and was trying to be brave. He told me that mom was in the other room because he didn't want her to hear the emotional state that he was in. He told me that after sending off test results and her medical record to M.D. Anderson and discussing her case with other doctors, they had determined that she had Lou Gehrig's disease. Her issue wasn't the standard form either, but probably a rare form of ALS called Bulbar. I immediately told dad that I would be moving home.

At this time, I was already scheduled to come and visit for Christmas and told him that we could discuss arrangements and plans when I got there for Christmas. Dad tearily told me "thank you thank you thank you" and then we hung up.

Less than five minutes later my phone rang again and it was dad calling back. He apologized and told me that when he talked to me earlier, he had been calling not as my father but as a desperate husband. He told me that he and mom could get through this without me. After he hung up he had started thinking and he told me that as a dad he wanted what was best for his daughter and he knew that I had recently started a job with Boeing and he didn't want to hinder my career and my future by having me move home to help him. He reminded me that I was the kid and not the parent and that he had to remind himself of that after he had called.

Let me just stop right here to point out that this is an amazing dad thing to do. A man, who has just heard the love of his life is dying, STILL has time to consider the future of his daughter over his ease and convenience and through his fear!

I lovingly but kind of laughing at him said "that's all well and good dad but I'm still moving home" and we'll discuss the arrangements at Christmas. He choked up and cried a little bit and told me "thank you." He said that after he called the first time he felt convicted to call back as a dad and give me the opportunity to have an out. Once again, I can't state this enough - I appreciate that about my dad. In one of the hardest moments of his entire life, faced with his wife being diagnosed with a terminal disease, he was still able to think about me as his daughter and not just about himself. However, that just made me want to help and be there for them even more.

Christmas that year was a little rough as all of us wondered if it would be our last Christmas. We tried to make the most of it and had all three of us kids together since, for the first time in years. After Christmas, I flew back to Washington and turned in my two-week resignation. That was a hard resignation to turn in because I had only been working for the company (Boeing contractor) about six months - a large portion of that was training. I felt like I had robbed the company by leaving so quickly after they had spent so much time training me. I was also informed that I was on the fast track for team-lead from a couple of the other leads who were disappointed that I was leaving. (In retrospect I wonder if that "carrot" was dangled in front of me to tempt me to turn my back on my parents. The deceiver is sneaky that way – tempting us with what is worldly when we are trying to do what is right)

Proverbs 16:3 (ESV)
3 Commit your work to the Lord, and your plans
will be established.

I knew I was doing the right thing when I walked into that manager's office to tell him why it was that I was turning in my resignation. I didn't know this him very well, as most of the time I just worked with the team leads. Honestly, I can't even remember his name (I think it was Steve) but I can remember the impression he made on me that day in his office. After I sobbed my way through telling him that I had to quit because my mom was going to die and I needed to go home and help care for her and that I felt bad because the company had spent so much money training me but there was no choice and I wouldn't make any other choice even if I thought I could (it is run together here because I am pretty sure I ran it all together, tears and snot dripping down my face).

He looked at me and said – "you're doing the right thing. Don't think twice about leaving this company". He confirmed that I was being considered for the next team lead position, but he admired that I was leaving to go help my mom. He also told me that he would be a reference for me and that if ever I came back, they would rehire me in a second.

What a relief to get that kind of reaction from somebody who owes you nothing. He made good on his promise as well. When I went to a recruiter in Oklahoma City they checked my references, including this gentleman. They told me that he had given me a glowing recommendation and that was one of the reasons I was referred to what later became a permanent position at Dobson Communications.

The last week in January mom and dad flew up to help me move. We decided to make it a family affair and to enjoy each other's company on the way home. Mom and dad rented a moving vehicle and we loaded everything I owned into a 15-foot truck. Including the cat. The company we rented from had a truck cab with a bench seat (instead of two buckets) so that all three of us would fit. Typical of these moving trucks, it was quite a bit off the ground. At this time mom's right leg was movable but she tended to drag it. Her right arm hung down at her side with her fingers beginning to curl but she could still move it at her elbow and wrist but couldn't grip very well.

Off we went driving south to Portland then heading east across northern Oregon, where we stayed the first night having gotten a late start. Then we headed into Idaho and down towards Salt Lake City -cutting east again over the mountains and into Wyoming. The weather was cooperating nicely. I had made this trip with my mom once before, right after I left WSU, and we had horrible snow the entire time. This time it was clear and cool and the snow was already on the ground, not falling.

We pulled into Cheyenne fairly late. We were all tired of being cramped in the rental truck. We had discovered along the way, at the first stop, that mom couldn't climb into the high cab of the truck without a lot of help. She couldn't get a good grip with her hands, so pulling herself into the cab of the truck was out of the question. We had purchased a wooden two-step folding ladder and we used this for her to get in. She could turn sideways on the front seat, dangling her legs out the open door and, using gravity, slid her butt down the seat to get out (with one of us in front of her to stop her from pitching forward if she wobbled or lost balance).

This was just over a year after she first began having voice difficulty and her symptoms were becoming more noticeable. Her speech was slurred so that you could understand about 7 out of 10 words, which meant she was still easy to communicate with. She had to clear her throat a lot, and her voice tone was flat, with very little inflection.

All of us, being tired, wanted food and the bed, in that order. There was a restaurant right across the street from the hotel, so we checked in and dropped off our travel bags, then drove across to the restaurant. It was a busy, four-lane road near the highway, and it was COLD, I think in the teens, and bitterly dry. Too cold, dark, and busy to walk across the street after we were done eating.

When we sat down to order, dad, who had done over half the driving of our slow moving truck (governed to not allow us to go over about 65, downhill) said: "I want a beer". Well, I was 26 and wired from the stress, so I decided to order a drink also to help me unwind and sleep. After all, I was having to spend the night in a hotel (as an adult) with my parents. To our surprise, mom decided to order a Long Island Ice Tea. (She didn't understand what she was ordering). Both dad and I just looked at her. She just smiled at us, said "WHAT?" all innocently, then proceeded to order the drink when the waitress came.

-TIME OUT of the book for an explanation-

I want to explain that I was not raised to drink much. While we are Southern Baptist, who tend to endorse abstinence from all alcohol consumption, my parents hadn't raised me that way. They had said that nothing, absolutely nothing, should ever take the place of God in my life. If anything prevented me from living a God-centered life, then I should cut that out of my life.

Matthew 22:37 (ESV)
37 And he said to him, "You shall love the Lord
your God with all your heart and with all your soul
and with all your mind.

They also taught me that anything that impaired my judgment or my ability to reason and be a testimony to God, was not good, and this could include alcohol consumption. Therefore, we were raised that legally drinking at a very moderate rate was okay, with some conditions (not being a stumbling block, not if you have a predisposition for alcoholism in your family) but drunkenness, was not.

Romans 14:13 (ESV)
Do Not Cause Another to Stumble
13 Therefore let us not pass judgment on one
another any longer, but rather decide never to put a
stumbling block or hindrance in the way of a
brother.

Proverbs 20:1 (ESV)
Wine is a mocker, strong drink a brawler,
and whoever is led astray by it is not wise.

I think I saw my parents drink about 4-5 times a year growing up – Christmas or Thanksgiving, Independence Day, maybe when we went to a gourmet burger or pizza place. Never had I seen mom drink more than one or dad drink more than two in a single sitting. So, I am not advocating drinking alcohol. I want to explain how I was raised and acknowledge that some Christians reading this have different views on alcohol consumption. I believe any substance with the potential to seriously harm you or others should be approached biblically, prayerfully, cautiously, and with knowledge. I was raised to view any substance with the ability to distort reality and take the focus off of God as bad. I was also raised and came to believe even stronger after an experience I will relate later in this book, that some things aren't worth the risk; and also that we need to make sure we do not do anything that would harm our testimony or lead others to fall into habitual or lifestyle sin, which alcohol is very prone to do. Therefore, having a drink after this drive was not a common occurrence for my parents, and the telling of this story is not me encouraging drinking. I want to be as transparent as I can be, and this story helps lead into a lesson learned which is valuable.

-TIME OUT over, flashback to the restaurant. -

We all ordered our drinks, including mom. We had a nice meal and headed out to the car. This is where the challenge began. Mom, after one drink, was seriously impaired. She was stumbling and dragging her leg more and she was, as my grandma would say. "tickled". It very dark and the parking lot was not even or well lit. She was already losing her balance from ALS but adding alcohol and it was like she was drunk, not like she had only one small drink.

Picture us, in the parking lot, bundled up in the freezing cold, trying to get her into the elevated moving truck, using a two-step ladder. Dad was behind her, pushing on her bottom, I was on the driver's side, leaned across the bench seat, holding her hands and trying to haul her up and in the truck cab. What was mom doing? Giggling. You read that right, giggling. She was laughing so hard she couldn't even help us. She fell face-first across the seat, with her feet still planted somewhat on the stool, just laughing and laughing.

Dad and I were not amused. We were so afraid she was going to get hurt, that the ladder would slip and she would fall backward, and she just kept laughing. We finally got her in, then had to try and set her upright. She couldn't use her arms to push her weight up due to the loss of movement, and her hands were curling and couldn't be flattened to give her a grip. We just couldn't seem right her in that small space, so Dad climbed over her and kind of crouched in the cab and let me drive across the street.

Then, we had to get a still silly mom inside the hotel and ready for bed. She wouldn't stop giggling. She even got the hiccups. Finally, we got her stripped down to undershirt and undies, and she was doing her nightly ritual (more on that later) of cleansing and creaming her face, and dad and I were just exhausted. Being in a hotel room, I was on one of the beds, unpacking, dad was at the sink brushing his teeth, and mom was using the mirror on the hotel wall.

Then all of a sudden…THUNK. She had just fallen over backward, like something out of a cartoon. Most people try and break their fall. Bend at the waist and sit if you are falling backward. Stick out your hands if you are falling forwards. Not mom. She fell straight back. Dad and I were so shocked, we just stood dumbfounded as we watched her slide to the floor. The only thing that broke her fall was that she fell into the hotel closet and the wall caught her.

Guess what? You guessed it she was giggling the entire time. She just sat there, while dad and I rushed over, *freaking out*, worried she was hurt. Dad and I got on either side of her (she was all floppy) and stood her up and put her to bed "as is". We had checked, and there was just a small red streak down her back where she had hit the wall and slid, but it didn't break the skin. She was asleep in moments and we were just shell shocked.

Lesson Learned: This one should be fairly obvious. Alcohol has many side effects. It is a depressant. It can cause numbness, irregular gait, loss of memory, loss of inhibitions, sleepiness, anger, increased urination, slurred speech – and all of those are normal possible side effects. Throw in the possible complications from medications, and the possible side-affects, and the degree those side effects manifest themselves!!! Well, read the story above. My recommendation is not to drink alcohol while taking medication or when seriously ill. You might not be prepared for the side effects. Also, often terminally ill people are depressed, and alcohol is a depressant.

Needless to say, mom never had another drink for the rest of her life. We also found out that one of the experimental medications she was on *very very very* clearly stated, do not take with alcohol. Lesson learned. That is the main reason for this memory. Make sure you understand side effects and interactions with medications. Also, be aware that certain illnesses may change tolerance levels.

Dad and I were able to retrospectively view this incident with the humor it probably deserved. It is just that sometimes the caregiver loses the humor in the situation, out of concern and fear for the person with the illness or condition. We probably could have helped her just as well and been as cautious with mom during this instance, but shared her humor, instead of being ruled by the fear we were feeling.

We continued the next day towards Oklahoma City, and my new life, intertwined with theirs. I am so thankful for that trip. We talked, we laughed, we cried. We shared a cab with my cat Phoenix and my beta fish.

I didn't know at that time, but that was the beginning of a phase in life (not a short season, as I had thought) as a caregiver. What I thought was a brief move to Oklahoma to help dad with end-of-life care for mom and to spend every chance I could just being with her, turned into 13 years of caregiving, first with my mom, and then with dad.

Chapter 6 - Enlisted or Recruited:

Being a Caregiver is a Choice...or is it?

1 Peter 4:10-11
As each one has received a special gift, employ it in
serving one another as good stewards of the
manifold grace of God. 11_Whoever speaks, is to do
so as one who is speaking the utterances of God;
whoever serves is to do so as one who is serving by
the strength which God supplies; so that in all
things God may be glorified through Jesus Christ, to
whom belongs the glory and dominion forever and
ever. Amen.

Is being a caregiver, if you are a Christian, a choice? This might seem like an odd question. I think that many caregivers would say they had no choice, but that isn't true. They might have felt like they had no choice, or there was no better choice, but the truth is, at some point, you make the choice (consciously or unconsciously) to be a caregiver.

There are so many options out there. There are short-term and long-term care facilities. Rehab facilities. Assisted living facilities. Even wards of the state, if no one steps forward to care for someone who can't care for themselves. Family member options. Paid companion options. Group homes, institutionalization or hospitalization options.

I think that most people who say they had no choice, really mean that, there was no other right choice but to be a caregiver. Caregiving might involve a combination of the above options, too. Being a caregiver means you take primary lead and accountability for the welfare of someone other than yourself. Someone who can't do it on their own and might be in a dire situation without someone else being accountable for them.

To me, there was no way I was ***not*** going to take care of my mother, and later my father. I didn't stop and think about who else might do it, I just knew I had to be involved. My upbringing and my faith dictated it, but it wasn't like I weighed any options. I just knew, thanks to the Holy Spirit, that this was my path. My sense of right and wrong, given by the Holy Spirit that lives inside of me, dictated it. I am thankful that I felt this way. God spared me from having to wrestle with my conscience, for which I am thankful and believe I can take no real credit. I will never have to live with the guilt of wondering if I should have done something. *Now, the guilt of wondering **whether I did a good enough job**, that is another matter, and we have to talk about that at some point later in the book.*

I was asked by many other caregivers why they were so alone in caregiving or why certain members of their family didn't help (often siblings). First, we can't really know why someone does or doesn't do something, and thinking you know someone's intentions can be judgmental. I don't' want to skip this discussion, though, because many caregivers spend a lot of time thinking about and wondering why they aren't getting help and support. I can't tell you WHY someone isn't helping you, caregiver, but you should know that you aren't alone in feeling unsupported. I can discuss what has been shared with me from other caregivers, or experienced by me.

While I was writing this chapter, I talked to my husband about what the theme of this chapter is (embracing caregiving or running from it). He said that being a Christian Caregiver is a calling, and that might be why others don't embrace caregiving. His opinion is that you had to be called by God, gifted by Him, and enabled by the Holy Spirit, for caregiving.

At that time, this didn't make sense to me, because I know other people who are caregivers that aren't Christian, and I think I know people who are Christian but aren't participating as caregivers, even when needed. He asked me if I was writing this about nurses and doctors and people in the medical field. I am not – this isn't geared towards those people whose career is caring for others. They get paid for their work. I am not saying that they aren't loving and compassionate and therefore drawn to those fields (or even called by God), because I believe many of them are. Reality is that they are monetarily compensated for the care they provide, and in the case of some, very handsomely. A caregiver, the type I am writing about, are not paid positions. They are those who have a loved one who is no longer capable of fully caring for themselves. Someone they are moved to care for, regardless of the challenges.

My circle of caregiver friends is small, but they are fellow Christians. I know there are others out there who aren't Christians, who are devoted and loving caregivers. My faith and the Bible lead me to believe that everything good comes from God – and since mankind was made in God's image, everything good that manifests in Man is because of the capacity to do good that God has given mankind. Therefore, a person doesn't have to be a follower of God to do good, as God has given us the ability to recognize and act on both good and evil. I don't know how someone, without knowing God, can make it through a prolonged period of caring for someone they love who is so dependent on them, without falling apart.

I struggled so much even having my faith to lean into and I am 100% sure I would not have made it through without that faith. Maybe it is because, to go through the process to be a caregiver; to mentally, physically, emotionally and spiritually survive some of these situations, you have to have God. Even as a Christian, with the Holy Spirit dwelling inside of me, I didn't come out unscathed. I can't imagine what I would have been like if I hadn't had God and His peace and comfort!

Isaiah 40:28-31
Have you not known? Have you not heard?

*The Lord is the everlasting God, the Creator of the
ends of the earth.
He does not faint or grow weary; his understanding
is unsearchable.
He gives power to the faint, and to him who has no
might he increases strength.
Even youths shall faint and be weary, and young
men shall fall exhausted;
but they who wait for the Lord shall renew their
strength; they shall mount up with wings like
eagles;
they shall run and not be weary; they shall walk and
not faint.*

My husband may be right (funny note, when Tony was editing this for me, he underlined the words *might be right* and put !! next to it. Smmph…silly). His point was that having the nature of a true caregiver, one that has submitted their will for God's Will and put someone else's wellbeing and needs above your own, is a calling as well as a ministry. In my case, it was also honoring my mother and father, which is a Biblical imperative. I know I didn't do it on my own, I did it powered by God. If that isn't the definition of a calling – *feeling as if you have no choice because there is no choice better than you sacrificially caring for the loved one, but knowing you can't do it on your own, only God can get you through it and equip you* - then I don't know what is. I didn't think about being a caregiver as a calling when the time presented the situation. I just knew, beyond any doubt, no hesitation, that taking care of first my mother, and then my father, was the thing that I must do, and I didn't even entertain another option.

Dr. R Albert Mohler Jr, a theologian and ordained minister, wrote an article called Consider Your Calling: The Call to Ministry (found on his website, posted July 15, 2004). I am not stating that being called to be a caregiver is the same as being called to be a pastor (he goes on in the article to describe a second call, which is more specific to being a church pastor). I believe every Christian has a call on their life to serve in ministry, so I believe these descriptions might help. He describes a call by quoting two other amazing pastors:

First, there is an inward call. Through His Spirit, God speaks to those persons He has called to serve as pastors and ministers of His Church. The great Reformer Martin Luther described this inward call as "God's voice heard by faith." Those whom God has called know this call by a sense of leading, purpose, and growing commitment.

Charles Spurgeon identified the first sign of God's call to the ministry as "an intense, all-absorbing desire for the work." Those called by God sense a growing compulsion to preach and teach the Word and to minister to the people of God.

I think if I were to write about what I felt in regards to caring for my parents, I could borrow from these two great men. I felt through faith a certainty that caring for my parents was what I needed to do. I also felt purpose in this and a desire for the work and knew that I was being used by God to minister to my parents in this situation.

So, that had me thinking because I still felt like there is a choice involved. If there wasn't, then all of the unsupportive people have a, to borrow from the Monopoly game "get out of jail free card". They can simply say – I didn't help because I wasn't called. However, I asked my husband, 'if your parent is sick and dying, how in the world could you NOT feel moved to serve and care'? I had a Christian friend whose dad was physically violent to her as a child, and had been estranged from him her adult life and she still took care of him when he became sick. It was hard for her, all of those memories of abuse, but she knew it was the right thing to do; and that if she didn't do it, no one else would and her father would suffer needlessly. She also knew that this would force her to confront painful memories and feelings and that it would take the Lord working through her to accomplish this task.

As mentioned earlier, my grandfather was not an easy father for my mother. However, it was never an option in her mind or heart to not care for him during the last few months of his life as he died of cancer. So how is it that some people, who don't have the excuse of scarred memories from their childhood, feel no obligation to help their loved ones? How can they, in some cases, actually hinder the process of caregiving for someone they love? Or hurt the person doing the caregiving?

We can't know. We are not God to see into their hearts and minds. Out of our conversation did come a few discussion points. For example - caring for others, especially your family, is bearing fruit and demonstrates your walk with God. Sacrificial service demonstrates your understanding of what Christ did first for us, and this is the Holy Spirit at work in you. This seems right, but I know some people that show fruit in other areas but haven't shown fruit in this area. We all have sin in our lives, or areas where we are not obedient, and that manifests in many ways. I can't point out someone else's issues without first pointing the finger inward, at all of mine, and the duties I have undoubtedly shirked over the years.

All in all, I can only write about what I believe based on my observations. Not only am I not a clinician, or counselor, I am also not a theologian (so you are getting all kinds of unqualified opinions in this book). I would say that I have observed and been told by other caregivers I have spoken to, that many choose to not be a caregiver. The reason I am writing about this isn't to try and guilt or shame those people – that isn't my right or my role. What I do want to do is let other caregivers know that this is a trend I have observed and spoken with others in a care capacity and that when they are frustrated and wondering why they seem to be the only one feeling the burden of care, they aren't alone.

Maybe if someone reads this who isn't helping their loved one, or the person giving care, if God wills it, they might be convicted to take a more active support role – but that is for God to convict and call, not me. I will say that based on my experience, and others who I know, that the caregiver would more than likely appreciate your willingness to be part of the caregiving responsibility.

Psalm 25:15-18 (ESV)
15 My eyes are ever toward the Lord,
for he will pluck my feet out of the net.
16 Turn to me and be gracious to me,
for I am lonely and afflicted.
17 The troubles of my heart are enlarged;
bring me out of my distresses.
18 Consider my affliction and my trouble,
and forgive all my sins.

This feeling of being alone and alienated happens to so many who are the caregivers, and can lead towards feelings of bitterness, frustration and anger. Relationships between your "patient" and others change. Also, your relationship changes with them as well. In the next few paragraphs, I will discuss some of the reactions I observed in people during my caregiving and speaking with other caregivers. I am sure this isn't a complete list, however, these reactions seemed fairly common. I will be addressing negative responses caregivers experience but I want to also include experiences with some amazing people who may come along, if you are blessed, as well. I am hoping to focus on behavior and avoid motivation or reasons for the behaviors.

One person you may encounter when you become either the caregiver and/or the care receiver is **a person who may remove themselves from the situation entirely**. Maybe they become more distant to the person suffering than they were before. They are no longer available for visits, calls, letters, or any contact at all. They might contact you briefly, to check on the person, but don't actually talk to or visit the care receiver. They may state that "it is too hard for me to see the patien in this condition" or "I don't know what to do or say" or "they don't know I am there anyway". Most of their justification for the behavior revolves around their thoughts and their feelings.

I would encourage you to remind them to think about what they have to offer their loved one. It may be very sad, particularly if the person you are caring for truly loves them, and misses them, and asks about them. I think these people need prayer and encouragement to stay engaged in the caregiving process.

Lesson Learned: I tried to protect my parents from the hurt that they were feeling when they weren't receiving calls/visits. I made much out of the smallest efforts made by others, to try and help my parents feel loved and valued. This only prolongs the realization for your care receiver. If they survive long enough, you will not be able to keep up a front or continue to exaggerate the efforts others put forth. I highly suggest praying for those people, honestly but kindly answering inquiries about them from the person you are caring for, and find other ways to bolster the spirits of your loved one. Lying (by deceit) to make someone feel better is still a lie, and lies have a habit of trapping you.

Another person the caregiver encounters is **one who doesn't engage in the actual daily work of being a caregiver but wants to be consulted and to advise** on the proper way of taking care of the person in need of assistance. For the caregiver this feels like someone who is a micromanager, someone who believes that they, despite not living in the situation, is better equipped to make the decisions than the person who daily gives care and companionship. This type may become upset if you do not follow their advice, ask for their advice, or show appreciation of their advice. They may use your reaction to their advice as an excuse to no longer interact with the person needing care. It becomes the caregiver's fault that they no longer come around or communicate and interact with the person who is ill.

> *Lesson Learned: This is hard to type (LOL) but listen to the advice. I have learned this lesson not by doing, but by maturing years later. If they are interested enough to offer advice, you can listen. It doesn't obligate you to follow that advice if it is not in the best interest of the person in which you care. I am glad I wrote this book years after my dad died because if I had written right away, these words of wisdom would not have come out of me. Bitter words would have come out. Angry and resentful words would have come out. Instead, be humble enough to quiet the objections and listen, and then, pray and do what is right in the eyes of the Lord.*

You may experience **jealous family members or friends**, who are wanting of the caregiver's time. These are the ones that complain about the amount of time you spend with the person for which you are caring. They may hint that getting a break from all of that hard caregiving would be healthy and beneficial to you, so they are doing you a favor by making you feel guilty that you aren't coming for a visit. In some ways, they are probably correct, the break would do you good. Also, I hope that you don't just assume that their motives are selfish because many will be encouraging you to take a break, out of a truly caring motivation.

However, this situation is when there is no consideration of the fact that a caregiver is a caregiver, despite holidays or weekends. That the stress of having to try and arrange appropriate, loving, competent care, not to mention the expense, may negate the benefit of "the break". Also, the feelings, concern, worry about the person you are caring for doesn't just get turned off because you went on a weekend getaway. Your anxiety and worry are ever-present (even when you trust the Lord, you will worry about your patient's care when you are not there).

A true break needs to be planned properly by the caregiver to satisfy their concern for their charge before they can truly let go and enjoy the break. Someone who is trying to guilt the caregiver into a visit is not doing the caregiver any good, only adding another burden and sense of obligation on top of the already steep duties. Caregiving will often become the top priority for a time, but others might not understand. Caregiver, don't feel that guilt. Those relationships, if strong, will be there on the other side.

> *Lesson Learned: If you can create a break for yourself, do it. It will take a lot of planning. However, caregivers don't shy away from a cause simply because it is hard work!*

What happens **when someone you are caring for was also supporting someone** else? Do you become the proxy supporter of that person? An example would an adult child or grandchild of the patient who wants the caregiver to continue to support them, even though the care receiver is no longer making independent decisions or capable of caring for themselves. There may have been some sort of understanding between the two, or just a burden felt by the patient to the person they were assisting. Do informal support relationships affect your care, or should they? The caregiver may continue to support them like the person you are caring for was, believing they are keeping their charge's wishes intact. Perhaps you intend to help, to honor the person you care for, by continuing in practices they had established. What happens though, if the care receiver is no longer able to make these decisions, or to offer the same type of help due to the change in circumstances? At what point does the person who is accustomed to assistance, if he or she is old enough to be independent, stop relying on the person who is themselves in need of care? What if, as a caregiver, you must withdraw the expected assistance to properly care for the person you have been placed in charge of, and to conserve their resources?

What if this practice was not outlined in the directives you were given (formal directives, such as a trust), and there are other relatives or organizations that you have been instructed to honor in the trust you are enacting?

Lesson Learned: It is good to establish limits. You are not the person you are caring for (a replacement), or their substitute. You have been entrusted with much, potentially their health decisions, their home, their finances, and care in general but you are probably not responsible for every obligation that they might have obligated themselves to. If you are caring for someone, make decisions in the realm you have been given, what benefits your charge. If you are capable of having your responsibilities documented, this may help if this situation arises.

In the section above I spoke about potential negative interactions with those you encounter as a caregiver. I pray that God will provide for your needs, including with the people He brings you in your time of need! Not all relationships will be so complicated, I hope!

Psalm 34:17-20 ESV
When the righteous cry for help, the Lord hears and
delivers them out of all their troubles. The Lord is
near to the brokenhearted and saves the crushed in
spirit. Many are the afflictions of the righteous, but
the Lord delivers him out of them all. He keeps all
his bones; not one of them is broken.

Amazing People

Before this becomes negative, making you assume you have to hold everyone at arm's length in self-preservation, let me mention other types of people you may encounter. Those who are a positive force who help hold you up, comfort you, share the burden and share the joys. Those who through their love and generosity, truly become family, and if already family, closer than before. They seem equally called to support the caregiver as you were to be a caregiver.

There are **distant supporters**. People who can't be there physically, but wish they could, and try and do everything they can from where they are. In my case, I had some of my mom's cousins and aunts who were these supports. They became the caregiver's emotional caregiver. They were my cheerleaders, support, encouragement. These people are a true blessing. My aunt Nancy and Uncle Dick called nearly every day. It might only be for 3 minutes, but they checked in. Sometimes they asked to talk to mom, but often they were calling for me. When they were able, they came by every few weeks, which was quite hard considering they had health problems of their own, but they made the effort. If my phone rang at 9 pm it was usually Aunt Nancy, she was punctual. My Aunt Jolene would call every few weeks, also. She lived several hours away and was having health issues herself. It turned out, she had ALS too, but she wasn't diagnosed until after mom, even though her symptoms began long before mom's. Her ALS seems to have been the more traditional type, starting with the extremities instead of the respiratory and speech areas. She would share her struggles with me, encourage me, and ask about mom. She would tell me how she wished she could visit, but she couldn't. My aunt Clara and uncle Ron and their daughter Ronda and her family lived in Houston. The year mom was dying they drove up several times, bringing joy and happiness (and my cousins Kitty and Megan) with them. They would fill our house with conversation and laughter and little girls. They would talk to mom, dad, and I and always make sure we had a great Mexican meal out, usually on their tab. I looked forward to those trips so much, as did dad and mom. In a different realm entirely than family, my dad's place of employment (Computer Science Corp, which has dissolved since then), also supported us from a distance. They allowed my father to travel much less the last year my mom was alive so that he could be home caring for her. They also sent us a huge gift certificate for a home meal delivery company that would bring us food from many local restaurants (this was novel back in 2001/2). This came in very handy when we had people come and visit and needed to provide a meal for 15 instead of our usual 3. All of these examples of remote support helped carry some of our burdens.

I hope you also **have people who are right there**, *In the Muck* with you. These are those people, maybe family, perhaps not, who pitch in to help. Perhaps it is someone who cleans your house for you (thank you Cathy) so that she or he can take one less responsibility off your plate. Or someone who offers to make a grocery store run so that you don't have to worry about leaving your loved one alone (once again, grocery delivery and pick up has made this much less of a concern). Possibly, you are blessed with someone who just understands that your loved one grows weary of staring at the same 4 walls or the same few faces (I mean, my face is pretty cute but I am sure my parents didn't think so after so many hours and days LOL). This person might come just to chat, read a book, watch TV, do a craft, cook a special treat. I was very blessed when my mother was ill to have these friends in my life. A few were family, but most were from my spiritual family, church members. Which leads me into the next group, church family.

I talk about our **church family** later in the book, under Building Your Army. However, I want to talk about the importance of having a church family. My parents were members of a church when I moved to Oklahoma, and I attended with them when I moved home. They had not been there long when mom became sick (about a year) however, they had fully incorporated themselves in the church, which was their custom. They were not passive attendees. I believe this was God's design for them, as this church family very much loved them when they became ill and needed a church family. In my current church, we call Wednesday night class Koinonia (which in the Greek means Christian fellowship). This can be fellowship both among believers and between a believer and God. I don't think a Christian should forsake fellowship if at all possible, particularly in times of stress. Plenty of Bible verses (Acts 2:42 and 1 John 1:7 are two examples) illustrate our need for each other. If you are a Christian caregiver, do not forsake koinonia, with God or with your fellow believers, as it will truly allow you to enjoy sweet fellowship at the house of God (Psalm 55:14) as you walk among other worshipers. Also, take your loved one to church as much (or as long) as possible. They will benefit from this time of communion both emotionally and spiritually. Our church family visited, brought meals, sent care items, prayed for us and with us, encouraged us, served us in practical ways, and generally helped us to feel loved and supported while mom was sick.

Lesson Learned: If you are caring for someone who has difficulty being transported (my mom had a special wheelchair, dad couldn't bend well, so needed to be somewhere he could be stretched out), go to the church and find a "spot or two" where they can be accommodated in the sanctuary or a class. If you need to, talk to someone who works for your church facility or an usher, so that this spot is made available to you. Get your most persuasive friend to lovingly stake your claim before service. This will help you help your person participate in worship on Sundays (or Wednesdays or whichever day you attend church) with as little fuss as possible. I have noticed most of those who are having to be cared for can become embarrassed enough by the "hassle" they BELIEVE they cause others, to decide to forgo attending service or events. Take away their excuse by being very organized and thoughtfully remove barriers.

Hebrews 10:24-25 (ESV)
And let us consider how to stir up one another to
love and good works, not neglecting to meet

together, as is the habit of some, but encouraging one another, and all the more as you see the Day drawing near.

Finally, we have our **Loving Distractors** – friends and family who help you take your mind off everything for a while. For me, this was usually my co-workers and my cousins, and old college buddies. My co-workers were aware of the situation I was dealing with at home. After all, I frequently had to leave for doctor appointments, work from hospital rooms, make or receive frantic phone calls when something was wrong, and twice I had to take extended Family Medical Leave Act (FMLA) time off to care for my parents. They invited me to lunch, where we were goofy and relaxed. They invited me out after work on Fridays and weren't upset when I said I couldn't go, and were happy when I said I could. More importantly, if I said I couldn't for multiple weeks in a row, they didn't stop asking, assuming that the answer was no. They were lovingly persistent. They invited me over for dinner to watch American Idol (Thank you Tammy, Tom, Justin) where they made me, I mean, *allowed me* to cook <grin> and then loudly enjoyed my food. This gave me a creative outlet (cooking was a joy), a willing clientele, and some much-needed diversions. This meant that when I went home to dad, I wasn't so pent up. It was an aunt and uncle (miss you Uncle Gary) and my cousins who made me food, listened to me talk for hours or instead watched silly movies with me. I pray that you have these delightful distractors who don't treat you like a victim and expect you to be sad all the time. They let you feel how you needed to feel without expectations. They also occasionally played a very rousing game of spoons where laughter and spoons flew around the room, lifting the spirits of all.

Not a Victim

Why are these last few types of people so important to have in your life as a caregiver? You are not a victim and you don't have to be sad all of the time, even when going through very sad circumstances. The Bible says:

1 Thessalonians 5:16-18 (ESV)
Rejoice always, pray without ceasing, give thanks in
all circumstances; for this is the will of God in
Christ Jesus for you.

When people expect that you will be sad and depressed all of the time because of your circumstances, they don't understand the power of the Christ that lives within believers. True sometimes in my circumstance I got sad, angry, and frustrated, but through it all I had joy. I was able to see my parents daily and I was able to continue to learn from them and with them until their end. I was able to see the testimony of Christ in them as they dealt with chronic and terminal illnesses. I was privileged to be their caretaker, and I was not a victim. I couldn't have acted out some contrived, extended depression if I had wanted to. I have the Holy Spirit living inside me and He compels me to rejoice, pray and give thanks in all circumstances.

You may be familiar with the hymn, "It is Well with My Soul" by devout Christian, Horatio Spafford? This hauntingly beautiful hymn, one of my favorites, was penned by a man who knew so much loss in his life. His business ventures burned to the ground in a great The Great Chicago fire. This came soon after the death of a baby son. Planning a trip with his wife and daughters to help overcome the sadness of their tragedy, he planned visit to Europe with his wife and daughters in 1873. At the last minute, he had to stay behind for work, and planned to join them later. Their ship crashed into another vessel and sank. Only his wife survived (four daughters died). In a matter of year he had lost all of his children and the majority of his investments. It is believed he wrote this song on his way to join is wife as he approached the site of the collision. He later went on to experience both blessings (more children and financial success) as well as loss. What he saw in the midst of tragedy is God's strength. Song lyrics in this song about life circumstances include:

When sorrows, like a sea billows roll
Tho' Satan should buffet, tho' trials should come

and he speaks of his lot (what is given to him) and his sin. However, the hope and joy he knows exist in Christ also are shown in the lyrics when he pens (not in order of the song):

That Christ hath regarded my helpless estate
And hath shed His own blood for my soul.
My sin – no in part but in whole,
Is nailed to His corss and I bear it no more.

He declares that even has he is being buffeted and attacked and we must wait for the day for Christ to return, it is well with his soul and he must praise the Lord. I love one small nuance in this song, that I overlooked when learning the song as a child. The line is "*Whatever my lot,* **Thou** *hast taught me to say*". I put in bold THOU. God has taught this man to say that it is well with his soul. We learn this through the reading and the promises found in God's Holy Word, the Bible. When we are in the midst of tragedy God Himself gives us joy, peace, love, HOPE. Hallelujah! (Praise be to the Lord). I am so thankful for the Lord giving me strength and the relationships He sent me to help me through the hard trials of caregiving.

It was very difficult being around people who would constantly ask me, with pity in their eyes and voices, "are you okay, how are you holding up?" If I said 'I'm doing fine, or well", they would crowd in and ask if I was sure, or remind me that my mom was dying, or dad was in pain, and seem surprised that I could be doing well. It is exhausting to be sad all of the time. I don't know how people do it! I can't. I must listen to the Spirit within me, and the Spirit within me reminds me that all of life is part of God's perfect plan for my life, that I must have faith. So, I say again, a caregiver is not a victim. A caregiver is an instrument in the hands of the Lord.

Romans 8:28 (ESV)

And we know that for those who love God all things work together for good, for those who are called according to his purpose.

Chapter 7 - Going into Combat

Know the Enemy, Develop a strategy

As I caregiver, I find that the more I know, the better caregiver I can be. In my experience as a caregiver, I have had to learn a lot about issues that I might never have even heard, had God not used me in this capacity. These include ALS, attention deficit disorders (ADD/ADHD), pancreatic cancer, blood clots, and the co-morbidities that might come from these illnesses. Co-morbidities are related issues that are not the main disease or illness but are more likely to occur because of the main issue/disease. (Much like a hurricane will also spawn tornados and tidal surges.) This chapter is to show how I sought knowledge about the diseases I was encountering as a caregiver and to encourage you to do so as well.

Before I go into more details regarding specific diseases my family suffered from, I wanted to start with one that seems to be a co- morbidity of many illnesses. That is depression. Depression is an enemy that isn't "contagious" but can affect the caregiver and the care receiver both. Merriam Webster online dictionary defines depression as:

- *a state of feeling sad: dejection*
- *a mood disorder marked especially by sadness, inactivity, difficulty in thinking and concentration, a significant increase or decrease in appetite and time spent sleeping, feelings of dejection and hopelessness, and sometimes suicidal tendencies*

As you combat the obvious enemy (specific diseases and illnesses) be aware of depression, sneaking up on you and your care receiver. The only true way to combat depression is with the love of God (I am not saying that there aren't other good treatments of depression, but I do not believe we can determine or treat the root cause of depression without God). We find hope by being grounded in the scripture and the promises that God has given His children. Those promises hold true, even (or especially) in the midst of our battles. It might be necessarily as a caregiver for you and your patient to remind each other:

Philippians 4:8 (ESV)
8 Finally, brothers, whatever is true, whatever is
honorable, whatever is just, whatever is pure,
whatever is lovely, whatever is commendable, if
there is any excellence, if there is anything worthy
of praise, think about these things.

If you can't remind each other, then surround yourself with those who can point you to the Lord and all the good that He has done for you.

Early in dad's sickness, when things were at the darkest, I took a black marker and wrote all over a mirror in his bathroom, where he had to see it daily, the blessings he had been given. He was ready to give up, I was frustrated, and we both needed to focus less on our current circumstance and more on the abundances God continued to provide us. It helped me as much to write these for him as it did (I hope) him to be reminded of them. Dad also took medication to combat depression, as his body's ability to regulate his hormones was compromised by his surgery and other medications.

Medicine and constant reminders of blessings helped the care receiver, but I needed help as the caregiver as well. I had friends who helped me through my depression – with love, encouragement and even moments of diversion and fun. I was not always as receptive to this as I could have been, but I appreciated the efforts. I just wanted to take a moment and share about this enemy which can attack all involved in the care process, before moving onto the specific disease enemies. I love what King David wrote in Psalm 40. I think these are some of the true, honorable, pure, and lovely words that you dwell on when you feel the weight of adversity. This is what will allow you to lift up a praise when going to battle!

Psalm 40:1-3 ESV
1   I waited patiently for the Lord;
he inclined to me and heard my cry.
2 He drew me up from the pit of destruction,
out of the miry bog,
and set my feet upon a rock,
making my steps secure.
3 He put a new song in my mouth,
a song of praise to our God.
Many will see and fear,
and put their trust in the Lord.

My first two experiences with caregiving, as mentioned before were through my mother and her caregiving for her parents. Her dad, my grandpa, had lung cancer. What I did know was that this type of cancer was largely preventable. He had been a smoker for most of his life. I do remember that he had a quick decline and one day near the end my grandfather had his daughters bring in his older grandsons to make them promise not to smoke (I heard this from my older brother, who was one of them).

My next experience was in college when my maternal grandmother was diagnosed with pancreatic cancer. She lived a few months after she began showing symptoms. During that, I learned how some cancers show very few symptoms until it is either too late or nearly too late for treatment. The long weekend I spent giving mom and Aunt Marsha some respite I also learned that pancreatic cancer can change your taste for food. This had caused my grandmother to not want to eat, or only eat a few, select foods. In her case, fried eggs on buttered toast. I also learned at this time that illness can also bring out some peculiar behaviors in people.

Grandma only wanted my mom to make her egg, not my aunt. My aunt had lived closer to grandma her entire life and they were very close (and I know for a fact she was a great cook). For some reason she thought my aunt couldn't cook the egg the same so my mom needed to do the egg frying. When I came to visit, I wanted to give mom and my aunt time off. This meant I got to make the egg. My aunt warned me she wouldn't like it because mom didn't make it. Mom told me exactly how she wanted it, and I gave it my very best. My egg was determined by grandma after much scrutiny and a taste, to be acceptable and nearly as good as my mom's. This irritated my aunt. She, however, told me that even though she didn't like that her egg wasn't good enough, she understood that what was important was the comfort of her mom, even if that meant being humbled by a fried egg. This taught me to look at the mental state of the patient, as well as the physical.

Lesson Learned: Ill people aren't always rational or reasonable. Some of this may be caused by actual physical results of their illness and some may be manifestations of the emotional anguish that comes with their physical state. You can spend your time being frustrated and arguing with them, or you can just choose to love and abide together (Romans 12:10 and Ephesians 4:32). I have done plenty of all three (frustrated, arguing, and abiding), and I highly recommend the abiding option. It doesn't mean you can't try to reason with them, just don't try and grind in a point to the extent where animosity is maintained, and bitterness has a chance to flourish and grow. Heed Proverbs 15:1 and let soft words turn away anger.

Remember chapter 2 and a legacy of caregiving? My aunt was also a wonderful caregiver, and her daughter also became an amazing caregiver to her parents years after this experience. I am sure that that watching our mom's experience this with their mom contributed to her caregiving call.

Only about a year and a half after my maternal grandma died, my paternal grandma (biological) became ill. My aunt and uncle had recently moved her from Minnesota to Oklahoma so she would be close to family. I was spending my college summer break in Oklahoma on an internship at the zoo, so this was my first experience truly caregiving, with my cousin Dawn to help.

What was frustrating about this experience is that we didn't have a diagnosis. Grandma was type 2 diabetic, which I learned more about that summer, but there was something else "wrong" that we just didn't understand. She had gotten what seemed like a virus sometime in the spring, and just never seemed to recover. That summer we struggled with understanding what was going on. We struggled together to help her all that we could, with our limited knowledge and experience. I learned to give an injection for insulin (before that I had given many injections to animals, but never to a human). When she lost her appetite, I learned to try different types of food to find what appealed (we found that she also wanted an egg, only this time boiled). I learned how frustrating it was to try and get a doctor's appointment for someone on Medicare who had just moved from another state and so hadn't completed a transfer of care.

The biggest thing I learned that summer was to be still and listen. You see, my grandmother knew she was dying. She didn't know from what, but she knew it was the end. The problem was we were so busy trying to make her well, that we were bullying her into treatment that she didn't want. After one particularly frustrating day, when we came over after work to find her trapped in the bathtub, in cold water, unable to get out, I finally started listening. She hadn't eaten her food that morning. She had gotten in a tub, even though she was weak and "should have waited for us to help". I was in the middle of chastising her when I really looked at her. She was respectfully paying attention to my lecture, but I could tell there was something different in her attitude. I stopped, looked her in the eyes, and then asked her "Are you dying grandma?". She met my gaze and calmly answered "Yes". I truly believe it was the Holy Spirit that gave me discernment to stop railing at my poor grandma and instead see her.

I learned that day to respect the patient and listen to them. I couldn't research a disease I didn't know about, but I could learn from the patient how the disease was affecting her. I stopped browbeating my grandma and just started caring for her needs and enjoying the time I had with her. One bonus of this was that my cousin and I got to spend a few hours with grandma while she gave us some of her jewelry. She didn't have a lot of expensive jewelry, but she had some pieces that had been her mom's, my great-grandma. She didn't give it all to us – we were aware that there were two daughters and other granddaughters, but what was most precious were the stories that she told us. I now know that royal blue was my great grandma's favorite color and that the broach and earring set I have (costume jewelry, colored glass) was one of her favorites. I know that the small ring I have, diamond long gone, was her mother's 25th-anniversary band. The missing diamond, I replaced with a tiny tanzanite, also a blue gem to honor Great Grandma Marsh. If I had continued to pressure my grandma to do my will, I might have missed that afternoon of stories.

Lesson Learned: Others have shared a similar experience or observation with me. Sometimes people seem to know when they are dying or getting close to death. If we do not listen to them, respect them, we might pressure them into a level of care they don't want. As Christians (my grandma was a believer) we don't need to fear death. We know what God has promised us. I believe sometimes the caregiver fears death more than the dying believer. If the person you love is a believer, and they are ready to die, consider asking their wishes, respecting those wishes, enjoying time with them, and comforting them as they make a dignified exit from their mortal life, into their eternal one. They know what is in store for them, and they have hope and peace.

Hebrews 2:14-15 (NIV)
Since the children have flesh and blood, he too
shared in their humanity so that by his death he
might break the power of him who holds the
power of death—that is, the devil— and free those
who all their lives were held in slavery by their
fear of death.

My grandma was finally diagnosed with pancreatic cancer. I lost both of my biological grandmother's to this sneaky disease. She passed away about 6 weeks after I went back to college. I have done some research on this disease because I have it on both sides of my family and I have had digestive issues for years. Knowing that this disease does not show symptoms until it is advanced will help me to request screening as I get older, or maybe even get genetic testing should it become available.

Lou Gehrig's Disease. ALS – Amyotrophic Lateral Sclerosis. This is a neurological disease that is progressive, often rapid, with a loss in nerve cell response. This leads to a lack of muscle action and control. What I learned about this disease is that you don't want to have it or be diagnosed with it, as there is no known cure and treatment is largely experimental and not overly effective. There is no known cure and until recently, not much known about the cause. They have made many discoveries lately around the genes involved in this disease, and have found some genes related to both the sporadic and familial (hereditary) versions, but do not believe they have found all of the genes that lead to this deadly disease.

I learned during mom's diagnosis process that they will try and rule out every disease before they deliver this diagnosis. At one time, mom was diagnosed with a similar, yet treatable disease, Myasthenia Gravis, in the hope to have some avenue of treatment.

We learned that while trying to find another disease to blame instead of ALS may give the patient hope, it can also cause painful and unnecessary treatment. In mom's case, they did both dialysis and removed her thymus gland, in an attempt to treat MG, which she never had. Both the dialysis and thymus removal brought pain and did nothing to slow or stop the progression of her true ailment, ALS. The reason they were looking at MG, is because it frequently affects the face, mouth and respiratory muscles, and mom's symptoms included weakness in these areas. ALS most commonly starts with extremity weakness, but there is a rarer version of ALS called Bulbar ALS. This version destroys the corticobulbar area of the brainstem early in ALS, which affects muscles in the face, head, and neck. This version of ALS progresses faster than typical ALS.

Lesson Learned: There is a reason they call it medical practice. Doctors do not have all the right answers, all the time. There may be periods of no diagnosis, misdiagnosis, partial diagnosis. This can be very frustrating. I highly recommend that you educate yourself on every potential as they are presented. That you learn what the diagnostic tests can determine, or not determine. That you begin to understand the use of specific blood tests, diagnostic tests, diagnostic equipment, and other tests such as lab tests and results. This will help you understand when it seems like the doctors and nurses and technicians are speaking a foreign language. It is my observation that being able to speak the same language brings respect and a better chance of them being forthright with you. This might take writing everything down that they say, asking questions, taking home and reading the paperwork, and hours of googling. But it is worth it!

Knowing you can't cure ALS and that it is 100% fatal, allows you to go about caregiving differently. We wanted to find ways to treat and understand the symptoms the best we could. We learned about potentially painful spasms, and what we could do if mom had them, which, fortunately, she did not. We learned about losing the ability to swallow, even the small stuff like the saliva naturally produced all day, every day. We were able to get a medication that reduced saliva production, to help keep her from choking. We were able to make home modifications, in anticipation of the disease progression. Some of which were: widening doorways to allow for a large wheelchair, moving in a hospital bed with a lift, getting her fitted for a BiPap (not just a CPAP) to help her breath, and removing the garden tub and replacing it with a shower stall that lacked a ridge at the threshold so we could roll the wheelchair into the shower.

All of these are battle preparation – preparing to do battle with the disease, the enemy. Dad was able to find a computer program that would allow mom, with minimal mouse movement and hand movement, to select pre-recorded and created phrases, so she could continue to communicate when she could no longer form words. This program even allowed for the use of a nose mouse – a small metallic, reflective dot that was placed, like a sticker, on her nose. A laser projector was clipped to her laptop lid, and tracked her small head movements, and moved the mouse pointer on the screen. She could then do a single click to select phrases, letters for spelling sentences, or to ring a call bell for us. I just have to read this to hear the sound of the computer say "a necessary bodily function must be executed" (that's "I need to pee or poop" in layperson terms).

Lesson Learned: Technology. There is an ever-growing reservoir of technology available that can help caregivers and patients. My mom had a mobile speaking device that she could carry, that she could type on and it would both display her message and speak her message. She was able to use the computer setup listed in the paragraph above to type 8 autobiographical single space pages of notes on her life before she became too exhausted and she couldn't type anymore. These words are without price to me! Learn what technology is available to meet your needs. For dad, I wish I had installed an alarm system with cameras in the house, and notifications when the door was opened. This might have brought me peace of mind when I couldn't be home with him during the early years of his illness before we hired an aide.

Knowing your illness also allows the making of particular decisions in advance. For example, mom decided not to do anything to prolong her illness. She was able to tell dad that she didn't want a respirator or a feeding (Peg) tube put in or used to prolong her life. She was able to get her medical protectorate and DNR drawn up and signed and notarized, as well as a Will and Power of Attorney.

I would like to point out that these types of decisions should be shared and if at all possible, discussed beforehand. In mom's case, she did not want a feeding tube. However, I was the primary person trying to feed her. She wanted to eat, she still felt hunger, so I tried to feed her. However, it was a slow and laborious process, and often she choked despite my best efforts to make the food soft and the bites small. She just couldn't chew and swallow well. It was not uncommon for us to be sitting, trying to get half a cup of food into her, for over an hour. She frequently choked and I had to use the suction device and tube to clear her airway. Once or twice dad even had to use the Heimlich Maneuver to clear her airway of food. After a few months of painful dinner sessions, where we would both end up crying – she in frustration and hunger, me in fear and frustration, she finally agreed to a feeding tube. Dad told her he respected her right to not die dependent on machines breathing and feeding her, but that this would not make the disease go away (the feeding tube) and would drastically increase not only her quality of life but ours as well. Mom loved and respected dad and listened to his reasoning. This made her last few months of life much more pleasant. I know this was a choice she had not wanted to make, as it would only prolong death, but she did it for me and dad, to bring us relief.

One of my fond memories of this time was when she asked for coffee in her feeding tube. She missed coffee. A Lot. We had just put chocolate Ensure down the tube, then flushed it. So, we thought, WHY NOT? We cooled the coffee and put it in the tube. A few minutes later, she burped, then a HUGE smile spread across her face, and she pointed to her computer. She then spelled out for us that when she burped, she got to taste the chocolate Ensure and the coffee mixture, and it was like drinking a Mocha, which I had introduced her to years earlier when she visited me at Washington State University, in the Bookie (Student Bookstore) coffee shop. She loved it, and from then on, she got a mocha every day!

Lesson Learned: They will probably tell you not to put regular food into a feeding tube. They gave us this warning with dad's tube. I am not going to tell you to ignore their statements (because we did have some scares where we struggled with a plugged tube)...but...if we had followed all of the rules, we never would have invented a feeding tube coffee shop special. Just saying!

Dad's Illness

Knowing your disease helps you prepare. When dad got sick, we learned about Chordoma cancers, and particularly chordoma of the clivus. Until then, I barely remembered studying the tiny clivus bone in the skull in anatomy. I didn't know much about bone cancer, much less a bone cancer that is caused by a remnant from tissue from fetal development! We learned that this was a rare type of cancer, a rare location, and a difficult surgery with a high percentage of something going wrong. Risky surgery, risky follow-up radiation, short post-treatment life expectancy, possibility of re-occurrence from metastases. All of this translated for dad to "get your affairs in order", which he did.

Dad was able to find an excellent surgeon and identify where Proton Radiation was offered; and make decisions based on his preferences, instead of not having a choice. For example, at the time, he had the choice of Proton therapy in Massachusetts or at Loma Linda, California. Loma Linda was about an hour and a half from his mother (Gigi, as we called her), so he was able to make arrangements to spend the four months there, instead of isolated in Massachusetts. The surgery to remove the tumor, at that time, often resulted in the severing of one carotid artery, which led to a higher chance of stroke. He was able to find a doctor who was performing the tumor removal endoscopically, through the nasal opening. This is performed more commonly now, but it wasn't at that time (2002) and this approach increased his odds of surviving the tumor removal surgery and faster recovery time with fewer post-surgical complications. (I believe his surgical intern/trainee told me that it was only the 3rd time it had been done this way, at least in the US, at that time)

Lesson Learned: Dad taught me that you have treatment options you might not be aware of. He advocated for these options directly with both his primary doctor, specialists, and the insurance company. They wanted to send him to the East Coast, simply because they typically sent patients there, but there was nothing in the "manual" that dictated they had to. Therefore, simply by stating his preference, he was able to have treatment close to family, and in better weather (I mean, would you rather spend August through December in Massachusetts or sunny Southern California?).

What I wish we had known more about was cranial swelling. We were so impressed by the Proton Radiation treatment capabilities, being able to target and radiate very specific areas, and spare surrounding areas, and brain swelling wasn't even on our radar, that we didn't consider the side effects. Cranial swelling from radiation is what caused the majority of issues in dad after treatment, and may have been preventable if we had known what to look for. When radiation was done, he seemed normal for about two weeks. However, the damage done by his brain swelling and the lesions forming throughout his brain (as well as a chunk of his brain being removed) caused short term memory loss, lack of ability to create new memories, lack of ability to make good judgments, loss of understanding of the passing of time, and extreme pain.

Unlike with mom, with dad I had to learn much more than the disease. ALS killed my mother. The nerves controlling the muscles of her diaphragm stopped communicating, and she stopped breathing. Dad didn't die from a Chordoma. He died from the deterioration of his body, over 12 years, after being treated for chordoma cancer. With him, we had to treat the "fall out", which kept changing over time. At one time during dad's illness we had his pain doctor look at us and tell him that he didn't have any other patients worse than dad. That dad's pain was the worse he had ever seen and he couldn't encourage dad by telling him that "others have it worse" than him. That was how bad the consequences of cancer and treatment were for dad. The final effect of this decline for dad was kidney stones and his body's inability to maintain proper blood pressure. Each of these issues had a list of causes, effects, treatments (side-affects), and complications. In other words, the longer you are a caregiver, the more you will have to "learn and adapt" to every changing needs of your charge.

I work in the Information Technology (IT) field. One methodology of software development is the Agile Approach. In Agile, you work towards small goals over short timelines (sprints of about 2 weeks). One of the goals of this methodology is to fail fast, fail often, learn fast, learn often. The same applies to caregiving. You are going to fail (or a treatment or medicine may fail) sooner or later during caregiving. The trick is to learn, adapt, and move forward. With all those I have had the privilege to care for we have had to adjust to trial and error. Dwelling on failure didn't help and it would have been just as destructive to have not learned from the mistakes. God cover's our mistakes with grace, compassion, mercy, forgiveness. While the below verse isn't about our mistakes in caregiving, we should know that our weaknesses and mistakes are something we should give to the Lord as we seek to serve the one we love and care for.

2 Corinthians 12:9-10 (ESV)
9 But he said to me, "My grace is sufficient for you, for my power is made perfect in weakness." Therefore I will boast all the more gladly of my weaknesses, so that the power of Christ may rest upon me. 10 For the sake of Christ, then, I am content with weaknesses, insults, hardships, persecutions, and calamities. For when I am weak, then I am strong.

I am currently a parent. I wasn't a parent during my mom's illness. I became a parent 6 years into my caregiving for dad, so after the worst of it was over (the first four years were consumed by a semi-coma, extreme short-term memory loss and then his battle with alcoholism as a form of self-medication), I began the adoption process. Being a parent is being a caregiver. Most of the time this is standard parenting. Our daughters have some different medical needs as a result of the care they received in their primary years. I have applied what I learned during the above caregiving opportunities, to learn more about their diagnosis, and how it manifests in them. This involves research, observation, and specialists. It involves trying different techniques or medications and changing as needed to best suit their needs. It involves a village, or a team, to monitor and help them achieve the best they can with the help of prayer, medication, structure, counseling, communication, help in school, extra monitoring and attention, etc. Building a team is important, and I would love to talk about that next.

Chapter 8 - Building an Army (Team)

Proverbs 27:17-18 (ESV)
17 Iron sharpens iron, and one man sharpens
another.

The last chapter was about knowing your enemy when you go into combat. This one is about building an army. We need help in caregiving. We need to be sharpened by others spiritually, emotionally, and physically. It is easy to become isolated as a caregiver. Your focus changes and your life can come to center on the person you are caring for. This can almost become inevitable, depending on the level of care needed, but I am not saying this is right. God should always be the center of your life. Chances are if you are a devoted Christian caregiver, He already is. Don't forget that your spouse, if you are married, and your children, if you have them, should still be your focus, after the Lord. This, of course, assumes that one of these is not the person for whom you have become the caregiver.

This is hard, establishing a proper set of priorities; as often it seems that you are so needed by the person you care for, that often it seems justifiable to let the others "fend for themselves". You might feel that this is only short term and that everyone will understand (and this might actually be a fact). However, you never know exactly how long you might be needed. My dad was given 6 weeks to 3 months to live in January 2003, and he survived 11 more years! Remember to keep your priorities Biblically based. That being said, as mentioned in an earlier chapter, my husband suggested that being a caregiver is a calling, and a calling should have the appropriate priority placed on it. You might have to remind others of this, or even yourself, on why this person requires so much of your time and energy.

That being said, look for help. Seek, recruit, and train up an army to help you. You will be tempted to go this war alone, be a brave hero (martyr), trudging through battle after battle, collecting scars and wounds for your valiant effort. You may feel that no one understands, so you can't share with them this responsibility. Don't fall into this trap. God will provide what you need, but you might have to look for it, reach for it, pray for it, and work for it! Don't grow dull trying to do this all on your own.

I want to start with the obvious. A **medical team**. Doctors and nurses. You are the advocate for your charge to the medical team. In the case of my dad, once the initial surgery and radiation was complete we had to move beyond the distant specialists and seek a local primary physician. Building a medical team has monetary and insurance considerations, so let's first segue to that topic.

Dad lost his company's insurance when he could no longer work. This is partly my fault because at 28 years old, I didn't know much about COBRA.

Lesson Learned: Consolidated Omnibus Budget Reconciliation Act of 1985 (COBRA). Per the Department of Labor website: "The Consolidated Omnibus Budget Reconciliation Act (COBRA) gives workers and their families who lose their health benefits the right to choose to continue group health benefits provided by their group health plan for limited periods of time under certain circumstances such as voluntary or involuntary job loss, reduction in the hours worked, transition between jobs, death, divorce, and other life events. Qualified individuals may be required to pay the entire premium for coverage up to 102% of the cost to the plan."

I paid the premium for COBRA continued insurance coverage a few days late one month (about a year after his surgery and 6 months after his radiation), and he was dropped immediately. This was at the beginning of my caregiving experience, and I was devastated about this mistake. Even though dad's insurance payment under COBRA was over $700 dollars a month, that was still better than the cost of actual medical bills and prescription costs. This left me having to learn quickly about Medicare and disability, and how to apply for early Medicare benefits, and have dad designated as permanently disabled.

I applied for disability for dad (so that we could get him on Medicare). I should have done this earlier, but with his private disability insurance payments and COBRA, I had not needed to do it prior to that time. This was a mistake. I filled out all of the paperwork (the package, really). I gathered medical paperwork that showed his cognitive function testing (loss of nearly all short-term memory and reasoning skills), loss of physical strength, being put on hospice, everything. We were still rejected. We had to hire a lawyer (I honestly called one of the organizations that advertised on television for disability claims), and about two years later, his disability, and therefore social security and Medicare qualifications, were approved. The lawyer fee was 20 percent of the back payments he received from Social Security Disability benefits, but it was worth the cost to us, to get him approved and medical insurance.

During this process, his primary care physician politely "fired" him. My mom and dad had both had the same PCP, and I have to admit I was very disappointed that this "history" was lost. I don't know for sure why it occurred, but the loss of private insurance and dad's extreme loss of health in a very complicated medical situation may have contributed to it. I don't know, what I did know was that now I had to get a copy of his record and start shopping for a new doctor to take him, with Medicare only. I found that doctor, and through the providence of the Lord, he was closer to home.

However, that is where I found out that PCPs don't like to do heavy-duty pain management. He explained that there was a liability with having a patient on high levels of pain medication, and complications that go with the medication, that he preferred not to manage dad's narcotics. Therefore, I had to go shopping for a pain management doctor. We found one of those also, however, not nearly as close to home. Actually, about a 25-minute drive from home (in the opposite direction of his PCP, naturally). This might not seem like a big deal unless you understand that pain management requires more frequent visits. To avoid losing their license, considering they are often giving out very dangerous, highly addicting medications, they require urine or blood tests more often and frequent office visits. This is for the patient's safety, as well as I believe, for their license/liability protection. This meant that about once a month I had to take off from work to drive my dad nearly an hour round trip to the doctors for his pain medication, and that didn't include the hour in the office. Just something to keep in mind. Even when we reached a stage where dad was more stable on his medications, and he only had to go in every three months, I still had to drive to the office to pick up the monthly medications.

Lesson Learned: Governance of controlled substances. States have different laws around controlled substances, such as narcotics. Your state might be different than mine, and I don't think any of them can be less restrictive than the Federal guidelines. Up until recently, my state (or at least most doctors in my state) dictated that to receive narcotics the patient, or a representative, needed to personally pick up the prescription in the office (and show identification). The doctor's office my dad was using for years also randomly did drug tests. Which meant that if I had driven down to get the prescription by myself, but dad was scheduled for a "surprise" drug screening, to get his prescription, I had to drive back home to get him, load him in the car (very difficult), drive him down, and hope he could pee in a cup. Frequently, he could not (swollen prostate issues), so we then had to get the doctor (who may or may not have been in the office) to write an order for a blood test, which we then had to wait while someone drew blood. All this is to say – know the laws in your state and the rules of your physician so that you are prepared for what it takes to help your loved one who takes pain medication.

So, now we have a PCP and a pain specialist, how about therapy? Dad qualified for occasional physical therapy, even in-home therapy visits. So, this is another agency. Occasional, you may ask? You see, you have to learn how the system works. Dad would qualify for, say, 6 weeks of physical therapy, 2x a week. They would come out, do the therapy, tell us what to do to keep the progress moving. Only, dad didn't improve. He got worse. Also, due to the short-term memory loss, they could tell him what to do, but he wouldn't remember, so he was considered non-compliant. I would work with him when I could, and later our aide, but still he didn't show improvement. So, the therapy would end....until *the next time*.

What is *the next time*? A change in condition or qualifying event would occur. This is where good record/chart keeping as a caregiver helps. To qualify for particular treatment, frequently, something must happen that shows a change in the patient's condition before care (such as physical therapy) can be covered again. In regards to therapy, this could be a fall or admittance into the hospital. This is something I didn't know until years into caregiving. Only then did I start keeping a journal, or asking our aide to do this. This is very important if you want to get the best care. Document any changes in condition, and share this with the care team. We had home health nurses, and when we told them of falls or UTIs or bruising and pressure points, all of a sudden, we would find dad qualified for something else to help with the care.

Lesson Learned: Keep a health journal. It should contain the following type of information:

- *Medication List*
- *Pharmacy contact information*
- *Insurance Contact information*
- *Physician List*
- *Hospital Visits (date, reason)*
- *Allergies*
- *Diagnosis Lists*
- *Changes in Condition*

Communicating condition changes really can help with care. For example, when we started having issues with dad no longer being able to stand on his feet, we could get coverage for a wheelchair, mobility device, and transfer board. When dad could no longer sit up long enough to sit in a shower chair, he qualified for weekly bed baths. When dad started to show signs of a bedsore on his coccyx area (rear end-tailbone), we were able to get a hospital bed. When he couldn't roll over very well, in came the air mattress that fluctuated pressure. When his feet started to pronate severely (turn in), he qualified for air braces for his legs. All of this might have been caught by a visiting nurse eventually, but was caught sooner because we communicated these changes to the nurse, who then helped with diagnosis and insurance coverage. Remember, these nurses are part of your army!

For the first 4 or so years, I tried to be the only caregiver for dad. (What is a general without an army...deluded, that is what!) That was while he could walk on his own. This worked for a while because we were fighting for disability and insurance, and he could bath himself and still had some mobility. As mentioned before, that was a two-edged sword, as he could also get substances he shouldn't have.

When dad began to have foot nerve pain, and severe spinal nerve pain, things changed. He no longer drove or did much walking. He started to not want to bathe because it hurt to be on his feet for that long. He started to have occasional incontinence due to his pain being prohibitive for getting up and getting to the bathroom (or sitting on a hard toilet). At first, I just dealt with it like I had for mom and also for him when he was really sick at the beginning. I cleaned him up, cleaned up the bed, helped him to shower or bath. This became a more frequent necessity, and it was becoming hard to do this and still function as a working person.

I would get calls in the middle of the night from dad because he had gotten diarrhea and was lying in it. This would be a 30 minute to hour ordeal to clean him up and the bed, and I would have to turn around and get to work the next morning, frequently after having cleaned him up again in the morning. Sometimes he would lie in his own waste because he felt bad about me having to clean him, which meant that he would get skin integrity issues (rash). He was more cognitively aware than the first year after his radiation treatment, so he was more aware that his daughter was cleaning his private area, and I was aware of his embarrassment also. Neither of us was comfortable, but because we loved each other and God, both of us accepted that this was how it had to be. After a time, however, we decided to get an aide and that restored some of his privacy and dignity, and some of my ability to be daughter, not just caregiver.

Lesson Learned: Find out what your insurance covers and doesn't cover. Some need very specific wording or diagnosis to qualify for services. Some services are only available to someone on hospice, some services are not available to someone on hospice. You must become an insurance detective (or find someone to help you) to track down what you can get for your loved one. In this ever-changing world of insurance, you can't be too diligent. I know for a fact that I paid for treatments, help, and supplies that I didn't have to because they were covered. I just didn't know how or who to ask. I was blessed and was able to afford this, and I know not everyone has that luxury.

I know that many insurances cover the cost of **nurse aides**. Sometimes, they are for specific duties, such as bathing or feeding. Sometimes, they are just to give medications or specific therapy. We needed someone more available and flexible, and because dad had a good income (thanks to long term disability) he had the means to hire someone privately. We had several aids over the first few years, but then we found Sandra – or she found us, or her service found her for us. Whatever it was, it was the perfect match.

Sandra was close to dad in age. She had been a nurse's aide for years but needed part-time work. We needed someone who could split a shift so that dad had company for a couple of hours at different times of the day, and she was willing and able to satisfy that. She also didn't feel that "caregiving" ended with just the patient, but extended to the entire family. She embraced my family, and we embraced her. Sandra helped with laundry, cleaning, and was a kind and open ear to listen to me, a sounding board. She truly loved our family, and we loved her.

Sandra was a Christian woman, and that was perfect. She and dad watched Christian programming together and praised God together. They formed a bond of friendship that was both beautiful and reassuring. She cared for dad for years, between 4-5, I believe, and still called him Mr. Toms, out of respect. When dad talked about Sandra, you could tell the respect and love was mutual. He learned all about her family and would relate their adventures to us. We knew that we could trust Sandra in our home and with dad. As the years progressed, she worked more hours, different hours, and had to learn different ways to care. We worked together on this and communicate issues and needs, joys and concerns. I don't know what we would have done without Sandra.

Sandra is one of the reasons we could take vacations. She would get the mail, feed the dogs and cats (who, incidentally, loved her too). She would pick up prescriptions if she needed to, as well as prepare meals for dad. When dad went into the hospital, which he did usually 1-2x a year, due to urinary tract infections, Sandra attended to him there, too, so I could work and we didn't worry about him being alone all day. Sandra even watched the girls when they had to come home sick – they would curl up in bed with grandpa, and Sandra would spoil them! I hope that everyone who needs a "Sandra", finds one. We know that God sent her as a blessing for our home. If I was the Admiral of this army, Sandra was the Captain! (Okay, I know that Army has Generals, the Navy has Admiral and my analogy is to an Army, but dad was a Naval Officer, so I HAVE to refer to my position as Admiral, out of respect for dad. I did say, Captain, which is an Army title!).

Even if you are blessed with a Sandra, that doesn't end your responsibility as a caregiver. Sandra wasn't there 24 hours a day, which meant that even with Sandra, we still had caregiving responsibilities. Medications, bedding and clothing changes, bathing, and doctor's visits. Plus, I found that sometimes I had to be the bad cop (caregiver) because dad and Sandra had such a tight bond that he could wheedle/talk his way out of certain things that were good and necessary for him. I occasionally had to lay down the hammer when he refused to do something for Sandra that I had asked. This usually involved me insisting that he do such terrible things as - eating well and doing therapy exercises, or bathing.

Family can also be an important part of your army. My extended family had limited involvement in direct care for my dad, but my core family, Tony, Jacob, the girls, were very much part of our army. When someone is bed-bound, there is no underestimating their boredom. Dad got very bored. There is only so much TV watching you can do. Also, for the first two years, he couldn't concentrate to read, and dad had always been a voracious reader. After about two years, the damage from the brain swelling and lesions lessened, and he began to read again. We kept him stocked up on books, but even this grows tiring when you are stuck between the same four walls. That is where the kids came in extra handy. They were a source of love, entertainment, and joy for dad. They spent hours with him, sometimes reading to him, him reading to them. Sometimes watching cartoons. Sometimes, they just chatted away with him about their day. The girls were also great about letting us know dad's needs. Their rooms were in the same hallway as his, so all he had to do was shout, and they would come and see what grandpa needed. Usually, this was a request for chocolate!

My son was older and could have a little more advanced discussions with his "new grandpa" (Jacob is my bonus son from Tony). They spent the occasional hour together, and of course, our family dinners. It was nice, all of us going to grandpa's room, for dinner. Each of the children knew what to do. Jacob usually carried grandpa's food and had his chair by the door. Tony usually sat close to dad's head on the walker that turned into a chair. I sat on the loveseat across the room, and the twins had a little table and chairs that we could carry in there, or leave in there. We would have dinner together several times a week, depending on dad's mood and sleep patterns, and it was nice family time.

Your spouse can and should also be a valuable member of the Army. Tony was of course a huge help with dad. First of all, he helped with dad's boredom, bringing not only a man's perspective and conversation but also one that was engineering/aeronautical in nature. Dad was an engineer by education and experience. Tony could spend a few minutes to hours talking with dad, and dad loved it. You see, dad had been praying for Tony for years. He didn't know it was Tony he was praying for, but he had been praying for a husband for me. Some might consider me an "old maid". I was 34 when Tony and I met, and I had never had a serious relationship in my life. After mom died and dad got sick, dad was really worried that I would be alone.

He prayed daily that God would bring me the right man. He was so glad that he was able to not only live long enough to see that happen but long enough to enjoy seeing Tony and my marriage.

Tony married me knowing I was a package deal. He signed on to be a General (there, I got the correct Army Title in there after all). I had adopted two little girls, who needed a father. I also had a live-in, disabled father who needed a "son". Tony accepted both of these challenges as joys.

I remember once when we were still dating and dad got sick and incontinent. He had horrible loose bowel after being constipated for over a week. He lost his stool all over the bed. This was not the first time this had happened, but the first time that Tony was there to witness. The stench was terrible and the mess, extreme. I had already begun to clean it up when he arrived from work (because we did dinner together every night while we dated), but there was still a lot of work to do. I figured that Tony would take one look (or smell) gag, and excuse himself – offering to watch the girls while I cleaned up. NOT SO. He stayed and helped. A truly godly man!

All I have to do is close my eyes to see the image of Tony, standing on dad's bed with the carpet cleaner, wet vacuuming up the mess that had seeped through the sheets and bed pads onto the mattress. Looking up at this man, keeping a cheery attitude, so as not to make my dad feel any worse or more guilty for the mess, vacuuming up the feces of a man he had only know for a few months, I knew I had a keeper! It wouldn't be the last time he had to deal with poop, either, but he has always done it with love and patience. That love and patience weren't just for me. He grew to love my dad as a father, and that is more than any woman can ever ask from her husband in this situation.

Lesson Learned: Poop. Get used to it. Being bed-bound contributes to constipation. Narcotics/pain meds, contribute to constipation. Dehydration (frequent for people who don't feel

like drinking because they aren't exerting themselves physically) leads to constipation. Learn how to track bowel and bladder output. I can't explain how vital this is. I have an entire chapter on poop coming up, it is that important.

I have had **other family members** help as well. I mentioned earlier my two aunts, taking me to the doctor when dad couldn't leave mom alone. One of those aunts, Peggy, worked close to the hospital pharmacy, so she would pick up medications for my mom when she was on hospice, and bring them to us. Her daughters, my cousins, would occasionally come and stay at the house for an hour or two when dad and I both had to run an errand, and mom couldn't be alone.   This family, my uncle Gary's, offered their home as a respite for me, as well. They lived less than 10 minutes away and frequently had me over to decompress, watch a movie, eat a meal, and just 'veg-out' away from the responsibilities. They also listened to me cry and worry and offered encouragement and comfort.

My aunt Di and my aunt Marsha were there for me and mom the last week of her life. Aunt Marsha helped with bedding changes and kept mom company, even though she was unresponsive. Aunt Di came over one afternoon and the three of us stood around mom and sang some of the hymns we know she loved. I can close my eyes and hear us lifting our voices to "In the Garden".   Mom, who as I said, was unresponsive, actually scrunched her face slightly as we sang. Worried that we might be hurting her ears, I asked her if it was too loud. She, who hadn't been able to open her eyes or do much of any response, slightly twitched her hands and scrunched her face when I asked if okay. I took that as a yes, and we kept singing. My aunt Marsha was one of those who also inherited the legacy of caregiving. As I mentioned, she cared for her parents with my mom, and she passed on this to her daughter as well.   Beautiful to see this within your family. I had the greats – my great aunts and uncles, and their kids, my mom's first cousins, checking on me, encouraging me, calling me. They made us all feel loved in our trials and hardships. These were our Specialists, our Privates, our Foot Soldiers, marching in our army, showing their support.

Speaking of family, our **Church** was like family too. Mom and dad were members of Canadian Valley Baptist Church. It was a small congregation, maybe 130 people, but a tight-knit community of believers. When I moved down from Washington to help with mom's care, they threw me into helping at church the first weekend I got there, with a youth winter retreat to Falls Creek. I had not been able to regularly attend church in Washington due to lack of transportation, and they wanted to make sure I got back in the habit of corporate worship and service.

This church loved on us. They brought us meals. They visited. They encouraged and checked in on us. Pastor Kevin was there several times a week, talking with dad, talking to mom, praying with us. I believe he called nearly daily to encourage dad. He also helped dad with a sense of connection and purpose to the church, seeking dad's advice in a kind of "elder" capacity. Judy, Kevin's wife, and their daughters welcomed me with open arms. I had a special status before I even arrived, being the daughter of Nancy. They allowed me to find my place in their congregation, and also me adopted into their family.

I was able to form bonds of friendship in the church as well. As a caregiver, I greatly needed community, but had just moved there. The church gave me this community. Mom and dad had a weekly Bible study group that met in their home. Mom made them dinner and I was able to take over for her in that capacity. By meeting at home, this allowed mom and dad to have that fellowship, even when they could no longer make it to church because mom became difficult to move as she lost control of her body. I was able to form bonds of friendship with this group, as well as other ladies at church. Becoming part of the youth sponsor group allowed me to have a social network of Christian women that I had been missing in my life.

I will forever be thankful for ladies like Cathy, Judy, Debi, Roberta, Sherlyn, Micki, Jean, etc….the list could go on and on! They supported and encouraged, laughed with me and cried with me throughout my mom's illness and after. I also formed some bonds with some amazing young women in the youth group, such as Katrina, Christine, Lindsay, Shamika, and some young men as well! Cathy particularly was a support, helping "watch over" dad when he was sick in the guise of the "housekeeper" when she was really my "Peace of Mind" keeper; knowing someone was in the house when I couldn't be, and helping me with the chores that fell to me when mom was gone and dad was incapacitated. She welcomed me into her family and her home like a sister and I was able to bond with this wonderful family. To this day, I know that in a pinch I can count on her and Billy in times of trouble. They are that type of rock-solid. I would hope everyone could find people like these to support during your caregiving period in life, and the best place to find those people is in the Body of Christ, the Church.

Hebrews 10:24-25 And let us consider how to stir up one another to love and good works, not neglecting to meet together, as is the habit of some, but encouraging one another, and all the more as you see the Day drawing near.

I have to take a moment to talk about one of the most amazing sisters in Christ I have ever known. Jean. I met Jean at Canadian Valley Baptist Church. She was the lady who always had a smile, a kind word, and a bag of candy for the kids. She was lovely and quirky. She didn't know my parents well before mom got sick. When mom stopped being able to attend church (and therefore dad too) someone mentioned that she needed home visits.

Jean decided to be that person who visited my mom, and that is how I got to know her better.

Jean could talk to a rock, and that is exactly what mom needed. You see, when someone can't talk back and hold up their side of a conversation, most people get uncomfortable and stop coming. Jean, however, was blessed by God to have the gift of conversation. She didn't need my mom to verbally affirm their conversation. She just offered her company and conversation freely, lovingly, frequently, reliably. On top of that, she was very crafty, as my mom had been. She would bring over a craft or project almost every time and show my mom. She would talk about materials, projects, her dog, the church – her ability to have a conversation with my mom, who could barely converse, was a joy to behold. I wish there were more people like Jean, because the world, and our life, is better for having her. Her husband, "Ol What's His Name" Virgil, was also chauffeur and companion, and as contemplative and quiet as she was communicative and outgoing. He brought her to our house without ever a complaint and would wait patiently as his wife weaved her gift of conversation around my mother. I can't express how thankful dad and I were for Jean. She truly was a gift for all of us. If we are keeping with the Army analogy, she would be the recipient of the Silver Star, which means that she displayed gallantry in action.

The 13th chapter of 1 Corinthians is used at weddings all the time. It is dubbed the Love Chapter. This chapter isn't really about marital love, however. It is about the love that is shared among the body of Christ, the Church. This verse is so appropriate to ascribe to Jean and her treatment of my family at our time of need:

1 Corinthians 13:4-8a (ESV)
Love is patient and kind; love does not envy or
boast; it is not arrogant or rude. It does not insist
on its own way; it is not irritable or resentful; it

does not rejoice at wrongdoing, but rejoices with
the truth. Love bears all things, believes all things,
hopes all things, endures all things. Love never
ends.

So, I have to confess. How did I treat this gift, Jean, after mom died, when dad became sick? I left Canadian Valley Baptist Church about 2 years after mom died, and left Jean too. I don't know that this was the right thing to do, but at the time I almost felt like I had no choice. Not because the church wasn't just as wonderful, but to heal. You see, sometimes, when people who know you well, know you have gone through some tragedy, they look at you differently. I don't know if pityingly is the right word, but there were knowing and compassion, and maybe some pity in their eyes and voice, every time they look or speak with you. This happened to me after mom died, and dad became so sick. I couldn't go to church without being reminded of my circumstances. It became overwhelming for me. Also, since mom and dad had taught the singles class, and now there was none, I was missing that spiritual feeding, at a time I needed it most. Pastor Kevin still taught in his sermons just as wonderfully as before, but I didn't have that small group interaction, that fellowship. Our home Bible study had broken up due to dad's illness, and I felt very spiritually needy.

One of the hardest conversations I ever had was when I called Pastor Kevin to tell him I was going to find another church, closer to the house I had purchased in Oklahoma City. He said he wouldn't tell me it was okay. That he wouldn't tell me it didn't hurt, as he felt for me like I was a daughter. He appreciated me being honest, and not just leaving, but that he was disappointed. I don't think any Pastor would take "I'm not getting what I need in your church" very well, but he loved me through it, and we still kept somewhat in touch. I am not sure he truly understood that going to church, and being treated like a victim (even out of love), and having the constant reminder of mom's death and dad's struggle, was hard on me. Once again, I am not sure what I did was right, but this is about honesty, not necessarily having the answers. I think there will be other caregivers who will understand that sometimes you have to distance yourself from the people and places and reminders of the trauma, to heal. Jean was another loss when I did this. She tried so hard to not let that happen because that is Jean. She called, she emailed, she visited, she invited me over, she did what she could to stay in touch, but I didn't do my part.

Lesson Learned: Be honest with your pastor. Leaving a church should never be an easy thing. It is best to stay and work out issues and concerns. However, I think to find the help you need, and it might be in another church, is not a bad thing. You should not leave or look without consulting your pastor, however.

You see, Jean was a constant reminder of what I had lost when I lost my mom. That is a horrible thing to say about someone who was a gift, a blessing. Unlike others, she didn't look at me with pity in her eyes, or constantly ask, in a sad voice "How are you?" expecting me to break down and wondering how I was still walking and talking. She allowed me to have moments of joy and fun, not just expected me to be overcome by grief like the other seemed to. However, every time I looked at her I saw my mom's, crooked, flat smile on her face, gazing into Jean's face with excitement and wonder, listening to every word she said…and it broke my heart. I couldn't pretend around Jean. I couldn't forget about mom around Jean. Jean was intimately tied to the last memories of my mom, and I was struggling - not to forget - but to keep the joy and the strength because I was still going through trials with dad and I couldn't dwell on the loss of my mom when I was fighting for the life of dad!

Slowly, I stopped answer phone calls from her, until they stopped. A few years later, when I was better, I reached out to her. She wanted to know why I had disappeared. Her reaction to my reason was a testament to the type of giving woman she just is. She wasn't mad at me, that wasn't Jean, she just wanted to know why. I was honest, crying the entire time, and told her that she was too much of a reminder of mom and that the hurt and the pain came to the surface when I saw her. In typical Jean fashion, she forgave me and put no expectations on me. This is the sign of a true gift, one that I am not sure I deserved! Jean (and Virgil) I love you, that is all I can say.

I had **co-workers** that also were comfort and help during this time, which was good since I frequently had to leave work to check on my parents or take them to doctor's appointments. Tammy and Keera and Cecilia would listen as I talked about what I was going through – three gems – Christian sisters – who also were co-workers. My boss had watched her mother die from breast cancer, so she understood when I needed to be there for my mom and was lenient, particularly for funeral leave and when dad had surgery. My supervisor, Debra, even stopped me from quitting. When dad got so sick he needed full-time care, I thought I had no choice but to quit my job and stay at home. When I handed her my resignation and told her why she threw it away and told me about FMLA. She then insisted I go directly to HR and get the paperwork, as she wasn't going to lose a friend and co-worker if it was unnecessary. I took 12 weeks off that time for FMLA, and dad improved for me to go back to work, I did. A year later, when dad started doing poorly again, again I thought I was going to have to quit, she anticipated what was happening and preemptively read the FMLA law and policy, found out when I had applied last time, and came to me to let me know if I could hold out for just a few days, that I would be eligible again for FMLA…and that I could take up to 12 weeks without it being consecutive. That time I took about 8-10 weeks, with bouts of me being able to work here and there when dad was doing a little better. Other co-workers exchanged weekends with me, when I needed to go to Arkansas for dad's surgery, and California for two weeks during dad's radiation.

Every time things got overwhelming, God supplied what I needed at church, at home, and work, through the relationships I had there.   If you can build up that kind of support, if you can trust and pray in the Lord, I truly believe that if you are doing the right thing for your loved one, God will do the right thing for you by providing the people in your life who will make up your Army of support.

Lesson Learned: I have mentioned FMLA before. Last time I checked, FMLA allowed an employee to leave their position for up to 12 weeks per year to care for a qualified person (parent, spouse, child) with the proper paperwork and supporting medical qualifications. This is unpaid leave, but it holds your position (or a similar one) while you are gone. This might not benefit everyone, as many can't afford to go unpaid for that long. It greatly benefited me. The second time I didn't have to take it all at once, so I was able to weave work into the hospital and doctor appointments, and work when dad had good days, but stay home when he had bad. This is good to know if you are afraid of losing your job while you do the right thing for your loved one.

It's hard to ask for support – at least for me, it is. I was raised to be very independent and self-sufficient.   In a way, this is sinful. You see, God didn't make us islands. First, we need to, in all things, depend on Him. Then, we need to realize that part of His provisioning is sending us people and resources that we need, during our times and trials of most need.   That is a humbling process. If we have too much pride and feel we can "go it alone" He might need to remind us of our frailness and weakness. I think God has done this and continues to do this for me. I struggle with the illusion that I can do it all and be in control and self-sufficient. That is lonely and hard.   Being God-sufficient is joyful, and satisfying, and brings peace and contentment. I am hoping I truly learn that one day…as I am a bit hard-headed in this matter. I am much like the Israelites in the Old Testament. They didn't want to be guided and they quickly forgot all that God had done for them. I hope that I can humbly learn to repent of this sin so that this verse doesn't always apply to me:

Acts 7:51 (ESV)
"You stiff-necked people, uncircumcised in heart
and ears, you always resist the Holy Spirit. As your
fathers did, so do you.

I think I am a bit of a coach in this aspect, as I want to encourage you to seek help; first from the Lord, and then from others, as you go about your caregiving experience…because going it alone is unnecessarily painful and hard and quite frankly, impossible! I am thankful that parts of my army hit me over the head with reminders every once in a while; about my arrogance of independence (talking about your reminders here Tony) and reminded me to reach Up and out and not rely solely on my own, broken self, when I have God and all His resources at my disposal, for the asking.

Chapter 9 - Staging the Battle Ground

We have discussed knowing the enemy – that which has attacked the person you are caring for. We have discussed building an army to help in the battle. Now, let's talk about the battleground, itself.

Care Facilities

I know many people who spend a lot of time and effort in finding the perfect nursing or assisted living home for their loved ones. That is great! Not all care facilities are the same. There might be level-of-care restrictions, accepted insurance restrictions, as well as quality and type of care differences. As previously mentioned, I worked for just over a year in the nursing home. I was employed in the Alzheimer's unit and worked as a recreational therapist. There, my job was to help present to the patients recreational opportunities that would help them maintain their cognitive and physical ability as long as they were able. I am a believer that care facilities, such as nursing and assisted care facilities, are a vital part of caregiving. My dad was admitted to nursing homes for physical therapy, several times. These stays lasted anywhere from a week to a month and followed episodes that weakened him to such an extent that they wanted to build back up his strength/endurance or monitor his recovery in a clinical environment, before returning home.

I will say that, from my observation, the people who did the best in these facilities, truly reaping the full benefits of their time there; did so because of the love and care and attention of their loved ones, not just from the treatment they received from the employees. I observed, over that year, patients with family members who visited daily, several times a week, or once a week. Their family was active in their care plan, reactionary when they saw anything of concern and had excellent bonds with the staff at the facility. The staff felt enabled to reach out when there was a change in the patient's health and knew that the family would be receptive to their suggestions for a plan of care. This truly was the ideal for a nursing home or assisted living situation, as the family and staff worked together as a cohesive team.

Sometimes the family members in these cases would express to me guilt that they were not caring personally for their loved ones, but they were honest with themselves and recognized that either their loved one needed more specialized care or that they were not in a situation to provide what that loved one needed, and recognized their limitations.

I also observed the opposite level of concern. These were patients who never, or rarely received visits from their family. Often, from my observations, these were the patients who deteriorated the quickest, or just seemed the most anxious or discontent. One gentleman, a wealthy man, was wearing 20-year-old clothes. He didn't have any children of his own and a niece was his estate manager. When I asked why he couldn't have more natural material clothing (instead of the polyester he was wearing), I was told that she only authorized new purchases once a year and that she had denied clothing allowances because his other clothes were not torn. This broke my heart when I thought of a man who had worked his whole life and could afford better but was wearing polyester pants that didn't breathe and stank. In the year that I was there, this gentleman never received a visitor. This contrasted with a woman who was in the unit whose daughter came nearly every day, just before dinner, to sit and talk to her mom, and eat dinner with her. This woman seemed happy and content. This was the woman I mentioned in the first chapter, as she made a big impression on me with her care of her mother.

When I spoke to the daughter who visited frequently, she would tell me of her observations and feelings. She did feel bad that her mom couldn't live with her, but she worked full time and her mother was prone to wander. She had a multistory house, as well. I asked her how she felt that her mother did not know who she was. You see, many of the sporadic visitors who came to see their family members with Alzheimer's said the same two things to me. One, "it is too hard to see them like this" and two, "they don't know who I am anyway". I love how she addressed this. Her comments, and I paraphrase, were that it wasn't about her and her comfort, it was about her expressing love to the mother who had raised her. That she could get past her discomfort and sadness to support her mom. Secondly, she said it didn't matter if her mom thought she was her sister, daughter, mother, or just some nice lady when she spent time with her mother, her mother knew that she was the center of attention and loved. I think that is the best way to look at caregiving. It isn't about you, your comfort, and your feelings. It is about the other person. There needs to be a level of selflessness to be the caregiver God would have us to be, just as Christ was selfless in his sacrifice for our salvation.

Working in the nursing home I learned that it didn't matter who I was, but how I could serve. To the residents of that ward, I was a mother, a sister, a daughter, that "nice/sweet girl" and occasionally a "meanie". Once or twice I even got to be the girlfriend and flirt with the gentleman who was old enough to be my grandfather. We had one gentleman who was quite the dancer. We had a player piano, and when I would put on "Sentimental Journey" he would sometimes sweep me into his arms and twirl me around the dining room, grinning the entire time, and at the end, dip me back with a chuckle. He was fairly non-verbal, just muttered, but he sure could remember how to dance!

Occasionally I would get a glimpse into a special moment. Anyone who knows someone with a form of dementia knows what I am talking about. That moment where the person you know and love, remembers and seems to be "back". These were the most precious moments of all. The woman and her daughter I spoke of earlier – I remember one visit that turned into hours because her mom seemed aware of who she was. She wanted to catch up on all of the news on her grandchildren and her daughter, and they just talked and talked. A couple of hours later, when the moment faded, her daughter walked out in tears. I imagine those tears were both joy and sorrow, intimately intertwined. The joy of having that moment with your mom, sorrow in knowing that the next day it would be as if it had never happened for her mom, and you would be reminded of your loss once again. Those moments made my heartache. While I believed in the facility I worked in, I vowed that if I had the chance, if I was capable, I would take care of my parents personally, not in a home. Little did I know, less than two years later, I would be deciding to move home and care for mom.

I consider that year at the nursing home a huge blessing. First, it helped me with some valuable skills such as how to transfer from bed to standing, standing to seat and back, and some ways to help with bathing. I also learned how to feed a patient with Dysphagia (difficulty swallowing), and how to truly observe how someone is doing and notice small changes in behavior, health, and ability.

Lessons Learned: As a caregiver, there are certain skills and knowledge that will benefit you to learn. These include, but are not limited it:

- *CPR and Basic First Aid,*
- *Transferring patients,*
- *Making a Bed with someone in it,*
- *How to clean someone bed-ridden,*
- *Proper mouth and foot care,*
- *Bathing techniques,*
- *How to check skin integrity,*
- *Ways to adjust someone to decrease the likelihood of bedsores,*
- *More than one way to take temperature,*
- *How to Crush Medication,*

- *Nutritional Supplements.*

I learned this information by taking classes, asking medical professionals, and observation.

It was talking with the speech therapist at the nursing home that helped me clue into what was going on with mom before she was diagnosed. I had watched the lack of movement in her tongue and her difficulty swallowing (constantly clearing her throat) that had me calling dad and telling him I thought it was a neurological issue and beg him to take her to a specialist, not just her primary doctor. God, without me even knowing it, provided some of the training I needed, so that I would be better prepared to care for my parents. We have all experienced seasons in our life we might not understand at that time, as my year at the nursing home, but occasionally we can look back and see the Hand of God clearly guiding us.

Ecclesiastes 3:1 ESV
For everything there is a season, and a time for
every matter under heaven:

Home Care

My experience was primarily being a caregiver in the home. I would like to take this time to discuss some of the lessons learned on how you can make your environment (aka the battleground) better for both the caregiver and the person in your care.

I moved in with mom and dad soon after mom was diagnosed with ALS. They had a large, one-story home, which made things much easier for caregiving, but still, the environment (battleground) could be improved. I know that some of what I write won't be possible for everyone. Often people have constraints – budget, space, time, knowledge/foresight. So, please don't feel that if you can't make accommodations for caregiving, that doesn't mean that your care isn't wholehearted, meaningful, and worthwhile. Remember, these are just suggestions and lessons learned.

Fairly early into mom's illness, dad had the doors to the bedroom, and to the en-suite master bathroom, widened. The rest of the house had wide pass-throughs or entries, but the bedroom had a standard door. The house was such that he could widen them without compromising the integrity of the home, or making drastic structural changes. When you anticipate a wheelchair being used, consider corners. Doorways where you have to go around a corner can be very tricky to navigate with a wheelchair, hallways as well.

I took this lesson and years later, when dad was wheelchair-bound, had the hallway entrance and the door between the kitchen and the living room widened, as well as taking out one wall between the dinette and the family room. This wasn't a perfect solution, but much better than what we had before. Dad's condition created particular difficulties in my house with movement between rooms. His legs "locked" into place from disuse and he had severe nerve pain in his feet, so we couldn't bend his legs or put pressure on his feet, so had to sit inclined with his legs nearly straight out in front of him. His bedroom was at the end of a narrow hallway, with a turn at the beginning of the hallway, from the entryway. If we had not widened this doorway, we would not have been able to get him around the corner in his wheelchair or the ambulance rolling beds when they came to transport him (actually, we still couldn't get him out with those, they had to carry him in a sling, which they gave us to keep for future use).

Lesson Learned: If you can make doorways at least 32-36 inches in width, this increases ease of movement. This isn't a "hard number" however, as some wheelchairs have larger wheels, they are deeper or wider than others, depending on the size of the patient and the type of support needed. For example, my mother's wheelchair had a headrest that held her head in place, armrests with ridges to keep her arms from falling, and leg rests that also held her legs in place. My father's wheelchair was more standard, but we had to put the leg rests straight out and recline the back, making it very long and difficult to maneuver around corners. Electronic wheelchairs or mobility units are also much larger and have different turning radiuses. All of these should be considered when making accommodations. I have known people to move their loved ones into the formal dining room, putting up temporary walls, simply because this was the only room in the house they could make accessible.

One thing we didn't take into great consideration was flooring transitions. That is the place where one type of flooring transitions into another, often where two rooms meet. Transitions are big fall hazards if someone is still walking, due to having to shuffle or having difficulty fully lifting their feet. In our case, particularly where we went from wood to tile, we had problems with dad tripping. Later, when dad could no longer walk, the wheelchair had difficulty going over the transitions, and it made for a bumpy ride. When you are working with someone with nerve pain or chronic pain, going over a large, bumpy transition causes lots of unnecessary jolting.

Lesson Learned: Here are two things that might make transportation better (besides, of course, having no or low-profile transitions). First, get a wheelchair with bigger wheels, if you can. Second, if the large wheel is on the back of the wheelchair, back into doorways with high transitions, instead of going forward. We had to do this for our front door, or else we ended up fighting and pushing the wheelchair, hurting dad the entire time.

As mentioned earlier another transportation issue was that dad being at the end of the hallway was difficult when we had to call the ambulance. Their rolling beds would not fit down the hallway, so he had to be carried out on a sling, and making the turn at the end into the entryway with him in the sling, meant opening the bathroom door or the kids room door, walking into that, then backing at an angle through the doorway. If you can, if you have the opportunity, please consider doorways and hallways before putting your loved one in a room that is not easily accessible in case of an emergency.

A good wheelchair was vital for both of my parents. When dad could no longer bend and fit into a car, we would take him back and forth to the hospital in the wheelchair. (The hospital is a block away). Near the end, it was the only time dad got outside, and he loved the wind in his hair and the opportunity to see the sun, hear the birds, and enjoy the outside. Tony and I have beautiful memories of pushing dad home from the hospital.

When both mom and dad were still walking with a shuffling gait, they had difficulty with changes in floor texture. Going from a carpet to tile, from tile to wood, back to carpet, etc., creates a fall hazard as well. It might be good, if you can, to support someone while they are navigating across these different floors. Some shoes shuffle just fine over hardwood but drag more on the carpet. The same shoe, with a rubber sole, might stick to tile, and pitch the person forward when they move onto the tile floor. We saw this frequently with my mom.

Lesson Learned: We found that walking backward, locking our arms with theirs, was a safer way to help someone walk across floor changes and transitions. If you are standing beside the person, holding only one arm, you cannot stop them well if they pitch forward or fall backward. They also could wrench your arm (or visa versa). The two-arm clasp seemed to be better. This would not be a solution for a lengthy walk, but navigating within a house or building it works well. One person on each side, if there is space, also helps.

Speaking of flooring. I would like to take a moment to discuss how much I learned to hate carpet. If you are a caregiver, you frequently encounter messes you might have never anticipated. Spilled food and drinks are the least of the worries. I have had to clean urine and feces off many a floor, as well as vomit (often, all three at once). The worst for me was blood. If I have the choice I will never install carpet in a house again.

One day, my dad fell into a built-in glass shelf in our home (going across one of those flooring transitions). When he tripped the closest thing to him as he fell was a built-in glass shelving unit set into my fireplace. The shelves gave under the force of his weight and momentum, and the glass shattered, and he was cut deeply, mostly on his face and neck. I was at work and had no idea. That was during his drinking phase, so I called frequently. That day, when I couldn't get a hold of him, I came home early to see what was going on. I walked into the house to find what looked like a homicide scene in front of me. Broken glass from the shelves, broken trinkets that were on the shelves, and a huge pool of blood soaking into the carpet. What I didn't see at first was dad! Dad had managed to drag himself onto the loveseat about 10 feet away and was sitting there with his neck slit open, his cheek and chin hanging in tatters, and covered in blood and urine. I live one block from the hospital so instead of waiting for an ambulance I practically carried him to the car and drove to the ER. He had to have approximately 150 stitches in his neck and face.

When I went home, I was confronted by a carpet that I knew would never be the same. Two weeks later, we had laminate floors installed in the living and family rooms. It wasn't long before the hallway and dad's bedroom flooring was swapped out for the laminate as well. I have removed all of the carpets from my house and much prefer the tile or wood (or even polished concrete) for cleanliness purposes as well as ease of walking and rolling. This might not necessary be for all, but for us; with dad's incontinence issues, unsteady gait and shakiness, the stains and smells, and the difficulty rolling a wheelchair, carpet just got to be too much. We have found that hard surface floors are much better for us as a family.

When mom died, and dad worsened, needing daily care, we sold our respective houses and I purchased a house where we could live together. The house my parents owned and the one that I moved dad and myself into were different. Theirs had been new and one story. The I could afford was older and two stories. It was a big house and might have seemed too big for the two of us, but I had hope for a future family. I also wanted room for my siblings and their families, as well as other extended family members, to come and visit.

The house I had a "mother-in-law type setup with a downstairs master bedroom with a bath as well as a small suite upstairs comprised of a bedroom, bath, and small living area. This allowed for a double master feel so we both had our privacy. It also had 3 other bedrooms, so there was pretty of room to grow. Once again, God's guiding hand was seen because it was one block from the hospital, 5 minutes from what became my church, and just enough rooms for the three kids that would appear in my life within a few years. I am sure that many people who find themselves in a caregiving situation can't move. I am thankful that we had this as an option for us. The proximity to the hospital was convenient the 12 years I cared for dad, 8 of which were in the house one block from vital emergency services.

Lesson Learned: I believe that there is often pressure for caregivers to move into the house of the one they are caring for so that this person has continuity and feels at home. In the caregiving support group I was in I heard arguments for this arrangement, but also the stress and pressure it put on the caregiver. I think you should evaluate seriously the condition of the person you are caring for (for instance, how long will they need your care), the condition of the home they are living in, and your condition. If that person has dementia, moving them might cause emotional trauma, or if they have a sight impairment, they might not be able to learn to navigate a new home. These should be taken into consideration. However, if you can openly and honestly communicate with your loved one, be honest. In my father and my case, a new home allowed both of us to have our own space, proximity to a hospital, and a fresh start. I think that denying yourself or not communicating your own needs is not the way to find the best solution.

There are more ways to make homes safer for someone with mobility issues. Most people are familiar with handrails in the bathroom. We didn't just put them in the tub, we also put them by the toilet and shower, so that everywhere someone might need to support themselves, there was a rail. We also made sure that they were very securely drilled into a stud so that they were firm and could take heavy impact and wouldn't come loose or pull out of the wall.

There are also rails for beds. Arm rails but also others that attach to the bed headboard and allow the person in the bed to help pull themselves up with a handle suspended over their head. Also, you can get lifts with slings that are designed to slide under the bed, so that you can lift someone out of the bed for transportation or transfer to a chair. We sometimes would leave dad in the sling in the lift, and "drive" him, as the lift was on wheels, into the living room, as it was easier than putting him into the wheelchair then lifting him back up and into a recliner. Even the recliners have lifts. We purchased one that was "pleather" or vinyl (ease of cleaning – antibacterial wipes). And we could use the lift to lay him in the recliner, then use the lift recliner to help him change positions.

On the subject of beds, often if needed, Medicare and other insurances will pay for a bed that makes more sense than a standard bed. When mom was sick, she and dad wanted to share a bed as long as possible. This was a level of intimacy they did not want to give up. Dad told me that while becoming a caregiver to his wife he didn't want to lose sight of the fact that this was his bride. Dad would sleep with his hand in mom's hair because he loved how soft her hair was. This was comforting and reassuring for both of them, so we avoided getting a hospital bed as long as possible.

When mom's breathing got worse, and she could no longer lie flat on her back without choking issues, we had a hospital bed delivered. Even then, we placed it next to their queen-size bed, so that they could lie side by side. This dual bed setup took up a lot of room, and made maneuvering a little tricky (had to move a dresser and climb into the bed over the footboard) but was worth it for them as a couple. This bed allowed mom to sleep with her head inclined so that the saliva and mucus that she could no longer swallow, would have the help of gravity to drain, and she wouldn't choke. Also, we were able to put a lift on the side of the bed, which allowed us to lift her in a sling for bedding and clothing changes, and bathing. The mattress was an air mattress that modulated the pressure so that she did not form bedsores, as she could not roll over by herself. Dad also tried staying in his standard bed, but it became too hard to keep clean and change. The hospital bed we got for him had a standard mattress, which we swapped out for a memory foam mattress, and allowed us to prop up his feet to help with the nerve pain. We could also raise this bed to waist height, which helped us with cleaning. Getting rid of a king-size standard bed also made room for rolling side tables, extra lighting, storage for bed pads/gloves/gauze pads/and every other type of medical supply you can think of. Having them in the same room saved time and energy and also was handy when there were "accidents".

We found that when dad and mom began spending all of their time bedridden, and having to be changed, our concept of appropriate clothing changed as well. First, consider dignity. You should not force the person you are taking care of to wear hospital gowns or scrubs all of the time just because they are easier on you as a caregiver. THAT being said, if you can have that conversation with the person you are caring for, and you can come to some sort of compromise, changing someone who is in a hospital gown, or pants that snap down the side, is much easier than constantly changing from regular clothes. Also, hospital gowns, which are open in the back, are much less likely to get wrinkled under them and cause sore spots.

With dad and mom, near the end, we had a system that provided ease in changing and comfort for the bedding and their clothes. Mattress cover. No fitted sheet, just a flat sheet tucked under. Another flat cloth bed sheet, folded in half and draped sideways cross the bed with the top at chest height and the bottom around the knees. The cloth sheet allowed us to shift mom or dad up or down in the bed, depending on need and comfort. Also, when trying to prop them up on either side to insert a pillow, or putting the pillow under their knees, the cloth pad help hold the pillow in place and keep it clean from urine or sweat. This is a trick we learned from the nurse aide. We also used disposable bed pads from mid-back to mid-thigh, which usually meant two.

We wanted to have the bedroom still be a bedroom, but also have what supplies we needed on hand. The supply closet in the corner held what we needed from bedding, lotion, bathing supplies, to pads. The mini refrigerator we used instead of a bedside table kept pudding, sodas, and Ensure close at hand. The rolling bedside table with adjustable height and angle worked as both a dinner tray and for a computer monitor and keyboard (clamped on for sturdiness). A larger TV was put in the room for ease of viewing and a lamp, within easy reach, for reading. The dresser, no longer needed because the clothing choices fit on a shelf in the supply closet, was replaced with a bookshelf full of books we purchased at the used book store. The bookshelf also had room for pictures and knick-knacks the kids made, to remind their grandpa how much he was loved.

Each situation is going to be unique. I just encourage you as a caregiver, to think about your environment and how you can make things easier, more comfortable, more hygienic, and safer for all involved (while still being home, not an institution).

Technology was our friend with mom. ALS, particularly Bulbar ALS, affects the nerves and muscles that control speech. This eventually led to mom's loss of ability to verbally communicate. She went from slurring 3 out of 10 words, to 5, to 7, to all words slurred, and then lost even the ability to make noises beyond grunts or groans. The way we communicated was with technology.

As mentioned previously, she was given a device that helped her communicate when she was losing her ability to speak. I think that for many, this would be a great tool. Mom only got a few months use of it, though, for a few reasons. One, it had to be carried. It was small enough to fit in a big purse, but with mom's issues, she stopped carrying a purse, so it had to be carried by others or it was left at home. Second, her ability to type became very hindered as one hand (and arm) lost all mobility quickly, and the other hand's movement was very degraded. What worked for mom was a computer program that acted similarly but could use a mouse. This obviously wasn't for when she went out, but for at home with the family or visitors. She could move the mouse much easier than typing. When she got to a point where she couldn't move the mouse with her hand, dad found a "nose mouse". This was a reflective dot sticker that would stick to the end of her nose (or forehead) and that with just the barest turn of her head, would guide the pointer. She could then click with one finger to select a letter or a phrase. Both the speaking device and the computer program also had "call bells", so when she needed something, she could ring the bell. My favorite phrase from the computer device was "A necessary bodily function needs to be executed". We could have changed it to "I have to pee, or I have to poop" but we all got a kick out of the phrasing.

With dad we went a little "old school" and we gave him a real bell to ring. It was a little brass bell that fit into the palm of your hand, but it had a loud ring comparative to its size. I have to admit, sometimes I hated that bell. He would ring it over and over...I could hear it in my sleep. Sometimes, because he was ringing it when I was sleeping, others just because it was a bad dream.

Lesson Learned: If someone is shut in an interior room all the time, they may lose track of time. Not knowing day and night, much less what day or season it is. If you can help with this, that is advisable. Open the curtains and close them at night to give a sense of the passing of the day, talk about the outdoors (especially if you can't take them outside). Show them pictures you take on your phone that show the passing of the seasons. A calendar that you advance together may also help.

I must admit to having hidden the bell once or twice, just for some peace (he was well monitored during this time – he was not left without help and care). When dad was ringing the bell constantly, asking for things, it was out of boredom or necessity. We had to learn to recognize which it was and act accordingly. The kids became great "bell answerers" and would help us get what dad needed or entertain him if it was lonely or bored bell ringing.

Most of everything I have written about in this chapter, I learned by observation or being taught. I think I will end this chapter by stating – learn from whomever you can. I had nurses in the nursing home teach me how to evaluate signs of illness or changes in condition. Nursing aides were the most valuable to me – teaching me how to lift, transfer, soothe, change bedding and clothing. The speech therapist helped me learn to feed people who had difficulty chewing and swallowing and now to check the mouth for choking hazards. Doctors who told me about the side effects of medications and treatment for sores. Don't be too proud to learn from anyone! Even the grumpy aide, who has been doing the roll for 30 years and might seem a bit unapproachable, can give you an amazing grain of experience when she shows you how to put a transfer belt on your patient before trying to get them out of bed.

I was blessed to also encounter Social workers and Caregiver Support Group leaders who told me about resources that would be available and the right wording to use to get the needed resource. Be a sponge, because you never know when that morsel of information can either be used in your situation or to help others!

Transportation

I nearly finished editing the book before I remembered to add a section on transportation. Transportation concerns are very important to the care-receiver and the caregiver. I know I mention some of our challenges in earlier sections, but want to dedicate a little to this topic about staging the battle ground.

Driving themselves (the ability and safety aspect) is a topic you may need to discuss with your care receiver. With my grandmother, she told us she would live on her own until *she could no longer drive*. My mother told me that she didn't think she could make the decision on her own to stop driving, as her desire to be independent would overrule her judgement. She told me to let her know when I thought she should no longer drive. With my dad, he didn't recognize his inability to safely drive, so I had to take his keys from him.

Others that need caregiving might not face an all-or-nothing driving scenario. I had an uncle who needed a lift in the back of his truck that would raise his mobility unit, and he could continue to drive himself for much of his life, despite health issues and having lost a leg years earlier. A co-worker's father had a retrofit minivan that he was able to roll into.

I encourage you to be open and honest with the person you care for and address the needs honestly and openly. Some transportation options are expensive. I considered buying a modified minivan that would allow me to roll a wheelchair in the back, up a ramp. New versions of these were expensive and cost prohibitive for me. I called a medical transportation company who told me that they sold their vehicles periodically. Insurance might pay for some options as well, such as the lift for a mobility unit or a ramp, it might just take effort to acquire insurance approval.

Transportation decisions are part of staging the battle ground. An army might need a tank to advance, and you might need a modified vehicle. Medical transportation services may also exist in your area, as well. MedRide in our area became our transportation option of choice, especially when dad came to a point where he had to be laying down at all times, unable even to sit in a wheelchair.

Mom handled my opinion that she needed to stop driving better than I anticipated. Her right hand slipped on the gear shift a few times one day after a shopping trip. She hadn't driven by herself for about 4 months. We got home and I just looked at her struggle to put the car in park (we had a center console shift, not a dash lever shift). We went inside, but I didn't bring it up until a few hours later. Not pointing out the obvious to someone struggling (during the actual struggle) is always a "good call". She lightly protested that she was just more tired than usual, but she never exerted her right to drive again. I hope everyone has this type of experience. With my father I am not too ashamed to say that I hid his keys. I actually had to "loan" his car away to prevent his driving, so not all experiences will be the same.

While on the topic of transportation, I want to mention handicap parking spaces. I never knew the value of these spaces until mom was in a wheelchair. When you experience wrestling your loved one into a wheelchair to get them outside. Then you wrestle them from the wheelchair to the car. Then you drive to a location and try and find a spot wide enough to get your car door totally open so that you can maneuver your loved one back into the wheelchair (which you had to fight into the trunk). The entire time you don't want someone waiting for your spot, because you need extra time. To get a close spot after this exhaustive procedure is wonderful. To have the extra buffer space in the spot and on either side is also a blessing. A typical outing with someone in a wheelchair requires at least 5 transfers from wheelchair to vehicle, and that isn't calculating for a bathroom break. It changes your perspective on handicap spots (and handicap bathrooms), and their necessity. It also makes you a little grumpy (or a lot) when you see someone abusing these spots.

If the person you care for needs handicap parking, make sure they speak to their doctor as it requires an application with doctor endorsement (at least in my state it did). If you need transportation modifications, also speak to your physician and insurance company. Please don't abuse the handicap parking privilege. They are needed!

This is my appeal to people out and about NOT while taking care of someone. My version of a Public Service Announcement (PSA) if you will. If you are in a public bathroom and all of the stalls are open, please don't use the big, handicap one (unless you KNOW there is no one who needs it). Many of these stalls are just big enough for a standard wheelchair. Also, be considerate for the amount of time it takes for someone with mobility issues to use these stalls and understand they might need assistance. When mom received her wheel chair it was much larger than standard. Dad took her for a trip to the old family farm, which is in a rural area of west Oklahoma. When stopping to go to the restroom at a gas station, they had either a man's or a woman's, each with a toilet and sink. Dad had to take mom into the women's restroom to help her get onto the toilet. When they exited the restroom, they were given very rude looks of disapproval. It had taken them a while to get mom situated on the toilet. The large wheelchair should have indicated to those waiting that this was not a case of inconsiderate behavior, but the sting of those looks affected my mom. She didn't want to go on trips over an hour (so she wouldn't need a bathroom break) after that day.

Transportation is a necessary topic to discuss with the person you care for. Consider cost and convenience, and be flexible, as needs may change over time. Mom and dad learned to laugh about the restroom incident, imagining they scandalized the small-town folks with their bathroom noises. So proud of them for braving the difficult and spending the time together.

Psalm 46 (ESV)
God Is Our Fortress
46 God is our refuge and strength,
a very present help in trouble.
2 Therefore we will not fear though the earth gives
way, though the mountains be moved into the heart
of the sea, 3 though its waters roar and foam,
though the mountains tremble at its swelling.
Selah
4 There is a river whose streams make glad the city
of God, the holy habitation of the Most High.
5 God is in the midst of her; she shall not be moved;
God will help her when morning dawns.
6 The nations rage, the kingdoms totter;
he utters his voice, the earth melts.
7 The Lord of hosts is with us;
the God of Jacob is our fortress.
Selah
8 Come, behold the works of the Lord,
how he has brought desolations on the earth.
9 He makes wars cease to the end of the earth;
he breaks the bow and shatters the spear;
he burns the chariots with fire.
10 "Be still, and know that I am God.
I will be exalted among the nations,
I will be exalted in the earth!"
11 The Lord of hosts is with us;
the God of Jacob is our fortress.
Selah

Caregiving is not necessarily a clean and easy task. One frequently has to roll up one's sleeves and delve in, not knowing what it is you are sticking your hands into. The term, in the trenches, refers to a long ditch used during warfare time. They would dig this trench to protect themselves from the enemy's weapons and give them a place of cover to return fire. It has come to mean when someone is really doing active work and labor, at risk to themselves, a full participant.

There is a lot of sitting and doing nothing but waiting when you are a caregiver. You wait for test results, you wait for doctor appointments, then you wait for the doctors. You wait for a diagnosis and you do more waiting for referrals. Once you have appointments, you wait in waiting rooms and you waiting in treatment rooms, and then in recovery rooms. Before and after surgery or treatment, you wait. When your charge is recovering, you wait for them to wake up, and you wait to see how successful the procedure or treatment was. Wait. Wait. Wait. Waiting is being a full participant in caregiving. However, it is enough to drive you crazy. It is an excellent time to work on patience and pray.

This is an excellent place to put the Bible verse from Psalm 46 that says, "Be still and know that I am God". Being still before the Lord is a good thing. It allows us to hear God when he is trying to tell or show us something. It is a good time to remind ourselves that God has everything in control. I love how the rest of Psalm 46 is about the activity of War – both nations and nature are raging, and God is also forcefully in the midst as well – He is breaking bows and shattering spears and setting chariots on fire, for His people's protection and for Justice. God is in the midst of it all, and He is in control and in charge. God is showing His might, while all around chaos is occurring. God calms and subdues the chaos so that He will be exalted and we will know that He is for us. When you are "stuck" being still (waiting), be still with confidence and with God.

The next chapter is about poop. Yes, poop. I don't want to steal any of the glory of this topic (har har), but I do want to tell a story. My husband entered the trenches with me when we began dating and later married. I needed him to know what kind of "package deal" he was getting, marrying a woman with adopted daughters and a live-in, disabled father. He strapped on his boots, rolled up his sleeves, and got down into that muddy trench with me, and I am so thankful. One example of this was when we needed to bath dad. He had gotten too dirty for a bed bath, we needed 'John the Baptist' emersion level of cleansing. I was not able to get dad transferred into the tub by myself, so I needed help. We ran the bath but needed to raise dad out of the lift's sling and lower him into the tub. The easiest way to do this was for someone to climb into the tub with him. My hero, my husband, volunteered. He cuffed his jeans and got in. As we lowered dad into the tub, "something" slipped out of dad, from the exertion. There was my husband, standing over my father in a tub, a piece of poo circling around his ankles in the water, propelled by jets.

My dad was embarrassed. I was both embarrassed and amused. My husband, who had every right to be grossed out, instead started cracking jokes. This is what a soldier-at-arms, shoulder to shoulder with you in the muck, in the trenches, does. He looks adversity in the face rolls up his pants and cracks a joke.

Getting into the trench is what caregiver's family, and friends, and church often do. My kids were active members of the caregiving team. They read to their grandpa. They snuck chocolate into him, even though he, and they, were told not to. They answered his bell when we couldn't or couldn't hear it. They took him food and watched TV with him. They ran and got me medicine or cleaning supplies and helped clean up his tray when he was done eating. Sometimes they would come and get me and say, "mom, grandpa is dirty and needs to be cleaned up." They didn't come and say…" oh gross mom, grandpa has poop on him…or oh gross mom, it stinks in grandpa's room". They showed him love and treated him with dignity.

We have neighbors who have behaved like family. They have been kind to us from the time we moved in. They watched my family grow from just dad and me, adding the girls, and then adding Tony and Jacob. Before Tony, more than once I had to go and get help when dad fell. Dad wasn't very large or heavy but picking someone off the ground who can't help you is difficult, even if that person is only 5'11" and 180lbs. I tried to pick dad up by myself a few times but I hurt both him and myself trying. I was so grateful when Larry would come over and help me. This neighbor also found other ways to bless our family. He would frequently take our trash to the curb and pull the bins back to the house if we forgot. A few times he mowed the lawn or trimmed and cleaned up. He and his amazing wife Rose always had a wave and a kind word for us. These are the type of neighbors you want in the trenches with you!

When Tony and I got married, we were concerned we wouldn't be able to go on a honeymoon. We had three kids and dad to worry about. However, we had people climb into the trenches with us. Gigi came from California for the wedding and stayed for the honeymoon. Dad's brother Rick came from Texas and also chipped in. My other parents took care of the girls, which meant taking them to school on their first day, as we were in Costa Rica when school started. They helped alleviate anxiety and smooth out the details for us.

Sandra, Dad's aide, was more of a family member than someone there to do a job. I know I have mentioned her before and all she has done, but it can't be mentioned enough. She would house-sit, dog-sit, clean, you name it, she did it. Once, one of the twins was sick at school – she went and picked her up and brought her home because I was stuck at work. Another time she took clean clothes to one of the twins who had gotten soiled at school. If we had to go on a weekend or overnight trip, she would split her schedule so that she would work a few hours in the morning, a few hours in the afternoon, then come back at night, just to make sure that dad was okay.

Trenches are dirty. They can be cold and muddy or hot and dry. They can be lonely and scary, with shrapnel flying overhead. It is much easier to be stuck in a trench when you have good company! The opening paragraphs of this chapter talked about waiting. Even just having someone wait with you is like having a compatriot in arms, waiting in that trench side by side with you, sharing the burden of the wait.

Ecclesiastes 4:9-12 (ESV)
9 Two are better than one, because they have a good reward for their toil. 10 For if they fall, one will lift up his fellow. But woe to him who is alone when he falls and has not another to lift him up! 11 Again, if two lie together, they keep warm, but how can one keep warm alone? 12 And though a man might prevail against one who is alone, two will withstand him- a threefold cord is not quickly broken.

When you are in the trenches, it is good to keep your humor, as well. Make inside jokes, share a laugh, don't lose that sense of joy that you share as children of God. Mom had a routine, and we tried to help her keep it (that is part of climbing into the trench). She wanted her face cleaned (with a particular cleanser) and lotion applied (with a particular lotion), every night. Dad and I had to take over. I had a metal hairband, that had "teeth" that worked very well to hold mom's ultra-soft hair out of her face. I joked that it looked like a medieval torture device, securing her hair back from her face. Dad joked that it looked like something a cyborg might wear. We are big sci-fi fans, and mom and dad had been watching Star Trek Voyager, with a character called 7 of 9 (a Borg, for all our fellow geeks and nerds), because she was 7 of 9 of a group. We began calling mom 2 of 5 when we put in the metal hairband, and the name stuck. Every night, we asked 2 of 5 if she was ready for her torture (the face cleansing routine) and she would get a big grin on her face and chuckle. When you are down, on your belly, in a trench, shrapnel raining around you as the enemy tries to take your strength and your loved one's health and their dignity, don't forget to laugh in the face of the enemy.

Chapter 11 - Rules of Engagement between Combatants

The truth is, we don't always get along, even when we are on the same team. Caregiving can be stressful, and stress can strain relationships. If you are like me, at some point in your caregiving journey you will be at odds with at least one person you love. If you are more like me, you might find yourself at odds with multiple people, all at the same time! These might be family, friends, medical persons, even the person you are caring for.

When mom was sick, dad and I didn't always see eye to eye on her care. One time, when we had family staying with us, I got really upset with dad regarding mom's care. I don't remember what we disagreed about. All I know is that I used words to deliberately hurt him – stressing over and over that mom was MY mom, My mom, My mom. I was trying to exert control over the situation by implying that my relationship with mom (and therefore my opinion) was greater than his relationship, and therefore his opinion. First of all, how dare I? In retrospect, I see how disgraceful my actions were. Second, as a married woman NOW I see how incredibly wrong that assumption was. The Bible says:

Genesis 2:24 Version (ESV)
24 Therefore a man shall leave his father and his mother and hold fast to his wife, and they shall become one flesh.

My parents were one flesh, how could I have thought that my relationship trumped that of my parents with each other? I did, however, and acted terribly. The Bible also says the way a husband should love his wife:

Ephesians 5:25-30 (ESV)
25 Husbands, love your wives, as Christ loved the church and gave himself up for her, 26 that he might sanctify her, having cleansed her by the washing of water with the word, 27 so that he might present the church to himself in splendor, without spot or wrinkle or any such thing, that she might be holy and without blemish.[a] 28 In the same way husbands should love their wives as their own bodies. He who loves his wife loves himself. 29 For no one ever hated his own flesh, but nourishes and cherishes it, just as Christ does the church, 30 because we are members of his body.

Dad is a Christian man and husband who was actively loving his wife as caregiver, and I tried to interject myself between the care he though she needed with my opinion. I write this also to remind children that if one of your parents is caring for the other, to remember their role and your place. As long as there is not extenuating circumstances (known abuse, mental incapacities, physical incapacities, etc.), that couple is one flesh, and their opinion should matter most in the care of the other.

My dad, who was under tremendous strain, usually was not prone to react when pushed but had reached a breaking point. He left the house, just walked out. Seeing my dad, who was so calm, patient, wise, supportive reach a point that he would walk away and not engage was a shock. It was only then (and the very justified looks of disappointment on our family member's faces who were there with us) that I began to grasp how terrible my behavior was. They also kindly (kindlier than I deserved) reminded me of the strain and pressure that dad was going through. They reminded me that he was a husband watching his wife die, with no power to stop it, and that was a terrible thing to face.

Dad came back a few hours later. He sat me down and talked with me. He told me to never speak to him like that again. That mom was his wife, and that their relationship was sacred. He told me that he appreciated the help that I give them, but that if I ever tried to exert control like that again, that I would be told to leave. That my help was not more important than his and mom's relationship, and that I had better understand that. Then, as only an amazing and godly father can do, he forgave me and moved on as nothing had happened. We went back to caring for mom, and each other as well. I am so grateful for the forgiveness he extended to me, and for the lesson I learned from this situation.

In Ephesians chapter 4 we are told (commanded, really) to live in peace with one another. This is in response to our gratitude for the salvation we have in Christ. The reality is that this doesn't always happen. In any relationship, conflict is inevitable because it involves two flawed humans. Being a caregiver doesn't give you the instant ability to abide with one another in love. Learning to do this, and living out the *bearing with one another*, are part of our sanctification process.

My husband and I attended a marriage conference with speaker Pastor Marcos Peña (Pastor of Iglesia Bíblica del Señor Jesucristo in the Dominican Republic). He spoke of **_Six Ways to Combat Conflict_**. These were given in the context of marriage, but I felt that they could apply to relationships with others in general as well. You need to establish and maintain good relationships as a Christian, and as a Christian Caregiver, this comes into play even more due to the stress you and your charge are under.

Six Ways to Combat Conflict

Here are the 6 Ways to Combat Conflict:

1. Make sure God is always the center of your life.
2. Remember that as a Christian you have the Fruit of the Spirit.
3. Don't take everything (said or done by others) so personally.
4. Resolve Conflicts in such a way as to Glorify God.
5. Show discernment - when is the right time to resolve conflict?
6. Try not to assume you know the motives of the other person.

God as the Center of our Life

I have heard multiple times, from multiple different pastors, that when we are in conflict with someone else it is because there is a vertical (up and down) issue with our relationship with God causing a horizontal (side to side) relationship issues with other people. In other words, extreme conflict with someone else is always a spiritual issue. Therefore, if we are having issues with others, we need to work on our own relationship with God. The pastor said that we are dealing with wrong desires and motivations and that we need to be in the Word of God and work on our relationship with the Lord. I suggest reading the passage, James 4:1-8, which states we should resist pursuing our wants and desires and instead, draw near to the Lord so that He will draw near to us.

As a Christian you have the Fruit of the Spirit

As Christians, we are told to work out our faith. The fruits of the spirit are desirable characteristics we should pursue in our lives. Galatians Chapter 5 reminds us that Christ has set us free (we are no longer slaves to death and law) but should *through love serve one another*. We are then told to keep in step with the Spirit.

Ephesians 5:22-23
[22] But the fruit of the Spirit is love, joy, peace,
patience, kindness, goodness, faithfulness,
[23] gentleness, self-control; against such things there
is no law.

Therefore, when we are in conflict, we should remember:

Ephesians 5:25-26
25 If we live by the Spirit, let us also keep in step
with the Spirit. 26 Let us not become conceited,
provoking one another, envying one another.

We need to not provoke each other, not put ourselves as more important than others, and instead keep in step with the Spirit and pursue the characteristics of the fruit of the Spirit: love, joy, peace, patience, kindness, goodness, faithfulness, gentleness and self-control.

Don't take everything (said or done by others) so personally

The next method to combat conflict Pastor Marcos listed was to not take everything so personally. As we bear with one another, we might become easily hurt by what others say and do, feeling as if it is a personal attack. If someone offers advice or suggests an alternative treatment, you may take it as a criticism of your caregiving. If someone negatively appears to observes the housing situation you have provided for the person you are caring for, you may take it as in inference that you have done something wrong. Resist the urge to do this, as it could bring conflict into your relationship.

1 Peter 4:7b-10a
...therefore be self-controlled and sober-minded for the sake of your prayers. 8 Above all, keep loving one another earnestly, since love covers a multitude of sins. 9 Show hospitality to one another without grumbling. 10 As each has received a gift, use it to serve one another, as good stewards of God's varied grace:

As yourself - Are you fully using your gift, received by the Lord, to serve the person you are caring for? Do not lose self-control and love earnestly, both the person you are caring for and those who may also want to participate in the care. Their comments might be out of concern for the care receiver and might not be an attack on the care you are providing, but a need to understand. Even if it is said with insensitivity, your need to be self-controlled isn't trumped by their lack of sensitivity.

Resolve Conflicts in such a way as to Glorify God

Resolving conflict can be hard. It requires confrontation and I, for one, struggle with confrontation. I have been known to avoid confrontation for fear of escalating conflict. I have also stepped into confrontation and lost self-control and failed to be kind and gentle. However, the 4th way suggested for resolving conflict is to resolve conflict in such a way as to Glorify God.

So, how do we do this? Once again, we go to the Holy Scripture in the Bible. First Peter chapter 1 tells us to be obedient children and not to be conformed to our former passions and ignorance (what we want, how we want it, when we want it) but to be holy in our conduct. Matthew chapter 5 reminds us to let our light shine before others so that our good works give glory to our Father. 1st Corinthians chapter 10 beginning in verse 23, while speaking about practices that offend others, reminds us that whatever we do, do it all to the glory of God, not seeking our own advantage but trying to please others. Finally, Psalm 115:1 says that nothing should be for our glory, but the glory of God's name because of His steadfast love and faithfulness. Therefore, when (not if) we must confront someone else in the process of being a caregiver, we should do it to glorify God. I believe the way to do this is to refer to the other conflict resolution methods and demonstrate the fruits of the spirit, have a right relationship with God, and the last method listed above, do not assume you know the other person's motives for their input and actions.

Show discernment - Right timing in conflict resolution

Discernment. This is the ability to perceive and understand in the light of God's Truth. This is having a keen insight and good judgment. In the Bible, we see that the ability to show discernment comes from being wise.

Proverbs 16:21 (ESV)
21 The wise of heart is called discerning,
and sweetness of speech increases
persuasiveness.

The fifth method Pastor Marcos mentioned for conflict resolution is having discernment on when to address conflicts. We know in James chapter 1 that God will give us wisdom if we ask for it. So, once we have prayed for wisdom, and used this wisdom to have discernment, we can prepare for the conversations we need to have when we experience conflict. In Ecclesiastes chapter 3 we read that there is a time for everything, including a time to mend, to build up, to weep, to embrace and finally, in verse 8, a time for peace. There is a time for addressing confrontation and misunderstanding, for differences in opinions and methods. To know when, is to be wise, seek the Lord's guidance, and have discernment.

Don't assume you know the motives of the other person

The final conflict resolution method listed was to not assume you know the motives of others. This spoke to me – so much so that I had to re-edit parts of this book to make sure that I evaluated if I was doing this in my writing. The truth is that I feel I often believe I know why someone does or says something, but *I* cannot see to the heart of a man like God does (1 Samuel 16:7). By assuming I know someone's motivations, I am passing judgment on them, not simply seeing their actions and addressing these.

Pastor Marcos told us in the marriage conference that the differences in our natures are an opportunity for us to grow. In conflict, we may forget that the disease, including the symptoms and side effects, is the true enemy. Not each other, the people who love and support the person you care for, or who love and support you.

I often assume that my motives are pure, but others are not. Proverbs 16:2 says:

Proverbs 16:2 (ESV)
2 All the ways of a man are pure in his own eyes,
but the Lord weighs the spirit.

My own heart deceives me, so how can I perceive the heart of someone else? Only God knows what is in the hearts of others. Instead, I need to address the actions. How should I address the actions that I have found offensive, and am I at risk of judging their motives? James chapter 1 tells me to be quick to hear, slow to speak and slow to anger. Also, Ephesians chapter 4 tells me to not have corrupting talk come out of my mouth, but to build others up so that my speech gives grace to those who hear it. Finally, according to the book of Proverbs I should tattoo on my heart (15:1) that a soft answer turns away wrath. My prayer should become Lord help me because I need help in guarding my mind against assuming and my tongue from running when dealing with others and our differences in opinions.

I am thankful that the marriage conference occurred when it did, a few weeks before I wanted to prepare this book for publication. I address conflict occurring throughout the book with stories, but I had not included a productive way to address conflict. This message, on marriage, spoke to my heart as a wife, but also as a caregiver. These rules of engagement, I feel, may benefit caregivers who are struggling with their relationships, as did I.

Chapter 12 – Evacuation: Let's talk about POOP

If you are a caregiver or have ever been a caregiver, the title of this chapter probably doesn't surprise you. If you are not a caregiver, then, you should know that poop is a very valid and important topic. Not saying that urine isn't important too, but poop - that takes an entire (brief) chapter.

I bought my dad a T-shirt that said "I pooped today" and had a stick figure holding his arms up in a victory movement as if someone had just scored a field goal. In our household, a successful poop is like kicking the winning field goal in the Super Bowl.

Poop (Poo, Feces, dump, number 2, whatever you want to call it) is waste. Something your body didn't need, or couldn't use, which now needs to be evacuated from the body. So, it isn't too hard to understand why getting rid of the poop is healthy. Most bodies take care of this naturally, with very little help. We know when a system isn't working well also - what it is to get a little backed up, or possibly the opposite, and have diarrhea. What happens when your body stops being able to effectively rid itself of this waste? Often, caregivers find out. I know I did.

Mom had ALS. This meant that the brain was no longer communicating with the nerves, which would no longer move the muscles (or something like that says the layperson). What does that have to do with poop? Waste is pushed through the intestines via *peristalsis*. This is a contraction of the smooth muscles in the intestines, that slowly moves the waste along its digestive track, and eventually out of the body.

Mom's nerves began to stop communicating the need to contract and relax in her intestines, which meant that she was having difficulty pushing out the stool (pooping). For mom, who had been very regular, this was very disturbing, both physically and mentally. Physically, she felt full and bloated. Mentally, she was disturbed by the thought of not being able to poop. She constantly wanted to try to poop. The problem was, she had difficulty sitting on the toilet, as she had lost a lot of the core muscle function that allowed her to sit upright without being braced. We had to use chairs we had modified, that had arms and cushions to hold her upright and in place, and you can't do that very well on a toilet. There are toilet seat modifications, with arms and wider seats, but even these were difficult for her to sit in because they were so hard and not supportive along her entire body. She would use a bedside commode, but she didn't want to get off until she had pooped, so she would sit and strain, the entire time, dad or I having to stand by her and hold her up, watching as her face turned red with the effort.

The doctor prescribed medication to help make the contractions stronger, but that only worked on the muscles that were still receiving nervous system direction. Ultimately, for mom, the solution was to go to a liquid or soft diet, and finally, to a feeding tube, so that what waste she had was looser and easier for her system to move. We also kept her well hydrated, via the tube, to prevent constipation.

Dad had a similar issue, but with a different cause. Dad was on large amounts of pain medication, narcotics. The pain medication also slowed and lessoned peristalsis. He, however, continued to eat a regular amount of food, but while bedridden, he did little movement. Post-surgery and radiation had changed his taste preferences, he did not like the flavor of regular food but preferred super sweet, low nutrition foods. He also did not like drinking fluids anymore, so he refused. With dad, we struggled with severe dehydration and constipation. His constipation was so severe, that he sometimes would go 2 weeks without a significant bowel movement. I tried to keep track, but he would not report the issue or would forget if he had a bowel movement. Dad's constipation would become so severe, that he was constantly getting urinary tract infections.

Lesson Learned: This is based on my of the mechanics – but I am not clinical, please remember that fact. Constipation can lead to UTIs. Constipation can be caused by dehydration, slow digestion, poor fiber consumption, lack of movement, drug interactions. When your body is constipated, it tries to move fluid into the bowel, to help move waste along. This also takes fluid out of other parts of your digestive system. Your body also tries to start pushing (contracting) more to rid itself of the waste. If the bowel has become impacted, the squeezing can cause the mucus along the bowel (there to grease the works) out of your body. This mucus has bacteria and waste in it, and it can get caught in your clothing (underwear) or bedding, close to your urethra. This bacterium can cause infection. Also, someone who is severely impacted, that is a lot of pressure/weight in the abdomen, putting pressure on other organs and systems, causing issues as well. This was explained to me by various doctors. I learned that even some children's bodies remove too much fluid from their intestinal system, causing chronic constipation. Urinary infections, left untreated, can cause sepsis, which is very dangerous.

To put some perspective around how severe this problem was for my dad, here is an example. One time, we went to the hospital because he had a urinary tract infection. We could always tell when he got one because he went from fine to crazy (not a technical term, delusional is probably the correct term) in a matter of hours. The pain medicine masked any pain he might have felt from a UTI, and because he wore adult diapers, we couldn't always tell the amount of fluid coming out, so we usually didn't know the UTI was coming until he was septic. When they got him to the hospital, they started pumping him full of fluids. He was on one of those tables that has a weight scale, so they got his weight when he came in – incoherent from the sepsis. His stomach was distended, so they gave him something to help void his bowel. (Disclaimer:

this was the worst time this ever happened, and we learned so much from this experience. Honesty here, even though I am ashamed we let it get this bad. We just didn't know). He began to defecate – void his bowel (poop). I was horrified by the amount and stench. It just kept coming. The emergency room attendants had to keep changing his sheets. They filled one of those HUGE orange biohazard bags full of bedding and hospital gowns as he just kept pooping. The entire emergency room stank with it, it was overwhelming. His abdomen had been so full that they had to get some of it out before they could even put a catheter in to drain his bladder, and when they finally cleared enough out to get that catheter in, his urine was black with infection. At the end of about 4 hours, his weight had decreased by 20 pounds. This was not a neglected man who lived on his own "hermit style", but from a man with a daughter and a nurse aide who cared for him daily. You see, we didn't fully understand the importance of properly voided poop.

From that day on, poop became a daily topic. Daily. Have you pooped? Was it a big poop? Was it hard or soft? How much have you had to drink and eat today? Did you take the stool softener and laxative? I would gently compress his belly to see if it was beginning to feel distended.

We started to implement *Operation* "**Soft poop**". We talked to doctors and nurses and aides about ways to help with the bowel movement issues. For dad, we decreased the amount of food he was eating, and started paying attention to fiber. Even if we had to disguise fiber in Fiber One chocolate brownies, we would do it. We started paying more attention to how much fluid he was drinking, as well. For dad, who was bed-bound, it was a little more medication management. We discovered the beauty of MiraLAX – because we could mix it in fluid! He also received laxatives and stool softeners, but sometimes that didn't suffice. Then, one of the nurses told us about a "Brown Cow". Nope, not talking about chocolate milk, or a cute little heifer mooing beside the road and eating grass. This was a serious anti-constipation tonic. It was

Prune juice, MiraLAX, castor oil…all mixed with a little soda (we used Coke) to thin it and mask some of the flavors. It looked disgusting but it worked. The best thing about it was that my dad hated it so much, that the very threat of having to drink a Brown Cow had him drinking more fluid, including the MiraLAX spiked Diet Coke. Later, a few months before he died, a feeding tube was put in, which made fluid management much easier and decreased some constipation. Unfortunately, it was too late by then to reduce the kidney stones we didn't know had begun to crystalize his kidneys, probably from dehydration, infection, and 12 years of pain medication.

This might be a short chapter, but it is important. If you care for someone, care for their poop…cycle. Find out what you need to do to make sure that their bowel movements are regular. Too much can go wrong when the poop doesn't come out! After a while the talk of laxatives, quality and quantity of poop, timing, enemas, and Brown Cows will just become regular dinner conversation…I know, sounds crazy, but I promise! You'll be thankful it has, as the alternative is just not pretty and can be downright life-threatening.

Chapter 13 - Friendly Fire

Friendly fire doesn't sound bad. I mean, it has the word friendly in it, so how bad can it be? However, friendly fire as a military term is when those working on the same side inadvertently attack their own members, while trying to attack the enemy. In terms of caregiving, I am defining this as when you (the caregiver), one of your care team, a treatment, or even the patient them self, causes harm to the patient.

Let me start with an example of my patient suffering under friendly fire delivered by me. When dad went into his "semi-coma" after his radiation, we were told he was dying. I was told his survival expectancy was between 6 weeks to 3 months. That his brain was full of lesions and he would not recover. I was told to take him home and make him as comfortable as possible. He was put on hospice and I brought him home.

For 17 days dad did not eat. The only liquid he consumed was what I could get down him with his medication and a little when I dampened his mouth with swabs. We gathered around (his family) and waited for him to die. Not knowing how much he was aware of we still talked to dad. (He was only occasionally roused enough to talk or interact somewhat coherently for very short time periods) We moved him into the living room hoping the stimulation of daily living would rouse him, onto the couch. We sat by his bed, talking to him and each other. On the 17th day, we brought him to the couch and sat down at the table to eat dinner. Suddenly, he spoke, commenting that the food smelled good and he would like some.

This began dad's miraculous recovery but also where he fell victim to my friendly fire. Dad, while recovering, was in terrible pain. They still believed he was dying, so he stayed in Hospice. I spoke to doctors on the phone, to tried to get his pain under control with medication. However, no matter how much medicine they gave him, his pain level was still beyond what he could tolerate.

One day dad asked if he could have a glass of wine. He thought maybe this would help him sleep (as he was having difficulty falling asleep due to the pain). Due to the medications, he was on (and my earlier lesson learned on medication and alcohol mixing), I called the doctor first. The doctor responded that he was dying and that anything that would make him comfortable was okay. (The doctor actually seemed incredulous that I would even bother to ask) This reassured me, so I gave my father a glass of wine. I gave him glasses of wine several times over the next few days, and then weeks, to help him rest and combat his pain. It seemed to help.

However, what I didn't know was that dad wasn't going to die in 6 weeks to 3 months. Dad didn't die for another 11 years (as this was about a year after his diagnosis). What I also didn't know until 3 years later was that the portion of his brain that had been removed and radiated was also the portion of the brain that housed the ability to control addiction. I found this out when I had to take him to an alcohol rehabilitation center because his addiction had spun out of control (and I was totally at the end of my rope to try and help) and he had nearly died several times from alcohol poisoning and falls. According to the specialist, he had probably become addicted with the very first drink we gave him when I thought he was dying.

The friendly fire mistake I had made was helping my father self-medicate with alcohol. I, and the doctors, didn't see the harm in giving a dying man a drink that would help with the pain. Only what I really did was start a tailspin for both of us. While drinking my dad drove (thank the Lord he never injured himself or anyone else), he fell many times, he got so sick that he urinated, defecated, and vomited all over himself and the house. He ended up in the hospital many times from falls. This resulted in broken ribs (on two separate occasions), concussions, and more stitches than I can count. Years later I was told most of dad's nerve pain was probably caused by this period of alcohol abuse (although, with the work done on his brain and the radiation damage, no one was truly sure what was caused by the post-cancer treatment).

Dad also abused prescription pain pills. He was desperate for pain relief. I was so frustrated. Some of this time we were living separate and I had to work to pay my bills and we didn't have a full-time aide. I couldn't monitor him all of the time. I tried to hide his medication and take away his transportation, but he could call a cab and get a ride to the liquor store. I even tried to go to local liquor stores, show them a picture, and ask them not to sell to my dad. Let me just say, that didn't go over well. Dad's alcohol addiction did not disappear until his back became so damaged from falls and nerve pain, that he could no longer walk. I confess that while I was mourning dad's inability to walk, I was also secretly thanking God. This is what got us out of the spiral of alcohol abuse. It also ended his prescription pill abuse, as he could no longer walk and get them. That was when I hired a full-time aide. In retrospect, I should have done it earlier. I could have used the help, but I was so embarrassed and ashamed of dad's addiction. Dad wasn't the only one inflicting friendly fire upon himself, I too took shots at my dad in anger over his abuse. In the chapter on Battle Scars and Festering wounds, I discuss an instance where my angry reaction to dad's behavior, coupled with his depression, led him to try and take his own life. This could have been a tragic incident where friendly fire didn't just lead to injury, but death.

I am glad to report that dad and I both recovered from this friendly fire. It illustrates how something or someone, even with the best intentions, can hurt your patient. Be on guard about compromising what you know is right, because of circumstances. I know that mixing alcohol and narcotics is wrong, but I did it anyway, thinking that it couldn't hurt an already dying man. I was wrong, so very wrong. The consequences of this lasted for years. Please keep in mind these words of wisdom from the Bible.

1 Peter 3:17
For it is better, if God should will it so, that you
suffer for doing what is right rather than for doing
what is wrong.

Friendly fire doesn't always come from the uneducated and uncertified. Clinicians can also hurt the patient, even though they are trained professionals. Two instances of dad being harmed by a medical professional occurred because of his alcohol abuse. One time, because he smelled of alcohol and was filthy, the other time because the medical record stated he was an alcoholic, so he was given treatment based on old information.

When dad was drinking, he wasn't an angry, sad, or aggressive drunk. He was happy and friendly. The problem was, he was very unsteady and made poor decisions, which put his life at extreme risk. He frequently forgot to eat food or take his regular medications, and he fell. A lot. I can't count the number of times the first few years I came home to find him on the floor covered in urine, feces, vomit, or a combination of all three. Frequently, there was blood mixed in from knocks to his head or hands.

One such time dad hit his forehead, about 2 inches above his brow line, right in the middle. It was laying open about two inches, and you could see the white covering of the skull, the periosteum, stretched over bone. He was covered in urine, alcohol, feces, and blood. He smelled bad. Normally, I would have tried to clean him up before taking him to the hospital, but with the bleeding from his open head wound, I called 911 right away.

The first argument came when the ambulance wanted to take him to a hospital we had never been to before, about 15 minutes away. Let me just state, this is crazy. We live one block from one of the top hospitals in Oklahoma City. One Block! I bought this house for this very specific reason so that in an emergency, we would practically be in the backyard of the hospital.

The ambulance drivers argued that the hospitals had an agreement, that they took rotation for these types of injuries, and that the hospital they had mentioned was the one they needed to take him to. I protested, telling them that it would be faster to get him to the hospital a block away. They then told me that for head injuries, they had been told to take people to this specific, small hospital.

Lesson Learned: I have since learned a few things about ambulance transportation for emergencies. For example, insurance might dictate where you go and what is covered from the ride standpoint. You should know which facilities and circumstances your insurance covers.

Ambulances may have zones in which they have to transport you to a specific facility within that zone. This did not apply to our situation, as they wouldn't have sent an ambulance to our house if the hospital a block away was not in the same zone.

Coordinators may direct their drivers to specific locations depending on the type of injury. If you have a burn, for example, it doesn't make sense to take you to a hospital that doesn't have a specific burn department if it is available to you. One hospital might be better at dealing with different levels of trauma, is another example of why you might be transported to a specific location.

Dad's head wound might have qualified to be directed to a specific location. However, every website I have read, and every clinician I have spoken to, has told me that if a patient (or advocate) vocalizes that they want to be taken to a specific hospital, usually the ambulance drivers accommodate that request unless it is extreme circumstances. I believe that the level of dad's injury (head wound, but not at risk of bleeding out), our proximity to a major hospital (1 block) and my request (patient preference), should have resulted in dad being taken to our neighbor hospital. It did not. Dad was instead taken to the hospital that had none of his records. Due to this, instead of riding in the ambulance with dad, I had to follow in a car.

Lesson Learned: Advocate strongly for your patient. Speak up if you have preferences. Remember that time is saved (and time can be valuable in case of an emergency) when you go to a close facility and when that facility has a history with your patient, including a recent medication list and diagnosis codes.

When dad got to the hospital, I had to spend time filling out paperwork on medication. When I came into their treatment room, I was shocked at the treatment he was receiving. Every other time he had gone to a hospital, they had removed his soiled clothing (to help treat and also to prevent contamination). They had not in this case, he was still in his clothing. There was a lot of stench in the air from his clothing, and I had a jab of sympathy for them when I first walked in. That quickly left me as I watched how they were treating him.

Dad was not responding well to their care. They were being very rough with him. He was confused, hurt, and still under the influence. If he tried to move, they would jerk him back to the table, shoving down his arms. They were speaking very harshly to him – saying, don't move, quit doing that (which would have been fine words if the tone had been less hostile). I immediately stepped up to him and tried to calm him down. When I did this, they wanted to know who I was. When I told them, his daughter, they seemed surprised that he had a family member with him, but then made a remark about the lack of care he was receiving, and that they thought he was homeless.

I am not going to lie, comments like this hurt. I was trying my best to care for my dad. My care wasn't perfect, but his current state didn't reflect his care. He was fed, housed, cleaned regularly, given proper medication, taken to doctors' offices. What they were seeing was the results of our struggle with alcohol and the fact that my dad lacked reasoning and short-term memory (to learn from mistakes) due to a massive chunk of his brain having been removed, both with surgery and radiation. They were making assumptions with no history and without asking any questions.

They cleaned up dad's scratches, and then held him down and stapled the wound in his forehead shut. I was shocked at the staples! There were only a couple, and they hadn't lined the edges of the wound up, so they were overlapping, with a flap sticking out. I asked them why they hadn't used stitches and what would happen with the flap of skin that was sticking out of the wound?

Their reply: This is our standard care for someone like this, who might not be brought back to have stitches removed because the staples might just fall out or pop out if he doesn't come back. (once again, they were assuming he was homeless and didn't get much care). They also said that the flap of skin was dead and should fall off on its own when the wound healed. I was shocked. I couldn't understand the level of callousness with which they were treating my father.

They very quickly finished up with him and then loudly called for people to come in and clean the room because it stank so bad and they weren't sure how long until they could use it again without a deep clean. Saddened, and embarrassed, I took my father home.

I write this to let you know that medical professionals are people, have flaws, make assumptions, and can fling friendly fire with the best of them. I was on my dad's side, fighting for his life. They didn't know the battle I was in, and they were supposed to be on his side and my side, but instead, they aimed weapons at their patient and their patient's caregiver with very little care.

Lesson Learned: As a caregiver, you might be judged and persecuted. Jesus was perfect, blameless, righteous, and he was persecuted. We are not any of those things, even when we strive to do our best, we can't live up to that standard. If our Savior can endure, we can too. God will strengthen us in our trials and tribulations. Don't let the opinion of Man take away your drive to do what is right in the eyes of the Lord and serve the person you are caring for with lovingkindness. Matthew says in chapter 5 that we are blessed when people insult us, persecute us and say false things because of Christ. Your caregiving, my Christian brother or sister, is a service "to the least of these" and it comes from the love of Christ. Be encouraged!

The wound did not heal as they said it would. It was not a dead flap of skin to fall off, and it continued to grow, creating a large, ugly, red, flap on his head. It grew to be the size of a quarter, and round, sitting in the middle of his forehead. (We tried to use humor to combat the ugly growth, calling it his unicorn horn). Dad and I were both embarrassed as it drew attention wherever we went. A few months later I had to take dad to the doctor, and they had to surgically remove the growth, creating a new wound and then properly stitch his forehead. The doctor who performed that said that he never would have put staples in that part of the body and that using too few staples was poor care. We had known that, but it was nice to get confirmation.

Lesson Learned: Not every care facility is equal. Do your research. Voice your preferences. Fill out surveys. I later found out that patient feedback surveys matter for community recognition, referrals, and awards.

The other situation was at a different hospital. This hospital did have his record and had treated him before, including for an overdose. The assumption, in this case, was that when we brought him in, he had taken too much pain medication. I assured the physician on-call that that was not so, because at this time dad was no longer drinking (3 years, no alcohol because he was bedridden and could not walk) and his medication was not within reach but was given to him by myself or a nurse aide.

The physician didn't believe me, and administered Narcan, even though I begged him not to and asked him to call dad's pain specialist to confirm the levels of medications dad was on for his pain. The doctor didn't want to take the time to do this, or didn't believe me, I don't know his motivation for disregarding his caregiver's testimony. So he administered the drug to counter all of the narcotics in dad's system. Within minutes, dad was awake, confused, crying out in agony, and shaking (not gentle shakes, body jerky trembling). At about the same time, they were able to put a catheter in dad, and his urine came out nearly black! The doctor took one look at this and called for samples to be taken to the lab and medication for infection via his IV. This was the first time we had taken him to the hospital for a severe UTI, but it would not be the last. This is the experience that taught us dad's symptoms for a UTI – loss of cognitive ability (confusion, hallucinations) and then the loss of consciousness. We came to recognize and quickly seek treatment going forward, but this, being the first instance, we were unaware of his condition.

In this case, I give the doctor's friendly fire a mild pass. Dad did have a history of abuse (although, it had been 2 years previous) and dad had not yet had a septic level UTI history. The doctor didn't listen to the caregiver (myself or the nurse aid, both trying to reassure him that dad had not overdosed) and made assumptions, but quickly rectified the situation when the true cause of the problem became known. He also took the time to explain why UTIs were so easy to happen to people bedridden, to discuss the dangers of allowing UTIs to become septic, and to encourage us to keep dad well hydrated and clean.

The next friendly fire type to discuss is non-compliance. This is a term I learned while caring for my dad. Non-compliance is when the patient does not contribute to their own recovery. We struggled with this with dad. Before he could no longer walk at all, he was supposed to walk more, exercise his legs, to keep up his range of motion and mobility and muscle strength, but he did not. He was supposed to consume healthy food, but as mentioned earlier his tastes had changed drastically after radiation.

Lesson Learned: This isn't the first time that I noticed illness or treatment causing a change in taste. Both of my biological grandmothers (pancreatic cancer) and my dad experienced this. For dad, we snuck in fiber using Fiber One brownies and blended veggies and fruit into smoothies with ice-cream. Don't be afraid or ashamed to sneak in healthy food whenever and however you can. It is for their benefit. I am not saying lie if they ask you if there are extra veggies in the brownies (yes, I did put spinach in homemade brownies), but I am saying you don't necessarily have to go into detail about the food you are serving them. Wink Wink

Dad did not want to do the exercise therapy exercises in bed either, and he did not want to drink enough fluids. We had difficulty getting him bathed enough (until our aid began bed baths) and he didn't want to brush his teeth anymore either. Medication side effects probably had a lot to do with this, as did depression and most definitely pain, but it was difficult to help someone who didn't seem to want to help themselves. All of these non-compliances were friendly fire against himself and his care team.

Even the people who care for your loved one the most can inadvertently lob some rocks into the trenches with their caregiving comrades. Our nurse aid was an amazing woman. She cared for my dad with kindness, love, and diligence. However, she fell victim to dad's charm! He didn't want to do basic hygiene, so he would wheedle his way out of it. She was his constant day time companion and caregiver, so it was hard to fight that fight daily with someone you care for! I know, I too fell victim to wanting to go easy on my dad, who had gone through so much pain and suffering. Even the girls would slip him treats when we weren't looking, or my son would bring him something that he wasn't supposed to have because grandpa would look at them with those big blue eyes, that kind smile, and charming demeanor, and he would get what he wanted. We finally had to lay down some laws and set some rules that needed to be followed, and then to follow up on their progress. Teeth brushing is a must! Cleaning is a must! Slipping chocolate and goodies is permitted, but you can't all be slipping him this on the same day…. rotate the spoiling.

Lesson Learned: Balance. I could sit here and tell you not to give in to your charge, not to let some things slide, but I won't. I will say you can't make the "sliding" by the majority of the time because that is dangerous for the long-term health and care of your patient. However, the occasional give in I think is okay. This person isn't just a "client", this person is your loved one who you are caring for from a holistic standpoint. Their heart, mind, body, soul.

Occasionally treatment will become part of the problem. Friendly fire can come from the medications you are giving to fight the enemy.

Lesson Learned: It is important to read about the medications, ask questions of the physicians and pharmacists, document changes that might occur when new medications are started. A medication journal/list with the date of the prescription start, any interactions observed, side effects, dosages, etc. will help track. More than once we have seen that behavior and physical changes took place within a few weeks of starting a new medication. Without the journal, it is hard to remember what changed and when.

We once had one such drastic interaction with dad's medications. I can't remember the medication that caused the issue, but I remember that the pain doctor said it was necessary. Dad started hallucinating. We didn't know what was going on at first, we just saw that he was scratching and picking at his arms and legs until they bleed. He was peeling his skin off (remember, he had pain medicine daily, so this meant that he didn't feel this as badly as what most people would). We kept trying to get him to stop, but he wouldn't. We tried putting socks on his hands, but he would take them off and keep picking.

One day dad finally told me what was going on. He said that he had worms, that he believed he got the worms when we got a new puppy (we had gotten our dog, Cuda, about three months before this confession). He said the worms were crawling all over and inside him, and he was trying to pull them out. He also called me in to speak to me alone. He said that he was concerned because he noticed that Tony had also become infected with the worms, but he didn't want to alarm Tony, so he wanted me to quickly get Tony treated.

This would not be the first- or last-time dad hallucinated. It is hard to tell what was caused by the damage done to his brain and what was caused by a decline in health, and what was caused by medication. We took him to the doctor and the doctor, upon very close inspection, noticed his eyes seemed to be shaking back and forth. We believe this shaking was causing dad to see hairs as worms, and try and remove these hairs, thus, peeling away the skin. Tony had facial hair, so we believed that is why he saw the worms on Tony too.

The doctor was able to prescribe a medication that was an anti-psychotic, and this decreased the number of hallucinations that dad experienced. A few years later, dad's hands also began to shake, and he was diagnosed with Parkinson's disease just before he died. We still don't know if the eye shaking was Parkinson disease or a medication side-effect, but the medication helped, so we are assuming that it was medication-induced hallucinations.

As you can see from this chapter, friendly fire can come from every direction. It can be intentional, it can be self-inflicted, and it can be done with the best intentions. You can spend your entire time being a caregiver doubting yourself and your team of care, becoming discouraged, or you can pray and do the best you can. I recommend prayer and moving forward. Unfortunately, we hurt those we care for the most, or they hurt themselves under our care, but I can tell you that my father forgave me when I faltered. More importantly than that, we have a Heavenly Father who sees our hearts and intentions and forgives us when we repent. Do not give up doing good deeds; do not become paralyzed by the occasional mishap. You are serving the Lord with your service.

Jeremiah 17:10 (ESV)
"I the Lord search the heart
and test the mind
to give every man according to his ways,
according to the fruit of his deeds."

Chapter 14 – Battle Scars and Festering wounds

3 John 1:2 (ESV)
Beloved, I pray that all may go well with you and
that you may be in good health, as it goes well with
your soul.

You might think this section is going to be about actual festering wounds. After all, if you are a caregiver, this is a very real physical danger for those in our care. And, there will be some of that talk. However, I am using this as a metaphor (or is it analogy) for damage to the caregiver during the practice of caregiving.

Physical and emotional wellbeing are important for the caregiver, not just the care receiver. While it is true that our spiritual health is most important (1 Timothy 4:8) our physical well being is also important in our pursuit of godliness (1 Corinthians 6:19-20). After all, we are called to love the Lord (and display this love as action) with all our heart, soul, **strength** and **mind**. This chapter is about the need for the caregiver to exercise proper selfcare.

Emotional Wellbeing

All of us bring with us our baggage. Those things that we have experienced as we go about our lives, but don't process and leave behind, instead carrying it with us. Some of us, the things in our suitcase get lighter the longer we carry them (hurts fade, perception changes, issues are worked out), or we just build up our muscles enough so that these don't weigh on us as much. However, some things just get bigger, and heavier, and begin to drag us down as we try and continue to haul these issues around with us. This can be both physical and emotional, so first I am going to talk about emotional baggage, once again, from my own experience and perspective.

I have two types of wounds I want to address. The first develops while you are being a caregiver, directly related to that experience. I am likening this to a bedsore. A bedsore isn't always very noticeable at first, as it forms under the skin. It can form because we aren't properly taking care of ourselves, simple neglect that seems minor, but builds over time. From a caregiver perspective, it is important that our patients not lie in the same position for a long time, without being moved and rotated. The body is not made to have its own weight be supported by the same pressure points for a long period of time. Bedsores starts under the surface...a bruising not from a hit, but pressure, that if not relieved, will develop into an open sore, breaking the surface of the skin. The problem with this is that by the time this takes place, the damage is deep - multiple layers thick and serious.

For bedsores to heal, you have to start the healing where the damage began, deep under the surface, and heal from the inside out. The problem is that the sore was probably caused because the way the patient was lying feels natural for them. This is how they want to lay, or how they feel comfortable laying, or maybe the only position their body wants to be in. So now, instead of having them only lay that way for a quarter of the day, we tell them they can't lie in that position at all....in their comfortable position. We now have to break a habit, which is hard to do for healthy people, but very hard to do with those who aren't healthy or under stress.

Lesson Learned: For people who spend a lot of time in bed or a chair, it is vital to prevent bedsores (pressure sores). Use pillows, rolled towels, sheets or blankets, to prop them into different positions. In the hospital, nurses have a routine schedule to change their patient's position, and this is a good routine to set as a caregiver. Often the patient resists, but be persistent. Some mattresses help with this as well, and frequently your provider can help you acquire one if you qualify. I also found medical supply catalogs and websites selling affordable mattress toppers that would accomplish nearly the same effect as hospital air beds, using air to distribute the patient's weight and move them into different positions.

So how does this apply to the actual Caregiver's emotional state of mind? I can only speak from my own experience, so let me share with you something that I actually feel was my bedsore that had to break through the surface…and it led to the discovery of another festering wound.

In the previous chapter I mentioned friendly fire, and dad's alcohol abuse. When dad "woke up" after 19 days of a semi-coma, I was so relieved that he woke up that I didn't think about what kind of condition he would be in when he woke up. Dad woke up in pain, lots of pain. I unintentionally made a mistake (after consulting a doctor) and compromised common sense because I was desperate to help him. I didn't know the future and the ramifications for that type of assistance. As a caregiver, I made an unknowing choice to do something for what I thought was the right reason – help dad control pain - that I never would have done in any other circumstances. I justified this with what I knew. This led to a big problem, however.

I want to get back to the festering wound. My dad's alcoholism made me angry. I came to understand, from an intellectual level, that he couldn't control it. However, this was my dad, my spiritual mentor. The man who valued self-control and held me to a very high standard of control. This man, who I had looked up to so much, was out of control, and "seemed" unwilling to try and stop his destructive behavior. Part of me felt like he should be able to control his drinking if he wanted to.

This was my bed-sore. The pressure of caring for someone who I loved and looked up to so much, but was struggling with this sin, was a bruise that began small, deep inside my heart. A sadness and anger both that the dad I loved, who I was fighting so hard for his life, was doing this destructive behavior that was counter to all the hard work I was putting in to keep him alive. Notice, that was a lot of Is. I was trying, I was fighting, I was taking FMLA, I was treating, I was caring...I, I, I. Why wasn't he participating in his own care? Didn't he know how hard this was?

I can say now as I look back that my reality was not reality. I didn't truly understand dad's illness, the damage done to his body. So, inside me, anger and resentment and disappointment started to fester. The problem is, I kept laying on it, because the problems associated with his drinking and illness kept happening, and I DID NOT SEEK TREATMENT. I didn't even truly know I needed help. At this point, I wish I had known about Caregiver's Support groups, but I didn't. I thought I was all alone, struggling with a big problem, and not equipped. I needed to treat the wound before it got worse but didn't even know it.

One of the biggest contributors to this bedsore was that, as I mentioned before, dad was my spiritual mentor. I had put so much confidence in him, that I forgot how frail all people are. People will always let us down, but God won't. I let my disappointment in the behavior of a man take my eyes off of God and relying on Him alone. I grew bitter with disappointment instead of compassionate. This bitterness broke through to anger.

Jeremiah 17:5 (ESV)
5 Thus says the Lord: "Cursed is the man who
trusts in man
and makes flesh his strength, whose heart turns
away from the Lord.

Dad continued to drink until his body was so physically wasted, he couldn't drive anymore. This process took about 3-4 years. During those years, we both experienced a lot of trauma due to drinking. The combination of a damaged brain and nervous system from radiation, coupled with swelling and alcohol and narcotics for pain, led to nerve damage and nerve pain in dad's feet and then legs. By the time I adopted the girls and met Tony, dad could barely walk from his bedroom to the front room in our house. At our wedding, in August of 2010, marked the last time he walked outside the house. This was 8 years after diagnosis.

While he was drinking and falling more and more into the poison of alcohol, my wound was festering. Every fear when I couldn't reach him, every scare when he fell, every bottle I found hidden, made the bruise deeper and bigger. Once again, one side of me knew that he couldn't help this behavior but on the other side, the emotional side, felt that he should and could. I tried to get him help. I tried local rehab programs. My opinion of alcohol day programs, where the alcoholic drives themselves to and from sessions, is not very high. It seemed that the self-accountability level for these programs was too high. It might be that these are better for people who understand they have a problem and want to get better, instead of people like my dad, who hadn't recognized their problem. He just used the program as an excuse to get alcohol on the way home (because I would let him have his keys). A few falls, twice resulting in broken ribs, and we stopped trying these types of programs.

Next, I contacted Carron Treatment Center. Due to a lack of insurance, this was a very expensive option. I flew him out to their facility in Pennsylvania and prayed. Two weeks later I was able to visit. That is when I found out the extent of the damage and the importance of the location of cancer and radiation. They said his injury from the cancer and treatment reminded them of someone who had traumatic injury from a car accident. Carron referred him to another facility in Tennessee, and he spent a few weeks there as well. When I brought him home, I had high hopes, despite the information Carron had told me. I thought, surely, 6 weeks sober would mean he could kick this. However, once again, I wasn't truly understanding that he lacked that ability to kick this addiction.

This is about caring for yourself, so, I must say that not doing so causes issues, at least it did for me. Fester, fester, fester, and then eruption. Not his wound, mine. On his birthday, I had planned a nice outing to celebrate his birthday with pecan pie, which he loved. I went to church and said we would be going when I got home. When I came home, he was drunk. It took me an hour to find the bottles. One was in the toilet water tank, another was wrapped in a towel, under the mattress. I don't think he had gotten them recently. I think it was more of a search that had turned up bottles he had forgotten about. I exploded. I was livid – screaming hateful words and anger. I had raised my voice and been harsh before, but this is the first time that I had flown into a rage. After screaming, I stormed out. I left him alone for 3 hours. The entire time I both seethed and felt awful. Angry that he had ruined teh birthday lunch for him, angry at myself because I had missed the hidden alcohol, angry that this was happening.

Proverbs 29:11 (ESV)
11 A fool gives full vent to his spirit, but a wise man quietly holds it back.

Colossians 3:8 (ESV)
8 But now you must put them all away: anger, wrath, malice, slander, and obscene talk from your mouth.

When I got home, I went to check on him and he was asleep. I remember checking his breathing but was still mad enough to not want to deal with him, so I went into the living room to watch TV and brood. Two hours later, I checked on him again. This time, I noted that he hadn't moved at all. I was worried but felt he must be just in an alcohol-induced sleep. Two hours later, and I was really worried. This was about 7 hours after I had stormed out of the house. I started trying to wake him up by shaking him. I got no response and noticed he was cold and clammy. That was when panic set in. I called 911.

The EMTs came and took him to the hospital. They pumped his stomach. They gave him Narcan. He was admitted. Finally, after a few days, they moved him to another hospital with an in-house alcohol treatment program for observation. I wasn't allowed to visit very much there but did as much as I could. Three days into the program they called me. They told me that he had admitted that he was trying to commit suicide and had swallowed a bottle of his pain meds. They told me he had left me a note.

I was devastated. I went to his room and found the bottle. I hadn't even known he had it. I had taken to keeping his medication in another room, but somehow, he had this bottle. I looked and found the note. He had said that my life would be better if he just ended his and that he was sorry he had hurt me so much. I just sat there and cried. I knew that this was partly my fault. That my blow up, my eruption, had contributed to his attempt.

I don't tell this story lightly. This is one of my most shameful memories. I also wish I could tell you that after this I never blew up again, that I learned my lesson. That I got help for my festering wound. That would be lying. Truth is, when these bedsores under pressure, without treatment and care, these wounds keep developing and sometimes reopened. Please, don't let these wounds fester, seek help from the Lord, from your church, from mature Christians , biblical counseling. People who can help with the spiritual wounds festering inside of you.

Psalm 121: 1-3 (ESV)
My Help Comes from the Lord
A Song of Ascents.
I lift up my eyes to the hills. From where does my
help come?

My help comes from the Lord, who made heaven
and earth.
He will not let your foot be moved; he who keeps
you will not slumber.

This wound was probably inevitable due to the other type of baggage I discussed earlier. This other type of wound is more like a chronic illness than a situational induced bedsore. I brought this into the caregiving situation with me, but the situation made it worse. This chronic illness was control.

I have probably always needed to feel in control. I am sure someone with more qualifications than myself might say it stems from moving so much as a child and my parent's divorce. Or maybe, that is just who I am, my sinful nature. Let me tell you, being a caregiver means that you are not in control. Technically, God is in control whether you know it or not, but I am talking about the human ability we have to control ourselves, our surroundings, and our circumstances. When you become responsible as a caregiver, you cede over some of that control to the patient and circumstances of the person you are caring for. Their health, their wealth, their attitude, their "everything" becomes so paramount, that sometimes even the semblance of control is gone. If you are someone like me, this is very disturbing. Ironically, the very man who taught me to strive for control was the one whose illness took my feeling of control away, revealing my sinfulness, at no fault of his own.

I had these sins, control and anger from lack of control, in my life before becoming a caregiver. Caregiving merely illuminated it. God works in us this way. He sanctifies us with our circumstances. This has been a life long struggle and likely will remain a lifelong struggle, though I pray that I surrender to the healing of God so that is not the case. This is a faith struggle because anyone who struggles for self-control struggles with a lack of faith in God.

I am thankful for a husband, our pastors, Christians sisters, and counseling, which helped me to understand this struggle. I learned that I must combat it with God's promises, God's Word, God's Will and God's Way. I hope I grow in the knowledge and strength that being controlled in behavior, is good (a fruit of the spirit) while needing to be in control, is bad. The anger that comes out when I feel out of control is sin.

My ability to be organized and self-disciplined was very helpful as a caregiver. I was able to use it to keep a cool head in times of medical stress or emergencies. I was able to use it to handle estate and household matters. However, every time I felt a lack of control when my dad wasn't doing what I wanted him to do for his own well-being, my festering anger would start to peek through, and it was devastating to both myself and the person God entrusted to me for care. I pray that my honesty with my struggles will help you if you have any bedsores you are laying on or any festering wounds below the surface, waiting to break out. I urge you to seek the Lord, His Holy Word, and biblical help to work towards resolution. Just as you need to build a team as a caregiver for the betterment of your care receiver, you may need a team to help you emotionally and spiritually through caregiving.

I want to transition to physical health and wellbeing. I would be truly remiss in not discussing this, especially since caregiving can be very physically strenuous. The following were issues I encountered but are by no means a comprehensive list of potential physical ailments if you do not properly take care of your body while you are being a caregiver.

Physical Wellbeing
Back Problems

According to the National Institute of Neurological Disorders and Stroke, lower back pain is the most common cause of job-related disability, and around 80% of adults will experience it at some point in their lifetimes. Therefore, back health is undeniably important in ensuring wellbeing in both personal and work capacities.

(Why is Back Health Important? - The Health Lodge
www.thehealthlodgepractice.com/back-health-important)

My back problems began one day while taking care of my mom. She had gotten to a point in her ALS where she couldn't walk without someone holding her arm, or both arms, and walking backward as she walked. She also couldn't use her arms to push up out of a chair, or push up her weight with her legs, due to lack of strength and control. She used the speaking device bell tone to call us if we were in another room and she needed us to help her stand. One day she had been ringing the bell and neither dad nor I had heard it, and she needed to go to the bathroom. She tried to stand up on her own. That is when I walked in. She was trying to push herself up, but it was obvious she was about to fall. I didn't want this to happen because she was not able to use her arms to catch herself when she fell. We had discovered this a few weeks prior when she had tripped and fallen, and landed face-first onto a tile floor, because she couldn't move her arms fast enough, or have enough strength, to do what most of us do instinctively when we fall – brace ourselves. (This had blooded and bruised her face).

I ran over to mom and grabbed her around the waist, before she fell forward onto the floor, and possibly onto the brick hearth next to her chair. As soon as I had her, I started yelling for dad, who was in their bedroom. I was at an angle that I couldn't put her back down as her legs were crumpled and bent between mine, so I was just stuck, supporting all 180 lbs. of her weight, and yelling for help, hoping my grip wouldn't give out before dad heard me.

Dad arrived running and helped me get her back in her chair. We then quickly got her stood back up and to the bathroom. All seemed well, and it felt like we had dodged a bullet and so we continued our day. That night, around 11 pm, after putting mom to bed, I went to the garage to get dog food for my dog, Gromit. We kept the dog food in a tall, lidded trashcan, and the bin was nearly empty, so I had to lean down and into it, with my arm fully extended to scoop out the food. As I was leaning down, something snapped in my back. I was in instant agony, bent over, screaming and crying. I managed not to fall to the floor, but I couldn't straighten back up. I walked, doubled over, crying, to mom and dad's room. Mom had already fallen asleep, so I called for dad.

He walked me to my room and helped me sit down, where I continued to cry in agony and was having a hard time breathing, as every breath caused spasms and jabbing pain in my back and ribs and chest. We didn't know what to do. Dad couldn't leave mom alone to take me to the hospital. I was in too much agony to take myself. We didn't know what was happening and dad thought I was having a heart attack, because my chest hurt so much and I was gasping for air. My dad was nearly in tears of agonized indecision, watching his daughter in pain but knowing he couldn't help me.

We called my aunt Peggy, who lived about 10 minutes away. It happened that my aunt Diana was spending the night, so they both came and picked me up. These two aunts are my biological father's family, not my mom's or stepdads. It is amazing how supportive my "other dad's" family was to me. I am very thankful for their love and help! The aunts - with a lot of humor involved, got me into the truck, trying not to hurt me more. This was not an easy task. The truck was raised on large tires. I am 8 inches taller than one aunt and 4 inches taller than the other, and I outweigh them both by a significant amount. They then took me to the hospital, where I was treated with an injection for the pain, given a prescription for muscle relaxants, then sent me home. The ride to and from the hospital was a time of joy and pain. My aunts kept trying not to make me laugh, but were still making me laugh. I know their humor was both love and anxiety for me, and a genuine attempt to distract me from the pain.

This began years of back issues, first with mom, then with dad. I still struggle, and probably always will. So, after that story, here is my advice.

Lesson Learned: ***FIND OUT HOW TO TAKE CARE OF YOUR BACK. Find a nurse or nurse aide and ask them how to do transfers. Ask them how to lift patients. Even knowing much of this, I still did some things wrong. Maybe get a back brace belt. This was an unavoidable situation, but I had plenty where I did bad moves and sent my back into spasms or pain. Find YouTube videos showing proper patient lifts and transfers, do whatever you need to do, to try and protect your back. With my mom and dad, we ended up getting a lift. Find out how to use it properly, and use it! If Medicare or Medicaid won't pay for it, try and borrow or buy one on your own. They are worth the investment!***

I also suggest getting regular massages, if you can afford it. I only got one or two during most of the years I was a caregiver. Please, don't wait as long I did for this relief. Some massage companies will let you pay a monthly subscription that decreases the per massage cost. It helped to get regular massages. A heating pad helps also.

Weight Issues

Some people eat less when they get stressed. This can be a serious issue, so should be addressed. If you are a caregiver, you need energy. However, this does not apply to me, I was the opposite! I eat when I am bored and stressed. When you are spending hours taking care of someone who is home and/or bed-bound, that leaves lots of time to eat or cook. I gained lot of weight as a caregiver. While I have struggled with weight my entire life, dealing with two dying parents and a loss of the ability to do my normal activities, such as swim, hike, or walk, was devastating to my health.

This led to menstrual issues and edema – swelling of my feet and ankles. Wearing socks and tighter shoes helped, but not enough to stop the swelling. I started seeing veins in my calves and ankles as well, and sometimes I would go to sleep with swollen feet and wake up with my feet still swollen. Eventually, the weight gain also led to prediabetes.

I wish I had a solution to comfort-seeking that wouldn't lead to vice such as overeating. Self-control is a battle for most, in some form or another. Praying is always the first step in any area of your life that you struggle to combat temptation. The Bible says:

Matthew 26:41 (ESV)
"Watch and pray that you may not enter into
temptation. The spirit indeed is willing, but the flesh
is weak."

I can suggest finding something that isn't food that brings you comfort. Later, I tried making jewelry. It was something that kept my mind and hands busy, but I could do it at home or in a hospital room. I know others who knit. I wish I had known more about respite care programs when my mom was sick, and the beginning of dad's illness, as I might have been able to get out a little more and walk or hike. Do not think that overeating is the only vice. Over shopping is another one that I combatted. It is easy to spend hours browsing through online catalogs and ordering things, for that brief moment of pleasure when you get a package at the door. Then you have to live with the guilt of buying something you don't need, aren't going to use, can't afford, etc. Find comfort in the Lord, in friends, in gardening, in things that do not hurt you.

Skin Issues

There was a song in the 1990s called MMM MMM MMM by the Crash Test Dummies. One of the verses talked about a girl who wouldn't change in the changing room because she was covered by spots (birthmarks). When I was caring for mom, one way I handled my stress was with long, hot, relaxing, showers. This started when I hurt my back, and I would go and "decompress" in a hot shower. I didn't know it at the time, but I was hurting myself. I started noticing what looked like purple bruises on my stomach. I bruise easily, and, as mentioned before, I was doing lots of lifting and transfers with mom, so I assumed they were bruises. Then the spots, which were also a brownish-orange as they got larger, started spreading across my stomach. Then they started appearing on my thighs. Slowly, they started appearing on my torso and chest. I honestly thought I must be having liver failure! I figured, *well, there is something wrong, but I don't have time for there to be a problem, mom needs me.* When the first one appeared on my face – along my jawline and one on my collar bone, I knew I couldn't put off seeking medical attention.

When I went to the doctor, I was embarrassed and ashamed to show the spots. There were so many, and I knew she would ask me how long they had been there, and I would have to confess it had been months. That is exactly what happened. However, much to my relief, it wasn't liver failure, or anything nearly so severe. It was, per the doctor, the worst case of eczema she had ever seen! I was given special lotion and told to stop self-soothing with steaming hot showers for 40 minutes at a time. Within months, the spots had all disappeared and I have never had a return of them. I still dealt with skin issues, but those were mostly on my hands. When you are a caregiver, you wash your hands a lot (or you should) and frequently have to wear gloves, which can also irritate your skin. My hands were constantly dry and cracked. Please, take care of that skin!

Lesson Learned: Even if you hate wearing gloves, consider using them. Your hands will become cracked and dry from frequent washing. Cracked and dry hands aren't only painful, they can be dangerous for you and the person you are caring for. Infection can set in, and if you are cleaning someone, that infection can spread to the person you are caring for. Many people in need of caregiving have compromised immune systems. What might be an annoying infection for you, can turn into a severe infection for them.

Common Illnesses

When you are the caregiver, you need to take excellent care of yourself. If you have never taken the flu or pneumonia shot, consider it! If you are not the most hygienic person in the world, consider hand sanitizer and sterile gloves. That other person's wellbeing may depend on your health, and you not bringing in other illnesses that their immune system is too compromised to handle.

When dad got his shots, if I could, I got them too. This, of course, doesn't guarantee you won't get sick, but it might lower the chances. One year, despite getting the flu shot, I got the flu. This was before I had hired a paid caregiver, so I was on my own taking care of dad. I was sick for an entire week with both a respiratory and stomach version of the flu. I still had to make sure my dad had his medication, that he was fed, and that he was cleaned up. It was a HARD WEEK, to say the least. I spent as little time with him as possible, only spending the minimum time needed to take care of his most basic needs. We both had cell phones, so we had to talk on the phone, even though we were in the same house. I washed my hands constantly. Before I prepared him food, I took a shower.

I remember at my lowest that week wondering what would happen if I truly became incapable of caring for him. Who would know we were in this situation? Who would care? If I died, who would take care of dad? It makes you stare your own limitations and mortality in the face.

We got through that ordeal, and others similar, but I tell this to make a point. Take vitamins. Get preventative medicine. Have a contingency plan in case you get sick! Just know that sooner or later, you as the caregiver might temporarily be too sick to do your caregiver duties. Some nursing homes offer respite care. It might be worth looking into this option before you need it! Possibly look into a homecare service and have this as a contingency plan in case you become ill.

All in all, the caregiver needs to be diligent with their health, both mental and physical. When you are on your own, you have a certain level of leeway. When someone's wellbeing rests with yours, you have to learn to not ignore your mind, emotions, spirit, and body and learn to take better care of yourself than you might have done it if someone was not relying so heavily on you.

Chapter 15 – When Taps Plays - Death and Dying

There is only one way I know to soften this chapter. One Way. That is with faith. I don't know how people get through watching someone you love die, without the Lord. My honest belief and perspective are that without a relationship with the Great I Am, personally witnessing the death of first my mom, then my dad, then my grandma would have broken me. I was holding their hands as they took their last breath. I also lost two other grandmas before mom got sick, and during dad's illness, my biological dad's brother, my beloved uncle, died as well. Just over a year before this book is to be published I lost my older brother too No one who lives a normal life will go through life without losing those they love, but to have so much loss in such a short time really affected me. However, even amid pain and loss, particularly with my parents, there was joy and release.

John 14 (ESV)
14 "Let not your hearts be troubled. Believe in God;
believe also in me. 2 In my Father's house are many
rooms. If it were not so, would I have told you that I
go to prepare a place for you? 3 And if I go and
prepare a place for you, I will come again and will
take you to myself, that where I am you may be also.
4 And you know the way to where I am going.

This joy I was able to experience in the depths of loss was because I knew that for my parents to be absent from their bodies was to be present with the Lord. I also knew that our separation was to be short and that we would reunite in Heaven for eternity one day, as brothers and sisters in Christ, children of the Living God. I also experienced release, or maybe relief, because even though a selfish part of every person mourns when someone they love dies, if you have watched that person suffer, your mourning is shared with relief that the person you love no longer suffers. These two things go hand in hand, intertwined. If you are unsure of the salvation of the person you are watching die, the grief and mourning aren't tempered with joy and assurance of their release and your future reunification.

Mom

There are books and pamphlets about what to look for when the person you have been caring for is nearing death. I know this, because when mom got sick on New Year's Eve, 2001, I asked our hospice nurse for one. She gave me the booklet, and I read it. For some reason, I was very preoccupied with what it would look like, and knowing it (death) was coming. For some reason…I think we all know the reason. I am human, and I wanted to prepare myself for that eventuality. I thought that knowing the signs would help and, for me, it was something concrete to think about. Of course the book, which was good, couldn't tell me exactly what would happen and how I could tell but it was just specific enough to give me some reassurance. Dad and I were both worried that something would happen and that we wouldn't be there with mom at the end. For the most part, she was never alone for more than a minute or two at a time for the last two weeks of her life (and even the last few months). We didn't want to even think about her dying alone, about us walking in on her dead. We wanted to be there.

Brief-time out to discuss Hospice. Mom was on hospice several months prior to her death. She was a strong proponent of hospice and asked dad and me to call them around the same time she had her feeding tube placed. I believe her positive view of hospice came about because of their involvement in care for both of her parents. She had worked with two different hospice organizations and so she knew exactly which one she preferred for her care. Dad was also on hospice, but not at the end of his life, but periodically throughout the twelve years. More than once they thought he was dying, and he was placed on hospice, only to be removed when he had a recovery and we chose to pursue more aggressive care. Pastor Bill contacted me during the editing phase of the book and suggested I include a little more around Hospice, as he and his wife were being confronted with the decision to utilize or not utilize hospice as a service.

Lesson Learned: Here is my limited knowledge and opinion on when to decide to engage hospice:

1. Is the condition terminal, with little treatment or cure options? If yes, then hospice can help with end of life palliative treatment and care.
2. Does the care receiver have any mental, emotional, or spiritual conflict with the philosophy of hospice?

Per website www.uptodate.com

> *"Hospice care is a model and philosophy of care*
> *that focuses on providing palliative care to patients*
> *with a life-limiting illness, focusing on palliating*
> *patients' pain and other symptoms, attending to*
> *their and their family's emotional and spiritual*
> *needs, and providing support for their caregivers."*

3. Does going on hospice prevent the patient from receiving something that is seen as vital to comfort, either emotionally or physically? This includes counseling, particular medications, benefits, etc. The caregiver may want to check with insurance.
4. Does utilizing hospice GAIN the care receiver or the caregiver something valuable? This includes in-home assistance, equipment, respite care, etc.

You may also want to discuss hospice with other family members, as they might not understand the purpose of hospice. Some people may associate hospice care with "giving up" or an indication that death is imminent. Now I will return to the rest of the story.

Since mom had ALS, we were very careful about visitors' health, and our own. We had been told that mom would probably die because she would lose the ability to breathe or her heart would just stop beating. Mom had lost the ability to swallow or clear her throat, so the biggest risk to her was a respiratory compromise. Dad and I both got flu and pneumonia shots, as did mom, and if someone had respiratory symptoms, we asked them to stay away. There are no guarantees, however and around the holidays, with people coming to visit and family coming to stay, mom caught something.

On New Year's Eve, mom was sitting in "her chair" a glider we had modified by adding a wooden platform to raise it, when all of a sudden, she just slumpedover . We could see drool and phlegm dripping out of her mouth and hear her struggling to breathe. We had been provided a suction device a few months earlier and had used it to help clear saliva out of mom's mouth with a pipe-like tool connected to a tube, which runs into a reservoir in the suction device (I believe it's called a Yankauer). We used this to suction out her mouth and noticed a lot of mucus that was yellow and thick. We called hospice. Hospice came and brought a child version of the tube for the suction canister – one that was used on infants and toddlers, which allowed it to go down the throat and nose, not just in the mouth. That began 48 hours of exhausting care and fear.

Mom's sinuses were in revolt and producing copious amount of thick mucus. The fear was that she would choke and drown on this. Mom couldn't speak, but her eyes did plenty of speaking that weekend. She would fix her eyes on dad or me as we fought to rid her of the deadly mucus. Dad and I never left her side except to get something to eat or go to the restroom, and never both at the same time. We took turns suctioning her throat, down her nose. We found that I was better at getting the cannula down her throat and nose, so that was primarily my job. Dad would clean the canister and hold her hand, talking her through the feeling of panic as she felt that tub moving in and out of her throat and nose, feeling the gagging tickle, but lacking the ability to cough or clear her throat.

My mom's sister came over and helped as much as she could, spending time with mom, giving us a brief break to sleep (I slept in the room with mom, dad slept in the guest room because if he was in the same room, he got no rest. At the end of the three days, we had won the battle against the virus, but lost the war. The constant lack of oxygen from the mucus, and the exhaustion from the fight for her life, had taken its toll on mom. She slipped into what appeared to be a coma. She had lost her ability to open her eyes, we think, or she just was in that state where she was no longer truly conscious. We won't ever know. We treated her as if she could still hear us and was cognitively alert. We talked to her, we explained what we were doing, we listened to the radio with her and read to her, but there was very little response. She would sometimes scrunch her eyes, like when my two Aunts, Marsha and Diana sang to her, but there was no other response.

Before I tell about the end, I need to go back a bit and talk about end of life choices and decisions. Mom had spoken with dad and I about her preferences. She had told us that she did not want anything that would prolong her life or any devices that she would be dependent upon for life. She had compromised that for dad and I in one area. That was the feeding (PEG) tube. I think she finally gave in, for our comfort, even though she didn't want it. That, my friends, is love, when the person dying is worried about the mental state of the caregiver. She was very adamant about not getting a respirator. Her BiPap was the closest assistance she would accept for breathing, and had even asked that oxygen not be hooked to it, that it just be air. A BiPap is different than a CPap – a CPap pushes air one direction, into the body, to help keep the airway open. A BiPap, however, both pushed and pulled air, to assist with voiding air from the lungs. This helped in mom's case as her diaphragm, which is a muscle structure that expands and contracts to allow air to go in and out of the lungs, was losing its function because of her ALS.

Lesson Learned: Have the hard discussions. What form or level of life assistance does the person you are caring for want? Do they want to sign a DNR (Do Not Resuscitate) form? Do they have a Living Will and a Medical Protectorate? What do they think about blood transfusions, experimental treatments, palliative care and hospice? These conversations don't get easier if you put them off.

Back to mom's condition. She was no longer struggling to breath from mucus, but she was no longer able to communicate with us. Unknown to me, dad had started to enact mom's wishes. Since he usually did the medicine if he was there, I didn't notice when he stopped crushing and giving her medicine. At that time, there wasn't much in the way of treatment for ALS, mostly experimental, but mom did take a few other medications. We still gave her a liquid that helped dry her mouth. It was a few days before I noticed that he didn't seem to be feeding her the Ensure anymore, just water. I got upset and asked him why. That is when he reminded me of her wishes. He said that he was waiting to stop using the BiPap until he had spoken to me. I was upset, I am not going to lie. My first instinct was to *fight fight fight*. However, after cooling off, I agreed with him. At this point, we knew it was the end. We both just wanted her to be comfortable, and I was worried she was hungry. Dad told me that if he saw any discomfort, we would treat that…but, she didn't show any signs of pain. These conversations, both with the person you are giving care, and other family members, are vital. I am thankful that we knew what mom wanted, specifically, and that dad was strong enough to honor that.

They were able to tell us what mom's lung capacity was from her breathing (how much her lungs filled with air when she took a breath), so we knew that it was decreasing, and getting near the end (the last number we received was 17%, down from 25% in just a few weeks). The last few days were very quiet. Just each of us taking turns being with her, talking to her. My aunt Marsha was there too, so it was three of us during the day, and dad and I at night. Sometimes I slept in the room for the night, so dad could rest, sometimes he slept there, and a few times it was all three of us. Just being together. People would drop by, and we would go out and be social, but not both at the same time, and not very long. We just wanted to be with mom.

The last day, we were going to give her a sponge bath and clean up the small amount of bowel that was on her bed pad. We hooked up the sling and lift and were in the process of raising her out of bed when dad stopped us. "Stop, Stop, Put her down" he said. He had noticed a change in her breathing. We lowered her, removed the sling, and dad said, "Just wait". I was on her left side, holding her hand, Dad was at the foot of the bed, his hand on her feet and her sister Marsha was on the right side, stroking her arm, when she breathed her last breath. It was just one long sigh out. I was holding her hand with my finger on her pulse....it just slowly faded away. I let out a sob at first, but then started praying. Dad, Marsha, me; just sat there and praised the Lord, praying, holding her as she left this world. The brief stab of pain was quickly replaced with a sense of joy and release for my mom. I just knew at that moment, in my spirit, that she had been released. I had never felt anything like it in my life…it was like I felt her spirit leave her body and I just knew she was gone. She gave one last breathe about a minute later, which is common, as the body reflexively reacts, but then, she was still.

We had a call list. Mom had insisted on it. It was hanging inside a cabinet in the breakfast nook. I started making calls. First to our Pastor, Kevin. Then to the Hospice Nurse and then to the Funeral home. Dad started calling family, as did Aunt Marsha. We were able to sit with mom, and a few people came and say goodbye, before the nursing home picked her up.

Mom had planned her own funeral. I teased her, since she was such a good party planner, that of course she wanted to plan her own send off. So, all of the details were taken care of. The next three days were filled with sleeping (we were exhausted) and preparing a memorial with pictures for mom, as well as me writing a Eulogy. We laughed and cried over those three days, but mostly we just slept.

If I were to make a list of what you should take from this experience, it would be as follows.

Lesson Learned

1. *Know your loved one's end of life choices and desires*
2. *Make sure you understand those choices.*
3. *Ask for help from family, hospice and church.*
4. *Get rest wherever you can.*
5. *Make funeral arrangements beforehand.*
6. *Have a call list, and people who will help you execute it. This way you don't forget someone in your very emotional state.*
7. *Know the signs of end of life, but also know that there is no one who can tell you when and how.*

And the final suggestion from my experience with mom is if you are taking care of someone you love, take advantage of the time you have. Mom was diagnosed December 5th 2000, I moved to Oklahoma City January 2001, and she died January 2002. The year of 2000 I spent two weeks in the summer with mom and dad for her Thymus removal surgery and a week at Christmas in Oklahoma. Mom was in Washington with me in May 2000 (when my worry had really started, and set off the intensive diagnosis phase. I am so thankful for that time.

The year that I spent caring for mom, we worked through a lot of childhood mother to daughter miscommunications and misunderstandings. I loved my mom, but we were alike in some ways that caused conflict, and different in some ways that caused us to not "get" each other. I always felt like I disappointed her as a daughter, because I wasn't girly enough. Turns out, she felt intimidated by my differences, but was really proud. She just didn't know how to say it or show it and kept trying to relate in ways that she got, while I kept trying to prove that I was worthy. What a mess, right? We got to work through those misunderstandings, with dad refereeing.

Colossians 3:13 ESV
Bearing with one another and, if one has a
complaint against another, forgiving each other; as
the Lord has forgiven you, so you also must forgive.

Also, and something that I will cherish forever, is that we got to plan my wedding. I was the only daughter, and mom had looked forward to my wedding my entire life. However, there was no potential husband in the picture. I didn't want to lose out on that opportunity, and neither did she. She had always told me she would make my wedding dress, so we looked for and bought a pattern, even though we knew she wouldn't be able to make it. I told her about my desire to have lots of color, and a masked ball type of feel. She loved it, and we looked through Oriental Trader magazines and found feather Mardi Gras masks. We came up with a concept to have the table clothes all different jewel tone colors and to have the bridesmaids all wearing different colors, but the same dress. Not all our plans made it to the wedding, but many did. My table clothes were all different colors, I had only flower girls, not bridesmaids, and they all wore the same white dress with different colored sashes, and we invited people to wear fun masks for the reception, which was like a masked ball. While she didn't make the dress, and it wasn't the medieval high-waisted princess dress we had picked out, it was a high-waist Aline with a splash of color, which I know she would have loved! The entire day (which was 8 years after mom died) I knew her influence was there in our choices.

So, cherish and take advantage of the time you have. Work through issues, don't avoid them. That way, you can live your life with a level of closure and good memories, instead of confusion and bitterness. I also was able to encourage my mom to write out some of her life. I have a few pages of her autobiography. The writing has no punctuation and the words run together because she was writing it with her nose mouse and one working finger to click letters, but to me, that makes it more priceless, as I know the effort that went into those pages.

Dad

Most of my caregiving experience was with dad. Mom started showing symptoms around Christmas 2000, and had passed away just over 2 years later. Dad's journey was over twelve years, some of which he had kept hidden. Dad was an excellent example of the sacrificial love Paul told husbands in Ephesians they should demonstrate for their wives.

Ephesians 5:25-27 (ESV)
25 Husbands, love your wives, as Christ loved the
church and gave himself up for her,

Dad began showing signs of his tumor while mom was sick. In April 2001 they went on their annual trip to Palm Desert for grandma's birthday. Mom was still able to walk and, while her speech was slurred, she could still communicate fairly well. They knew this would be her last visit, so they had planned a lot of fun. They went off roading in the desert, mom and grandma had a spa day, and they spent the evenings by the pool, enjoying the dry, mild, desert twilight. Dad had begun feeling numbness in his feet prior to that, at first a quarter size spot on the bottom of his heels, but that had begun to spread up his legs. He later told me that it wasn't until he stepped into the hot tub, the first step, and couldn't feel the heat of the water until it reached up past his ankles, that he realized how bad it had gotten. At this point dad kept it all to himself, however. He told me later about the numbness, but not about the spreading.

When he finally shared his symptoms with me he told me that he needed to focus on mom, and he would worry about his odd symptoms later. Even the fact that mom and dad were in Oklahoma shows his sacrifice for his wife. Mom and dad had spent their married life moving around, not only within the US, but even out of the country; chasing dad's career. They had spent over a year in Moscow, Russia, and dad wanted mom to be close to her family for their retirement. He said the men in his family tended to die young, so he wanted mom to be surrounded by family in her old age. He gave up his high-powered job in aeronautics and took a lower paid project management type position in computer technology, that allowed him to work primarily from home. They moved to Oklahoma for mom. Little did he know (but God knew) that this decision would be so vital for their future, as it allowed mom to see her family in her last days, dad to care for her full time since he worked from home, and to bring me back to where I needed to be (unbeknownst to me).

After mom died, and the funeral was over, dad and I just both sat, worn out. However, I wasn't going to let dad continue to ignore what was going on with his body. I told him to get to the doctor right away, and he did. The doctor ordered an MRI and in February, we got the results. The first MRI showed the tumor, in his Clivus, a bone in the skull, but was read as probably benign. However, they wanted a second opinion, so in March he was sent for a second MRI. This report came back as cancer, a Chordoma. Not only was it cancer (flat bone cancer), but the location, being a skull base tumor, was very difficult for surgical removal, and there were only a few specialists who could perform it. Praise the Lord, one of those specialists was only 5-6 hours away, in Little Rock, Arkansas. As I discussed in the other chapter, dad had the surgery and Proton Radiation, and that began our adventure together.

While mom's experience was a steady decline that took place over 1-2 years, dad's experience was a roller coaster ride of ups and downs. He came through surgery and radiation extremely well, and initially we thought dad was going to be different than all of the statistics for his disease we had read about. However, the initial success was followed by years of decline and struggles. The first few years, dad improved in the memory department, as his brain swelling went down, but as mentioned before, the pain was so severe he struggled with self-medicating and addiction that damaged his body more than the surgery or radiation.

Every major infection or injury would cause more loss of his facilities, roller coaster dips in ability and emotional well-being. He would start to recover, but would never return to the level before, and then another change would happen, and he would plunge down that rollercoaster track again. Each time, his recovery never brought him up to the previous level, and the climb back up got harder and longer. Dad struggled with falls (broken ribs, cracked skull, bruising, and gashes) and urinary tract infections that always seemed to lead to sepsis before we knew what was going on.

The last year, dad started passing stones in his urine – like grains of sand. It was noticed in the hospital during a stay from another UTI, but never once did anyone suggest we treat it. We assumed that if it was a big problem, or worth treating, the doctors would have told us to do something, or referred us somewhere. It was never discussed, and since dad wasn't in pain, we just continued with our normal care.

We didn't know that he had kidney stones and we didn't know that he was going to get ones so big, and in a location that would block the function of his kidneys, and lead to toxic build up in his body. As in the past, dad went from fine to acting strange within a few minutes, hallucinating and incoherent. We called the ambulance (as we could no longer easily transport him as his body was frozen fairly stiff from years of bed bound-ness) and Dad was admitted for what appeared to be another UTI.

However, this time his blood pressure was all over the place, but mostly super low. As I mentioned in other chapters, Dad's urinary tract infections (and sepsis) had frequently been confused with drug overdose. His medical record also contained notes on his substance abuse (at this point that had not occurred in 9 years) but the ER doctor decided to give dad Narcan and counter the pain medicine – with the intent of countering the "overdose" be believed dad was suffering from.

I argued against this action strongly. I explained to the ER doctor that his pain management was very strictly controlled and that he could not take more than the prescribed amount as he couldn't walk and his medications were kept in another room, and his medication was given by an aide or myself. I told the physician that this was dad's classic symptoms of a UTI, to please check his record.

The physician did not listen to me and gave dad Narcan to counter his pain medicine. Well, just as before, this meant that dad woke up in pain and "crazy" from the sepsis due to a raging UTI. The doctor would not give any medication until the urine sample was analyzed and had them take blood. I was furious, as this was the second time this had happened in the same hospital and both times my protests had been ignored as I advocated for my father's care. My dad, who had been on prescribed and strictly monitored narcotics for years, had been woken into pain and refused relief, all because a doctor refused to listen to his caregiver.

That night was horrible, one of the worst in my life. I sat in the ER listening to my dad moan in pain, shake with the pain, and hallucinate. He appeared to be having seizures, as well. Dad had created an entire story in his hallucinations and was muttering and talking out this nightmare as his body fought pain and the effects of withdrawal and sepsis.

I tried at first to look at the story he was weaving as funny. However, the funny wore off very quickly. My dad, the man I had been caring for 12 years as his medical protectorate, was in agony. I felt helpless and angry. I sat on a hard, upright plastic chair – the staff had not offered to get me anything more comfortable and had even suggested I just go home. You see, they had been told the man lying in the bed was an addict.

Lesson Learned: Medical professionals are not perfect. They are human and subject to sinful thoughts and actions just like everyone else. Just because they have been entrusted with lives doesn't meant they are going to make the best or right decisions and choices. They are victims of their own prejudices and ignorance, just like the rest of us. When you are advocating for the person you are a caregiver for, do it with confidence and strength. I have found, particularly with physicians, that if I appear unsure, they will not always care for my loved one the way I believe my charge deserves. Be an advocate, what do you have to lose?

Let me be very honest here. Addicts deserve honor and respect when being cared for. Some care decisions made for an addict could be considered very difficult, painful, or hard by most standards, but they should be made in the best interest of the addict. In their case, addiction is the enemy. My dad, while dependent on pain medication, was not an addict. The enemy was the destruction to his body by cancer, radiation, nerve damage, and in this case, a raging infection. By treating him like an addict, and not listening to his caregiver, this physician caused my dad extreme harm.

I frequently questioned the nurse taking care of my father and anyone who came in for treatment, what was going on and why I hadn't seen the doctor since he had ordered Narcan in the ER (we were in ICU at this point). They kept telling me the doctor was on rounds, would come in later to speak to me, and we were still waiting for the culture to see if dad had an infection.

About 2am (many hours after we had been in the hospital) I saw the doctor come into the ICU. The beds in ICU were all in "glass boxes" which meant that the nurses sitting at the nursing station could see into the rooms, even though the doors were closed for privacy. I saw the doctor go to the nurse's station, sit at the desk, appear to pull up a chart, and put in orders. He briefly spoke to dad's nurse, and then he left the ICU. I want to remind the reader that I had been asking to speak to the doctor for hours. Everyone in that unit knew that I wanted to speak to him.

The nurse came in about 10 minutes later and, without speaking to me (they had been very cold to me, which wasn't my experience with this hospital or most any hospital before) and began administering something into dad's IV. This seemed strange to me because usually nurses tell family members what they are giving and why in if they are in with the patient, at least in my experience. I asked the nurse what she was giving and when the doctor was going to come and talk to me.

The nurse told me that the culture had come back, and that dad had an extremely bad urinary infection, and that the level of drugs in his system were consistent with what I had told them, and so they were giving IV antibiotics and also were going to give him pain medication. I asked again when the doctor was going to come and talk to me, and she told me that he wasn't going to come in, that he had been called to a situation in another part of the hospital and would be busy for at least 20-30 minutes, and then he was going home.

Readers, fellow caregivers, I am not going to lie. This was 100% not acceptable to me. I, in no uncertain terms, told that nurse that she was going to get that doctor back here to talk to me or she was going to get me her manager, or call whatever managing director was on-call! I told her that I worked for a hospital (which I did, their competition) and I knew what and how medical personnel were supposed to behave in this situation, and I would not be put off any more. She tried to argue a little, but her spirit wasn't in it, so she did what I asked, and I heard the doctor paged. The physician came about 20 minutes later. He walked in and demanded to know why I needed to see him.

Let me say right here that dad was still in the throes of pain and withdrawals. He was still muttering to himself, twitching and seizing in agony. His heart rate and blood pressure were all over. It was obvious that this man was in agony, even 20 minutes after giving him intravenous (IV) pain medication.

Before I explain my next actions, I want to put in a disclaimer. As Christians, we are not to seek vengeance. We should not react in anger, because anger is rarely justified. Vengeance is the Lord's. I hope that what I am about to do isn't seen as vengeance seeking. I was angry, so I did sinfully act in anger. However, my deepest desire was for this doctor to never do this to another person ever again.

I stood up and looked at that doctor, who faced me with what I interpreted as an arrogant challenging look on his face, and I let him have it. I didn't scream or swear or cuss – if I had done that I 100% believe that he could have written me off as low-class and crazy. I told him that he needed to stand here until my dad was no longer trembling in pain and agony. I told him that he needed to stand by and watch what he had done to his patient. The patient that was entrusted to his care, that he had callously blown off as an addict, against the input of his caregiver. I told him – You did this. You have caused him to go untreated for sepsis for 12 hours, because you wouldn't listen. You did this, you have caused him to be in pain and agony, because you wouldn't listen. You did this, in your arrogance. In your cowardice you refused to come and talk to me when you found out you were wrong. You sent a nurse to do your dirty work and tried to run away. This is your fault and you need to stand here and look at the consequences of your behavior. Maybe if you stand here and see this man shake in agony, you will learn something, and you won't treat anyone like this again.

Over the next half hour that doctor stood there in silence and watched my dad with me. I alternated between comforting dad, particularly when he would have a hard shake or tremble, and when he would cry out in anxiety. What did I alternate with? When I wasn't comforting dad, I told that doctor about the man on the bed before him. I told him how this man had survived a cancer where there were no statistics about survival past 5 years – because people didn't survive longer than 5 years, but my dad had! I told him how my dad had been an executive in a company but had lost all that because of the disease. I told him how my father had lovingly taken care of his wife who had died of ALS.

I wanted to make my dad a person to that doctor. I wanted that doctor to not forget, ever again, that he treated people and that those people deserved dignity and respect. I wanted that doctor to know that this man might be his patient, but he was my father and he deserved better than disdain. Once the pain medication kicked in and dad stopped trembling, I looked at that doctor and told him he could leave. He left, and I never saw him again. I have never planned on suing a hospital for malpractice or negligence, as I understand the difficulties when it comes to treating patients, especially patients as ill as my dad. I also did not want to give in to rage and anger, for the Bible tells us to leave that to God. However, if I had walked out of that hospital without at least trying to hold that doctor accountable for his actions, I do not believe I would have done the right thing. He could have victimized someone else, and that would have been partly my fault. Therefore,

I hope that what I did was not repaying evil with evil, but instead trying to help him.

Romans 12:17-21
Repay no one evil for evil, but give thought to do
what is honorable in the sight of all. If possible, so
far as it depends on you, live peaceably with all.
Beloved, never avenge yourselves, but leave it to the
wrath of God, for it is written, "Vengeance is mine,
I will repay, says the Lord." To the contrary, "if
your enemy is hungry, feed him; if he is thirsty, give
him something to drink; for by so doing you will
heap burning coals on his head." Do not be
overcome by evil, but overcome evil with good.

Dad never made it out of the hospital. The next day they told us that the kidney stones were blocking the function of his kidneys, and they would need to do surgery. They said that his body was in no condition to do surgery, so they would support him until he recovered from the sepsis, and then we could discuss kidney stone removal surgery, but they didn't think he would be up to that for a few weeks. They were worried about his blood pressure, as it kept going dangerously low, so they were going to move him into a step-up unit (usually means, a step up from ICU, but not ready to be on a regular floor, because he still needed lots of care). So, we moved to a new room and met new doctors.

It seemed like dad was going to recover from that infection like he had had numerous infections before. The antibiotics helped the infection, so he stopped hallucinating and began communicating with us. Sandra sat with him during the day, and I was able to go to work some and also get some rest. Tuesday evening, after the kids were in bed, Tony joined me and we hung out with dad, who was alternating between wakefulness and sleepiness. I planned on sleeping up there again, so Tony was hanging out with me, but planning on going home. This was my 40th "birthday eve". He hadn't left at midnight, so he was there when dad woke up around 12:20 am, turned to me and said, "Happy Birthday!". It was my 40th birthday, and he had remembered.

Lesson Learned: Learn to be thankful and celebrate no matter where you are, when you are, and your circumstances. I used to fantasize about my 40th birthday. I felt that reaching that milestone I deserved a party or a trip (the trip was really what I wanted). Instead, I was in a hospital, exhausted, sleeping in a hard recliner, next to my dying dad. There is no place I would have rather been than there! That last birthday with my dad was a gift.

James 1:17 ESV
Every good gift and every perfect gift is from above,
coming down from the Father of lights with whom
there is no variation or shadow due to change.

Thursday night I finally felt it was okay to go home, that dad was out of danger. He even had a great conversation on the phone with his brother, and his spirits were high. I stayed until about 11 pm, then went home to sleep in my own bed (the first time since Sunday night). What I forgot to do was take my cellphone off silent (I had kept it on silent in the hospital so that I wouldn't disturb dad when it rang).

I slept very hard that night – until just after 6 am when my phone started vibrating and I heard it. I had 4 missed calls when I grabbed up the phone and answered. The call was from a doctor at the hospital who said that dad had taken a turn for the worse and wanted me to come in right away.

I headed to the hospital right away. Tony stayed at home to get the kids up and joined me shortly later. Dad's blood pressure had begun to drop during the night and they couldn't get it stabilized. One of the doctors came in to give me information about dad's condition. I could tell that he wasn't trying to influence my decision on dad, but he told me that the only way to get dad's blood pressure stabilized in the long run was to fix the kidney issues. The only way to get it stabilized in the short term was to take him off of pain medication, as that was making his blood pressure stay too low for him to survive.

I looked at the doctor and asked him, very point-blank. If we take him off of the pain medicine, his blood pressure will come up but he will be in extreme pain and begin going through withdrawals. (Doctor answered yes). If we leave him on the pain medication his blood pressure will not come up and stabilize and he will more than likely die. (Doctor said, we can't know for sure, but probably). Then I asked the doctor, if we take him off the pain medication, how long until he can have the surgery to fix his kidneys? (Doctor essentially said, 3 weeks, if he survives that long without pain medication, but more than likely the kidney issue or withdrawal will kill him before then). I then said, what are the chances of dad making it to the surgery and then surviving the surgery? (At this point the doctor started hedging - saying that there was no guarantee and you could never tell, and it all depended on…). I asked the doctor to be blunt. I knew he couldn't tell me what to do, so I asked him what he would do if it were his family member. He wouldn't answer but said that dad's body was in very bad condition, the kidney stones were very bad, the surgery would be difficult, and even after the kidney surgery, he would not be able to take pain medication like he had been to decrease the chance of stones returning and to keep his blood pressure stable.

This is where I was glad dad and I had had the hard discussions. I knew dad's end of life wishes, and I realized this was the time to honor those wishes. I talked over the situation with my husband, who supported me and dad in any way we needed. Now, I just need to talk to dad. He was drugged enough to not be very alert (to remove the pain medication for his blood pressure they had put him into a medicated coma, so he wasn't in excruciating pain). I needed to talk to dad to make sure he understood the situation and see if he supported the decision I was making for him.

The doctor lowered dad's medication enough for dad to wake up. I leaned over very close to him and spoke to him. I told him about the kidney stones and failure, I told him about the need for surgery and the complications of the surgery and chances for survival. I told him about needing to remove the pain medication and that they would need him to stay off the pain medication until the surgery, and maybe after surgery. I told him everything. I then asked him he wanted to live the rest of his life in pain and through withdrawal, for the chance to have the surgery. He shook his head no. I asked him if he was ready to die, and he shook his head yes. I told him that we could decide not to take him off the pain medication (treat his pain) and he would probably slip away soon, without pain. Did he want that? Did he understand that his body was giving out? He shook his head yes.

This was painful. I had prayed and prayed before speaking to dad. I had gone to my husband for counsel. I had cried out to God to make sure I was making the right decision, the decision to not fight against his dying body, but to let his body die.

Dad was alert, so we wanted people to be able to say goodbye. My kids came in, to say goodbye. I had Jacob get some chocolate (dad LOVED chocolate), and against direction from the medical staff (who said, no food), we snuck a piece of chocolate into his mouth, so that the last taste he had on this earth was of the chocolate he loved. His aide, who loved him (and he, her) was able to come and say goodbye. The lasts words he spoke were to tell her he loved her! Sandra was such a blessing to us! My older brother's family was there, and they said goodbye as well.

While they were saying goodbye, I had to make two hard phone calls. One to my uncle, dad's brother, but the hardest one to my grandmother (dad's mom). I had to tell my grandma that her oldest son was about to die. I stood in a dark hallway, sobbing, trying to be strong, but I just couldn't. Telling grandma about dad was the hardest thing I have ever done. Grandma and Rick supported my care of dad and the decision that was being made for palliative care only.

Dad was getting agitated from the pain, so it was time to put him back under. The hospital transferred us to a larger room with lots of room for visitors, and dad was put on oxygen and pain medicine.

We received many visitors over the next few hours. My great aunt her family and many of our church family. We talked to dad and around dad, filling the room with love.

A few hours later, with family and our church family surrounding us, me holding his hand, and his oldest son on the other side of him, dad took his last breath. My husband had his hands on my shoulder and dad's leg, supporting me to the end. Our kids were there too. They had lived with grandpa and loved him, and they were with us to say goodbye. I was incredibly saddened but also so filled with joy too.

When he was gone, we called the nurse. She called the hospital chaplain. When the chaplain walked in, I think he expected to see people wailing and mourning. We were ready to praise the Lord. He asked what he could do, and I asked him if he wanted to pray with us! I think he was shocked that in this time, we were ready to pray and sing praises to the Lord. It was sad that a chaplain was surprised that Christians would praise God when their loved one was out of pain and with the Lord. I hope that our praise was a testimony to him about the love of the Lord when people lose those we know are believers and that he was encouraged to see us acting on our faith.

Romans 15: 12-23 ESV

12 Now if Christ is proclaimed as raised from the dead, how can some of you say that there is no resurrection of the dead? 13 But if there is no resurrection of the dead, then not even Christ has been raised. 14 And if Christ has not been raised, then our preaching is in vain and your faith is in vain. 15 We are even found to be misrepresenting God, because we testified about God that he raised Christ, whom he did not raise if it is true that the dead are not raised. 16 For if the dead are not raised, not even Christ has been raised. 17 And if Christ has not been raised, your faith is futile and you are still in your sins. 18 Then those also who have fallen asleep in Christ have perished. 19 If in Christ we have hope in this life only, we are of all people most to be pitied.

20 But in fact Christ has been raised from the dead, the first fruits of those who have fallen asleep. 21 For as by a man came death, by a man has come also the resurrection of the dead. 22 For as in Adam all die, so also in Christ shall all be made alive. 23 But each in his own order: Christ the first fruits, then at his coming those who belong to Christ.

Grandma, Gigi

I don't think you get used to losing people you love, but you do gain perspective each time you lose someone close. From a Christian caregiver's viewpoint, you hope that what you learn might help you comfort others who are in the midst of loss.

At the time I wrote this I had recently lost my stepdad's mom, my grandmother, Katy. In our family, she was known as

Gigi, our nickname for **great-grandma**. She was very much loved and appreciated, and we enjoyed all the moments we got to share with her. She was an amazing woman and had lived a life that many would find fascinating. She had experienced death at a young age in both her father who died from ALS and in her first husband who died within weeks of their marriage after enlisting and being sent to battle in World War II. My grandpa, her second husband, had battled chronic illness and she had supported him through that. All of these things made her hate going to the hospital and be very uncomfortable around illness and sickness. She would visit someone who was ill in the hospital, but you could tell that she couldn't wait to get out of there.

She came to see us regularly while dad and mom were sick. Often, because she hated flying, this would entail a three-day car ride all by herself (unless she was being accompanied by Melody, her trusted doggy companion). Do you get how amazing this was? This means that a woman in her a late 80s and even into her 90th year would make a 22-hour car ride where she did all the driving - from the San Diego area to our home in Oklahoma City! She didn't push herself, she just kept whatever pace she could, and stopped when she got tired. She did sightseeing along the way, enjoying the view and the solitude. She was a fount of knowledge for us and would tell us wonderful places to stop whenever we made our car ride adventures.

Watching her son die, my dad, was very painful for grandma. I hope I never experience one of my children dying before I do because I can't even imagine the pain. Her health had been amazing for someone her age, but she was starting to have more health problems after dad's passing. I think dad's passing took a lot out of her desire to live, but typical of grandma she seemed to look for the motivation to continue. She went from calling dad nearly daily to checking in on us every few days, and we tried to return the favor. I'm sure she called my uncle on a very regular basis as well because they were very close. However, about 6 months before she died, she developed pain in her lower back that radiated down her legs, making it very difficult for her to be comfortable walking, sitting or even laying.

Grandma was pretty stubborn – determined and stoic. She didn't like going to a doctor if she didn't feel like she had to. She wasn't a complainer and she didn't see the need to go to the doctor unless she had first tried to treat it herself (over the counter (OTC) medication, creams, stretches and walks). Often, she thought she could just power through it and wait for the problem to go away on its own. Back problems, however, really got her down, as it decreased her mobility. Her self-reliance was a source of pride. For many years she told me that she had chosen, and would choose, to live on her own until she could no longer drive herself; at which time she would move closer to us or my uncle. Her back pain began to sap away her ability to drive herself and she became reliant on her very best friend who lived next door.

Let me take it moment out of the story of grandma's last days to talk about her best friend. Her best friend Jean is an amazing woman. She's smart, she's fun, she's an amazing Christian woman who has a joy that has come from trial and experience; not from an easy life with no hardships. I am so thankful for the relationship that she had with my grandma. Jean's husband had died and soon after she moved in next to my grandma her twin sister died. Her family was not super close, so in a way she was alone. My grandpa had died and none of us lived near grandma, so she too was removed from family. However, I don't think this was the driving force behind their friendship. I think that if they had lived in other parts of the neighborhood and not as neighbors, they would have found each other and they would've been friends. They just had that "click" of chemistry that I think everybody knows when they see it in another person.

They did little trips together, they ate meals together, they shopped together. I thought it was wonderful how they, and a third friend and neighbor, had a cocktail hour a couple of times a week. Jean cared for grandma like a sister and I don't think she could've loved her any more if they had been related. Jean even got a little dog named Moses, and Moses and grandmother's dog Melody were fast friends.

Lesson Learned: Encourage relationships. If you are caring for someone, help them to keep and maintain relationships. Life is so much more fulfilling shared, and you might grow to have a deep friendship with their friends.

Even though grandma had Jean to rely, on she was not happy about her loss of independence from the back pain. She called the doctor several times about her pain and wasn't happy with his level of response; because her pain level was so high, she didn't aggressively pursue treatment and seek out other doctors. She called me one day and left a message that sounded a little bit strange; it said: "hey I want to talk to you about something call me when you get a chance". Most of the time grandma's messages were just checking in and ended with "you don't need to call back". This one was different, but I was so busy that I didn't catch it.

Later my uncle called me and let me know that Melody had passed and that grandma was upset that she had lost her doggie. She and Melody had a routine – walk time, treat time (she had turned Melody into a pug shaped like a football), bedtime. I knew that losing Melody was going to be very hard on her, particularly since it was just a year after she had lost dad, so I immediately called her.

This seemed to be a catalyst towards a loss of will to continue. I think that if she had been healthy, she would have been fine, but to be in constant pain and unable to move much, and then to have your companion dog pass away when you're 92 years old; it was just a little too much to take.

Grandma called the first week in December and told me she wasn't going to be able to come out for Christmas as we had planned. About three years earlier we had told her we didn't want her driving anymore so we had arranged so that she would be taking flights back and forth to our house in Oklahoma. She told me that with her level of pain there was no way that she would be able to take a plane because it was so uncomfortable for her to sit for any period of time, particularly in one position. We were sad, but more than sad we were very concerned, as grandma was crying! Grandma nearly never cried. We wanted to help in some way, even though we were over a thousand miles away – so we called a food delivery company that delivered frozen prepared meals and sent enough to feed a small village. OK, not a village, but enough so that her best friend and neighbor could come over and help her prepare it, and they could both easily eat together. I sent about 3 weeks' worth of food and called Jean (the neighbor who was like a sister to her) to help her unpack and asked her assistance in cooking. Jean, of course, was more than happy to help.

My husband and I discussed the situation, and our hearts were breaking with the idea that 92-year-old Gigi would be alone and in pain for Christmas. We felt that we needed to call Rick and let him know that grandma wasn't coming, as he was planning on coming up to see us. He had spoken to her and knew that she was in pain. About a week and a half before Christmas we could tell that grandma really wasn't doing well and so we called Rick and we all arranged for him to go and visit grandma for the week before Christmas as a surprise.

Mission "Surprise Gigi" was accomplished because she was shocked when uncle Rick appeared on her porch! I am so thankful for the week that my uncle had with his mom. He was able to go to an MRI with her and support her through the results when they found what appeared to be a growth or a tumor in her lower spine. Of course, she hid from both him and us about the scan results and told us that it did not appear to be cancer –she said that there was no chance it was cancer, just benign. However, how she was saying the results made my husband and me suspicious. Later we found out when we saw the paperwork and Rick spoke to her doctor that the doctor hadn't said that at all - that he did think that there was a risk that it was cancer. That was grandma; she was probably planning on protecting us and figuring things out before she worried or informed anybody of what might be a cancer diagnosis.

Lesson Learned: This is an important point for a caregiver to note, as my parents also hid thier symptoms. The person struggling with illness may try and hide or minimize the illness to protect their loved ones. This is bad for them, as they suffer alone, and for the caregiver, who can't help as efficiently and thoroughly without the big picture details!

We never found out if this was cancer because Christmas night after everything had settled down, she went into respiratory distress and had to be taken to the hospital. Her lack of mobility from the pain in her back had caused blood clots to form in her legs. She was admitted into the hospital for several days while they began blood clot treatment. She would never go home.

My uncle's job was fairly new and he had to get back to work so he was on a flight scheduled for the following day after grandma went to the hospital. I kept calling grandma at the hospital and calling the nurses at the hospital to check on her. I could tell that she was in a lot of pain plus she hated being in the hospital. They kept her for a couple of days and then decided to send her to a SNF (pronounced sniff) which is a **s**killed **n**ursing **f**acility.

That was where we lost contact with her. I called several times and my uncle called several times, but she never answered the phone nor seemed alert enough for an aide to get her to talk to us. I had a long conversation with my husband about how concerned I was with the fact that I wasn't able to talk to her and that this was very unusual for grandma. Grandma was very responsive when we called because one time she had allowed her cell phone battery to drain down and couldn't find it because her phone wouldn't ring. When I couldn't reach her after several days I had gotten so upset that I had not only called Jean but I'd also called other people within her housing development and even called my uncle because I couldn't reach her. She had been very embarrassed about that situation, not because she was upset that I had tried to track her down, she was grateful that I cared that much. She was upset that she had allowed herself to be unavailable for so long. So, I knew that if she was able to call me she would call me because she knew how concerned I would be. My husband and I kept talking about whether it was time for me to go out and be with her or if I needed to save my vacation time and go when we moved her to live with us (because there was no choice at this point). We planned to move her in with us as soon as she came out of the hospital. We knew that it would be a bit of a process, but we were ready for it.

A day after she was moved into the skilled nursing facility they called saying that she was unresponsive and they were having to take her back to the hospital. I was at work when I got this call and I immediately called my husband and said *please, can I get on a plane and go*? He supported me and I was on a plane within hours, because I had a very bad feeling. I hadn't been able to talk to grandma since Sunday, and here it was Tuesday morning, and that was just not normal. I knew that she had to be incapable of talking to me for it to have gone that long without returning any of my calls. This was New Year's Eve. I got to her hospital at about 10 o'clock that night (6-hour flight to San Diego with one layover, a cheap car rental, and an hour car drive north to Temecula).

Walking into Grandma's hospital room, I wasn't sure what to expect. Part of me expected to get there and just be relieved that she still looked like grandma, only sick. I *fantasized* that I would give her a hard time about giving us a scare, and then we would start planning her trip home with us in a few weeks after she had recovered enough for travel. *She would protest, of course, because she had been avoiding that for years – she didn't want to be a*

227 | P a g e

burden to anyone - but in the end, she would agree. After all, three weeks earlier we had started to have that conversation when her legs hurt too much for her to come out. We had started making tentative plans for her to live with us… cracked open that conversation, and for the first time the initial reaction wasn't NO, but a contemplation – she even suggested she might be able to help with watching the girls and give Tony and me some *us* time.

That isn't what I saw when I walked into her ICU hospital room. It's hard to explain unless you have experienced it yourself, the feeling when you see someone, whose body is still functioning, but you just sense the spirit is gone. That was the immediate feeling, and it was so heartbreaking. I realized I had probably waited too long and felt like I would never get to talk to my grandmother again. While that was the initial impression, I didn't want to believe that until I had spoken to her medical team.

Lesson Learned: GO. If you can, GO. Don't contemplate – should I wait until the person really needs me? What if I go and they are fine, but next time they need me and I can't go because I don't have the time or money? I know it isn't always practical, but PRAY, talk to your spouse if you have one, and if at all possible, GO. I do regret not going out the day after Christmas when they first put her in the hospital and my uncle left for home. How I wish I could have been there! GO…if you can GO!

This began several days in the hospital with grandma, working with her medical team to try and see what damage had been done. At first, they weren't even sure why she had been unresponsive, and tests were still ongoing when I arrived. It would take brain scans, EKGs, CT scans, and many lab tests to determine that she had a massive heart attack, more than likely caused by one of the blood clots in her legs breaking loose. While in the hospital I was communicating with my uncle – telling him her condition including the opinion of the physicians and nurses regarding her recovery. I was also trying to keep my husband up-to-date as I had run out of the house in a very short time. We hadn't made any arrangements for the kids (who were on Christmas break). We also wanted to prepare the kids as this might be grandma's death, and they loved their Gigi.

It is very difficult to explain to somebody who isn't there with you what you're seeing when you're dealing with somebody who's at the end of their life. If you don't see firsthand somebody's condition you might not recognize when somebody telling you about their condition is trying to be honest and forthright or is merely scared and confused. I wanted to be encouraging but honest about her chances of recovery, which at this time I thought was at zero. However, anytime you're dealing with somebody who might be or is dying, there is a huge burden you feel to do right by that person. It's a balancing game between wanting to carry out their wishes if they've told you what those are, between what is morally right, and battling your own emotions regarding letting somebody go. It's doubly hard when you're not the one who is making those decisions, but you're the person who's there onsite.

Grandma had set up her medical protectorate where I was an alternative to my uncle, but my uncle was having a hard time making arrangements to come back. I feel fortunate that my uncle showed a level of trust in my opinion and my understanding of the situation, and therefore was trusting in the decisions and choices that I was making for grandma. This didn't remove the burden that I felt to make sure that my uncle was involved in the situation. I wanted to make sure he was on board with all decisions and choices, and ultimately was the one to make the choices, as it was his mom.

My uncle arrived a few days later. We made the choice to stop extreme measures for grandma after they performed a second brain scan showing that she was having constant seizures. Essentially what this meant was that even if she could wake up, which she had shown no signs of doing, she would be in constant pain and agony due to the seizures and might have already suffered extreme brain damage. Even small noises or a touch of the hand would potentially cause her pain.

Grandma had left a very clear medical directive that stated that she did not want most of the things that we had already done to keep her alive. Unfortunately, the hospital had not had a copy of this directive when she came in from the nursing center unresponsive, or they may never have revived her.

Lesson Learned: Get multiple copies of Medical Directives, Medical Protectorate Designations, and DNRs that states the patient's desire in case of extreme situations. Make sure that the doctor has a copy, the hospitals have copies, the nursing homes, etc. This is the only way the wishes of your patient can be carried out.

When we stopped the extreme lifesaving care, it was a slow withdrawal, probably more for my uncle and myself then for grandma; it appeared that she was beyond most understanding of anything that was going on and could not wake up. Our biggest concern was to make sure that she didn't feel any pain, so they began pain medication and then slowly began removing support systems such as IV fluid, Lasix, antibiotics and anything else that was hooked up to her at the time. The one thing that I had suggested to my uncle that we not remove was a light level of oxygen, which was more for comfort than for actual breathing assistance (I had learned this with both mom and dad).

I was a little amazed how long her body held out after all of this was removed - approximately 15 hours. I never thought that with only pain medication, without anything helping her blood pressure, and without fluid, that she would last that long - but grandma had been stubborn in life and her body was stubborn unto death. Rick and I sat at her side in the room with her for those 15 hours, watching her heartbeat, watching every breath, waiting. If there had been any chance of her waking up, it would have been during this time.

I'm not one to quickly believe in so-called "miraculous signs and wonders" that people believe God sends to show them that everything is going to be okay. I believe the Bible is our wonder and our guidance. However, when we decided to remove the life-support system from grandma I was on one side of her, holding one hand, while Rick was on the other side holding that hand. I was facing the window looking out over the Temecula Valley, and a beautiful rainbow began to appear right outside the window. Over the next half hour, the rainbow grew brighter and deeper in color.

The previous few days I had sung songs of praise and had read to her from the Bible. I had prayed over her, not knowing if she heard. I still don't know if she heard anything that I said and I don't believe that seeing that rainbow is a sign from God. However, that rainbow did offer me a reminder of God's promises and that brought me comfort and assurance from my Heavenly Father as I was going through a time of turmoil. The rainbow is mentioned in the Bible (Genesis chapter 9) after the very first rain had ceased and Noah's Ark had come to a rest. God placed it in the sky as a promise to His people. I would encourage you to speak to your care receiver about faith and salvation. My hope and prayer is that one day I'll see grandma in heaven, and I clung to that hope. I also cling to the confidence that God's Plan is Good.

Grandma was the third person that I had seen pass away, so I was able to recognize the signs when it got closer to time. Her breathing slowed, her heart rate began to slow and there's almost an imperceptible change in the breathing, the sound that they make near the end. I was able to notify Rick because we had both been sitting and resting after the 15-hour vigil, and so both of us were at her side when she took her last breath and her heart stopped. I was really glad that we were able to share that moment and that we have been able to go through the last day or two with grandma because even if she wasn't aware, I don't like to think of her as having to be alone.

After somebody you are close to dies it's a strange feeling. In some ways, there's a sense of relief because this impending cloud, this storm, is over. At the same time, you've just lost somebody and you'll never see them again on earth. You are emotionally worn out, physically exhausted, and numb. On that day we waited a little while and then we headed to grandma's house, but I don't think either of us knew what to do.

It seems strange to start cleaning somebody's home when they've just passed, it almost seems disrespectful. In olden times I've read and remembered hearing that they had waiting periods, mourning periods before you would do anything. I think those periods were as much about respect for the deceased as they were also to give the family time to figure out what to do next! In our case, both of us had a timeline because both of us work and myself in particular, as I had a family waiting back home for me that I had abruptly left. This is where I'm glad in a way that I had been through this twice before as I could take off my mourning granddaughter hat and put on my dealing with the estate hat. Rick and I began to dig through some of grandma's items looking for what he would need to handle the estate, including paperwork and keys.

I write this because this was a different experience than what I had with my parents. With mom and dad, the decisions on end-of-life were either shared by me (as with dad and me for mom), or I was primarily responsible, such as with dad; but I was going through this experience with Rick, and he was the responsible party.

Lesson Learned: When dealing with having to make decisions about end-of-life it's very important to know your role in those decisions, and how you can support each other depending on those roles.

In one case I was daughter/caregiver and secondary in making the decisions. In another case, I was the daughter/ caregiver and primary in making the decisions. And in this case, I was granddaughter/secondary and was onsite for most of the final days of her life. So even though similar choices had to be made in all situations, my role changed. I hope that by writing about each of the situations I can encourage the caregiver and decision-makers and family to involve others in your choices even if ultimately you are the person making the decision. Also, to reach out for counsel and comfort from those who may not be part of having to make the decision but are concerned not only about the person you're caring for but also you as a caregiver.

Deciding to remove artificial life support is no easy matter. There's so much that needs to be considered that I am sure much smarter, higher educated, and certified people have written entire books and medical journal articles about this decision. All I can speak to is this from my own experience.

In the case of my grandmother, it was fairly apparent to me from the first night that I arrived that there wasn't a high possibility of her recovery. I also knew from previous discussions she did not want extended artificial support to keep her life going. However, I felt it was important that my uncle be the one making this decision (as did grandma, since she set up her protectorate that way).

After my dad's death I heard negative accusations from a small number of family members about my decision. While I 100% stand behind the choices that I made in dad's last day of his life, I didn't want there to be any opportunity or cause for my uncle to feel the same way. Also, my role was only the secondary or 'backup' decision-maker at grandma's request.

Caregiving and caring for somebody who is in this kind of situation doesn't always have to be in a vacuum and in grandma's case it wasn't. The decisions and choices were being shared and it is very important that when you're sharing these decisions and choices that you keep in mind the well-being of the other person. Don't forget to care for the other caregivers. In this case, even though it pained me to see my grandmother's body potentially in pain, it would have pained me more to try and forcefully influence my uncle into a plan of care that he wasn't ready to make.

Do your best to communicate the state your loved one is in and to also communicate any urgency for decisions if it exists. I say this so that people can work together in a state of grace, community, and family love if at all possible. Some will always question what you do as a caregiver and feel that they would have been better at the caregiving or the decision-making and that they would've made different decisions.

I hope that anybody making these decisions gets the love and support and understanding that they need. That might be hoping for *rainbows and butterflies and unicorn dreams*, though, because these situations aren't always reality. Reality is that what may be harder than making end-of-life decisions for somebody else is living with the repercussions of having to make those decisions.

As a caregiver, watching someone you love and care for die is painful. Having to stay clear-headed, use wisdom, and make difficult, informed decisions, is hard. I pray that everyone who has to carry out the desires of others in their position as a caregiver is given the strength to endure this difficult task. And, I look forward to being united with my loved ones in Christ, those who have gone before me!

Revelation 14:13 (ESV)
13 And I heard a voice from heaven saying, "Write this: Blessed are the dead who die in the Lord from now on." "Blessed indeed," says the Spirit, "that they may rest from their labors, for their deeds follow them!"

Chapter 16 - Preparations and Financial Strategy

Titus 1:7-9 (ESV)
7 For an overseer, as God's steward, must be above
reproach. He must not be arrogant or quick-
tempered or a drunkard or violent or greedy for
gain, 8 but hospitable, a lover of good, self-
controlled, upright, holy, and disciplined. 9 He must
hold firm to the trustworthy word as taught, so that
he may be able to give instruction in sound doctrine
and also to rebuke those who contradict it.

There were a few lessons I learned along the way when it came to be managing the finances of the person I was caring for, my dad. Some of these lessons were easy to learn because I reaped the benefit of the work my dad had done to prepare himself. Some of them were hard-learned, like when I messed up. I hope that this chapter, more practical than spiritual, will bless you so that some of the lessons I learned be passed on. After all, worrying about money is only a distraction from the real labor of love of caregiving but it is a necessary evil (as the saying goes). This chapter is primarily geared to the actual person who needs a caregiver, the "care-receiver", not the caregiver. However, if these matters are not addressed when you become a caregiver, you may be able to help with this as well. Also, for the caregiver, the Titus verse above is very important. You have been entrusted with much, and you, as a Christian caregiver, are called upon to be a good steward.

My father was a very organized man in most ways, and I reaped the benefit of his organization. Most of what I am going to write about dad had set the stage for, by modeling and providing me with the information while mom was ill. I am glad I get to share this valuable knowledge, as this took a lot of pressure off of me as the caregiver, and I hope that by being forewarned, you can also have that pressure valve opened a little. Here is another disclaimer. I am NOT a lawyer or legally trained. This information is informative and as hints and suggestions only not "the rule". Please consult with the laws of your state or land.

The first suggestion is that you should make the legal and financial decisions sooner, rather than later. This includes making sure that the loved one you are caring for has:

1. Created a Trust and/or a Will

I didn't know the difference between a Will and Trust before this began. Both are legal documents. A trust (my dad had a Revocable Trust, which meant at any time he had the right to revoke or cancel the instructions within it) takes effect even before someone has died. This means that you can transfer property to a trust, put the trust on bank accounts and as a benefactor for life insurance, and give someone, besides the person(s) setting up the trust, the right to administer the instructions in the trust, before death. Another important thing of note is that a trust doesn't have to go through probate, which is when the court is involved in settling an estate, which takes time and costs (court fees, lawyer fees, etc.)

My dad set up the trust (this can be done via a lawyer, or even with legal software or online services. You might be able to find forms to fill out as well). Then, he began the process of putting assets into that trust. Examples:

Bank accounts, house, vehicles, retirement and retirement funds such as CDs and IRAs, Insurance beneficiaries, properties, etc.

This meant that the trust owned these assets, not one person. Therefore, the trust managed the assets per the guidance put in the trust.

Dad also set up a Last Will and Testament. However, this just said, everything I forgot to transfer to the Trust, goes into the Trust. It was insurance for anything missed.

Note: You don't have to have all the specifics of the "things" to get the Trust drawn up. My dad referred to an Appendix in his Trust. In the Appendix he typed or hand wrote specific desires for the "things" that he wanted to leave to specific people. This way you don't drag your feet getting the Trust made because you haven't decided who gets what.

2. Choose a Trustee, and backup(s).

My dad was the head of the trust. However, he delegated equal power in the Trust to me, his daughter. He had backup trustees as well, but they were only if I choose not to take on the responsibility. I know of some trusts that give equal/joint trustee powers. In an ideal world, this would be a wonderful thing, because the choices and burdens and activity would be shared. We don't live in an ideal world, and I have heard and seen too many issues when it comes to the handling of estates, to recommend this.

3. Power of Attorney (POA) and Medical Protectorate and a DNR (Do Not Resuscitate)

A POA gives someone else the right to act on your behalf. It can be unlimited (in all matters) and limited, to particular matters (such as one transaction). This should be created to help your Trustee in cases where the Trust isn't enough.

A Medical Protectorate designates who can make medical decisions for you. This may or may not be the same person as your POA and Trustee. In my dad's case, I served in the capacity of all three, but in others, there might be situations where you want to split this up. For example, maybe someone is an excellent financier but doesn't understand medical issues at all, but you have someone else in your family or friend circle that is a nurse and can make good medical decisions.

DNR – this is a touchy subject. If you have decided that you do not want extreme medical activity to save or prolong your life, you need to have a DNR drawn up. This will tell your Medical

Protectorate and the Clinical Staff what your desires are for medical treatment. Include this with the Medical Protectorate paperwork and make copies so that you can file it (or they can) when you enter medical facilities.

4. Copies and Locations

Once you have all of the legal paperwork drawn up, make copies and get them into the hands of those who need them. My dad kept the "official copy" in a Bank Box (safety deposit box) and made sure I was able to access it. He then had copies supplied to his Bank, the mortgage company, given to me, his mom, and electronic. He also created a 3 Ring Binder that he had at the house for reference.

This Binder might also be an excellent place to store phone lists, for calling after death or for emergencies. My dad's binder also had account information in it for every investment. The name of the company, the account number, the phone number, the address. Contact names if he had one and the type of asset that was kept there. He also included a key to a fireproof box where life insurance papers, birth certificates, etc. were kept.

Oh, and the obvious. Make sure that everyone who needs to know where the information is located, knows where the information is located. Then safeguard it.

5. Get the proper authorization

Some states require only witnesses to Wills, Trusts, etc. Some require notarization. Some require both. Some require that these documents have to be filed with the state. Find out what your state requires and do it.

6. Inform your loved ones of your decisions and who you have set up as your Trustee, Estate Manager, Protectorate, etc.

This step, while not necessary, will help the people who have to enact your will. If they hear it from that person, they may hold grudges, be bitter or angry, or doubt the veracity. If you can, let your family know your desires and endorse the ones you have asked to make them happen.

7. Funeral/cremation arrangements (and finances)

If you can make funeral or cremation arrangements, before the need, this will greatly help your caregiver. This is an emotional matter. Everyone's choices and decisions are very personal. This is your opportunity to put your desires into action, or at least document them.

For example. My mom and dad had purchased a plot already. This was helpful, as I knew where they wanted to be buried. Mom had planned her funeral down to what she wanted to wear. Dad wanted to be buried in the cheapest box we could find; he would have been happy if it was a rough pine box.

Funeral expenses are high as well. Not everyone can pre-pay or set aside money for a funeral, but if you can, this will take a huge burden off the caregiver, the Trustee, the POA, whomever you have set in charge.

8. Looking for lost money

I know, funny section. However, each state has a website that is made for companies to inform the state if they have unclaimed money. This might be security deposits for utilities, mineral rights income, insurance that wasn't claimed, overpayments, etc. I found this out after mom and dad had passed away. I wish I had known before!

I found a few hundred dollars that were unclaimed for dad (and some for myself, YAY). Years later, I found some for my grandmother too! For dad, mostly it was easy to send them the Trust and Will and receive the money.

However, I ran into a problem. It turns out that my mom had unclaimed money, which had by default gone to my dad as inheritor. This doesn't sound like a problem, right? It should just go into the Trust, and be distributed according to that, right? Well, since it was for my mom, and dad hadn't claimed it, it didn't go into the trust, per my state's rules. The state rules said that it should be distributed evenly to the children of dad. Here is the problem. Dad had no natural children. He had adopted my older brother, but we other two are step-children. The Trust and Will stated that we were all to be viewed equally as children, but my state doesn't recognize step-children as children, even if a Will and Trust say they should be. Therefore, my mom's insurance payment, instead of going equally to all three of us (we are all her natural children), only went to one brother, because he was adopted. The point of this is to find the money before the person you are caring for passes so that A. They can use it for themselves (it is their money) or B. It can be included in the trust and the person whose money it is can decide where to distribute it, not the state you live in.

9. Long and Short-Term Disability Insurance

This is for any person who is still working and wondering how you are going to support yourself if you become sick or injured. Many companies offer both long- and short-term disability insurance. Consider these as good options for financial stability if you should become unable to work.

Some companies pay part of the premiums on one or both (my experience is they pay part of the premiums on short, but not long-term disability insurance). There are also different options of coverage (for example, short term might payout 40% of your salary for up to X number of weeks, while long term may cover 60% of your salary, after you have been not able to work for X number of weeks, for X amount of time/years (often until retirement).

I am thankful my dad paid for both of these types of insurance. It meant that as the caregiver I was not struggling to pay for his medical expenses, home, prescription medications, food, etc. It also meant that twice, when I had to quit working on FMLA for

12 weeks, dad was able to "pay me" as his caregiver (this was an outlined option in the trust), so that I could afford to do that (how you do this is either according to the trust or how you work it out with your care-receiver. I didn't take a salary, I just had my basic expenses covered only, which is far less than a salary would have been for full time care). It was something we discussed and he did for me, to take the pressure off me, and I am so thankful.

10. Post-death considerations

This is back to the caregiver. When your loved one dies, you will need to make many arrangements. You will need to contact banks, credit card companies, insurance companies, Social Security, utility companies, mortgage companies, investment companies, etc. They will need certain information from you. You might not want to do this right away until you have everything they will need. This will include

    a. Copies of death certificates (this can take a few weeks to receive). Make sure you order a lot of them (10-20) because just about everyone will want an official copy.
    b. Bank account numbers to route any insurance money into.
    c. Date, Location, Cause of Death
    d. Copies of the Trust/Will including who is the executor of those (they can't give you information about the accounts until you provide this – so, this should be the first thing you fax/email to them)

Also, make sure you know what the estate needs to cover expenses. I believe in paying bills. Unless dad's estate couldn't for some reason (which didn't apply, we were able to pay all the bills) I believe it is morally right to cover those costs and expenses. If the estate cannot, you need to consult with someone who can help determine what to do (probably a lawyer or legal help online), for guidance.

My suggestion is to not distribute money until you have paid all of the expenses/bills, determined what all monies/assets will be coming in, and do good math/accounting,

11. Keep excellent records

As the caregiver (or the Executor), you need to keep excellent records to account for your costs and expenses, income to the estate, distributions, etc. I am an IT Auditor by training, and I put those auditing skills to use. This is for transparency, and also to protect yourself.

A spreadsheet with tabs for Income, Expenses, Checklists/Tasks, etc. might come in handy, it did for me. I updated the spreadsheet every time I worked on the Trust. I had a tab for activities carried out (example: called this company, went to the Social Security Office, had to File paperwork at the court, mailed checks, spoke to this insurance company). I tracked my time and expenses as well. This may or may not be necessary depending on the dynamics of your situation, but it is good practice. It also allows you to quickly be accountable to those to whom you need to be, or simply want to be. Keeping a log of emails sent (or letters) is also a good idea and send letters with receipt notifications turned on (US mail and Email).

12. Email and Social Media accounts (and phones)

Just a quick note to not forget about these. If you can, get the logins and passwords for these so that you can monitor or close when needed. This might be a good notification method as well, as the person you care for might use this as a method to keep in track.

13. Taxes

Don't forget that someone will have to file the taxes for the estate, for at least one year, possibly more, depending on income to the estate. You will need to file for an estate tax identification number. We hired an accountant to do the taxes the first year, and this would be my suggestion. We did learn a few interesting things during this experience:

    A. Estates can file taxes, but not everything can be attributed to the estate

        i. For example, IRA income must be put on the taxes of the person who receives the money, not on the estate

        ii. Life insurance is tax-free (at least the amount that my father had, check with tax professional)

        iii. Many investments, if not reinvested immediately when you inherit them, must pay an early "cash-out" fine if the person inheriting them is not the spouse or of a certain age.

    B. Hold back the taxes the estate needs to pay, do not distribute until you have calculated those or have filed taxes the first year.

In Conclusion

I hope that this information will help both the caregiver and the care receiver to make good financial decisions during these stressful times. The type of practical issues and arrangements in this chapter have been asked of me many times. While you may want to focus all of your time and effort on the physical wellbeing of the one you care for, estates, taxes, planning, funerals, and other concerns can't be put aside. The Lord calls us to be good Stewards, and to care for others above ourselves. This type of planning, financial and end-of-life, might be part of your role as caregiver. It can be a heavy responsibility and one where you must guard yourself against your own selfish inclinations and the mechanisms of others as well. Good planning and record keeping may be vital.

1 Corinthians 10:24 (ESV)
24 Let no one seek his own good, but the good of his neighbor.

Chapter 17 - Am I ready for my own Battle?

After being a caregiver, I found myself thinking about my own death. As a Christian, I have the promise of eternity with our Savior, where there will be no more tears, no more pain. I hold tight to that promise and therefore I believe most Christians face death from a different perspective. I am human, however, so I also worry about pain and suffering here, before death. I worry about the hereditary diseases in my family –ALS, Frontal Lobe Dementia, cancers. I worry about my family having to care for me, and the burden that will place on them. Even though I look on my caregiving as a blessing and I am thankful I was able to care for my loved ones, I don't want my family to have to go through the same ordeal as I. As a wife and parent, I know that with the blessing of caregiving also comes the pain of watching your loved one suffer and the physical and emotional trial.

I have had episodes of worry where I would talk to my husband about what would happen if I got sick. Telling him we needed life insurance because of my high risk. Telling him how I would want him to divide things so the kids have an inheritance and memories. My husband would laugh and tell me he was dying first (because he is male and older) so no point in telling him these things. I would then remind him of my family history, and I would fret.

All these negative thoughts changed over a period of 3 weeks. Events and another death (this time my 46-year-old brother) led to my change in perspective, and I am so thankful.

I would love to tell you I bounced out of these worries within weeks or months after my dad and grandmother died, but that would be a lie. Four years after dad died, my brother developed pancreatitis. While most people are able to recover, his led to organ failure and a six-month ordeal that ended in his slow wasting away and eventual death. Once again, from a distance, I was trying to support and encourage a caregiver; this time, my sister-in-law. Due to the distance and having children in school, I couldn't be there for them physically. One visit was all I was able to make. Instead, my act as a caregiver was reduced to encouraging messages, text, phone calls and financial assistance. I was able to help her understand the medical conditions and test results, and be an emergency contact and sounding board, but that seemed so little when compared to their need. However, even in this little, I remembered the times I wished I had guidance when I was in the midst of mom and dad's illnesses – so hoped that what little I could provide was blessing them.

I digress. What changed me from dwelling on death by ALS or cancer was inevitable? I attended a True Woman, Revive our Hearts conference in 2018. This conference was about seeking truth, truth in God's Word. Truth in my role as a wife, mother, woman of God. Truth in my purpose, as a child of God, whose life is to glorify God. God was bringing me to a place of desperation where I would recognize how I had forgotten about God's promises. His promise of good plans for His children. His plan of support, comfort, hope in trials. The conference reminded me that God's truth is not in my own thoughts, feelings, emotions, but in the Word of God. I was also reminded of a woman of God at the conference who had influenced me in my teen years, Joni Eareckson Tada. As a teen, she became paralyzed but still found a way to live her life to glorify God.

Coming home with this knowledge reawakened in me allowed for the next realization. My husband had asked me to listen to Paul David Tripp's book, Eternity. I agreed and began listening to it in my car on the way to work after dropping the girls off at school. This was the second experience that snapped me out of my melancholy about dying. This book reminded me to view this life in terms of eternity. As Christians, we are taught to remember this life is just the beginning, and not the destination, but we forget. We tell ourselves we are focused on eternity but so often we really aren't, it is just a coping mechanism for disappointments. This can lead to discontent, and discontent to strife with our relationships.

I realized I was like the people in his book – trying to get out of this life as much as I could, as if this life was all there was. I looked at my Facebook friends and their vacations and was discontent. I thought – I have been so busy taking care of others, I don't get to do any of these amazing things. I am tied down with my responsibilities. I looked at my fellow pastor's wives and the conferences they got to attend and was discontent. I looked at homes on HGTV and was discontent as I stared at the water spot on the ceiling, which we had tried to get repaired three times! I thought about the years where I could have been living overseas but was home taking care of others, and was disappointed. All these things, in my head, making me think that this life was it. This life here and now was the goal, this was the one time around.

How had I allowed myself to forget that eternity was what God desired for me, not the possibly 84 +/- average years of life on this planet? I had been lured by the deceiver into a world view that ignored eternity. A wonderful Revive Our Hearts ambassador, Elena had been reminding me that troubles I experience are temporary, too look beyond the now; but I hadn't truly understood. It took her wise words in my mind, the reminder of the lives of women who had gone through so much more than I, and the book for me to begin looking FORWARD (and up to the Lord) and not down. Down at my current situation and circumstance. I needed to be reminded to consider the eternal view, of a life with purpose.

This is what I understand now. I have no idea how long I have on earth. I don't know if I will live to be in my 50s, like my mom. Or in my 70s, like my biological grandmothers or 90s like some of my great-grands. Maybe I won't make it out of my 40s, like my brother. I have no idea. Christ could return before I publish this book (Maranatha – come Lord, come). What I realized talking to Elena and my husband, attending the conference, listening to the book was this – However much time I have, Lord, I want to be your instrument. Use me, Lord. Help me to keep the eternal perspective. After all, I might never make it to the Galapagos Islands or The Great Barrier Reef, I may never get a "book deal", and I may not live to see all my children saved and happily married (and providing me with grandbabies). I may never...but, God has made me a promise. The promise of eternity praising and adoring Him. I know that God's Kingdom will far exceed anything this world has to offer. How can I mourn my lack of opportunity here, when I have a promise like that waiting?

James 1:12 (ESV)
12 Blessed is the man who remains steadfast under
trial, for when he has stood the test he will receive
the crown of life, which God has promised to those
who love him.

Fellow Believer, if you are a caregiver, and wondering what God has in store for you and your loved one, look to forever. Look at the time you have in providing care as time serving and glorifying God. Remember, even as you watch others suffer, with God as our Father, there will be healing. Remember, even as you struggle with physical, emotional and spiritual trials of your own, God is and will restore you, day by day, and eventually in eternity with Him.

The joy of the Lord is my strength. I hope you can have a prayer like mine. *Lord, whatever time you have given me, make me your instrument. If I have more people to care for, please help me to glorify you for that purpose. If I am the one destined to be cared for, help me to be a testimony even in my suffering. When I falter and hesitate, please, use me. Lord, into your hands my life is placed.*

In the next chapter, my husband (a pastor) is going to explain why it is that pain and suffering occur in our world. I think that during the caregiving process you (as the caregiver), the person you are caring for (who may be suffering or in pain), and others who watch the decline of those they love, question how a Good God can allow pain and suffering to happen to good people. It is important to know the origin and purpose of pain and suffering so that for the believer, we can have hope.

Death entered this world through sin. Romans 5:12 says

12 Therefore, just as sin came into the world through one man, and death through sin, and so death spread to all men because all sinned....

In 1st Corinthians we are reminded that death came through man (Adam) but that life will come back to man through Christ.

For as by a man came death, by a man has come also the resurrection of the dead. For as in Adam all die, so also in Christ shall all be made alive (15:21-22).

Since suffering, pain, and death are first introduced in the third chapter of Genesis, until the coming of Christ again or to believer's entry (through death) into Paradise, we must expect to witness and even experience suffering and pain. We must not give up hope, for ourselves, or for those we care for but encourage each other to remember the promises of God in our lowest times, because He is there for us, and has great and wonderful things in store for us.

This hard place in which you perhaps find yourself is the very place in which God is giving you opportunity to look only to Him, to spend time in prayer, and to learn long-suffering, gentleness, meekness - in short, to learn the depths of the love that Christ Himself has poured out on all of us.

- Elisabeth Elliot

Chapter 18 - Why Must there be a Battle?

Why do we suffer? By Pastor Tony Cordoves,

Tony Cordoves is both my husband and a bi-vocational Associate Pastor of Iglesia Bautista Central - Oklahoma City, OK

We live in a world full of illness and suffering. If you are reading this book, it is probably because you are going through difficult times due to being a caregiver; or you are suffering from an illness or injury. You may have asked yourself '**why**' does there have to be suffering? **Why** does God allow this, especially for His children?

When we see this pain in the world, we are frightened; especially when it happens to loved ones, such as parents or our children. Many then think that this is because God does not care, cannot do everything, wants to punish us or that He is indifferent to humanity or just bad. This is the reason why many say they reject God and the his message and live without hope. Even believers, when tested, think they are not saved or that God has abandoned them and therefore live without truly believing in the hope God has given them. C.S. Lewis said,

"Pain and suffering for some are reasons that they do not believe in God."

However, Charles Spurgeon said,

"Pain and suffering brings us closer to God and strengthens our faith in Him."

Isn't it interesting, this contrast? For some suffering is the reason they give for rejecting God, while for others, it is the reason they seek, trust and humble themselves before Him. Let me go back to the beginning of creation, *Genesis 3 vs.6 and 7 say,*

> *So when the woman saw that the tree was good for*
> *food, and that it was a delight to the eyes, and that*
> *the tree was to be desired to make one wise, she*
> *took of its fruit and ate, and she also gave some to*
> *her husband who was with her, and he ate. Then the*
> *eyes of both were opened, and they knew that they*
> *were naked. And they sewed fig leaves together and*
> *made themselves loincloths.*

For this reason, God told them in *v.13*, "*what is this that you have done?*" condemning them in *vs. 16 to 18* when he said.

> *"I will surely multiply your pain in childbearing; in*
> *pain you shall bring forth children. Your desire*
> *shall be contrary to your husband, but he shall rule*
> *over you." And to Adam he said, "Because you have*
> *listened to the voice of your wife and have eaten of*
> *the tree of which I commanded you, 'You shall not*
> *eat of it,' cursed is the ground because of you; in*
> *pain you shall eat of it all the days of your life;*
> *thorns and thistles it shall bring forth for you; and*
> *you shall eat the plants of the field."*

The Scriptures here show us that suffering began when Adam and Eve sinned and broke their relationship with God. From that moment they began to die. Disobedience introduced pain and suffering and the whole of creation was affected and corrupted; that is the reason for all suffering.

Perhaps most of us can accept this, but even Christians ask, *why does God allow suffering to 'good' people*? Notice I say good between quotes; this is because since Adam and Eve **no one is good**, we all deserve condemnation. However, God is Merciful with His people, and as we will see below, He pours out His Love on His chosen children.

Let us understand then that suffering is not the same for everyone. For the non-believer, it is the result of his separation from God through disobedience. For believers, who through repentance and God's forgiveness, are now at peace with God, these sufferings are tests that He orchestrates for our good. Even discipline is to make us better Christians. In other words, what the devil planned for evil God uses for good... we see it in *Romans 8:28*,

> *"... we know that for those who love God, all things work together for good, that is, for those who are called according to his purpose."*

We must understand that God allows suffering to his people to create in them a pious character. It is in the confidence and security of God's Love that He gives then Hope. It is this Love that we see in His Plan of Redemption, in the Justification that is the foundation for Hope.

To understand this Hope we first need to understand Salvation. It begins like this:

- God is Holy and Just, and for that reason, the sin in the world needs to be punished.
- Since we are all sinners, we all have a debt to God.
- Jesus Christ voluntarily became man, died for the sins of the believers, and paid the price (debt) for the chosen;
- He, therefore, justified the believers and, at that moment, (resurrection);

- God's progressive sanctification begins (Sanctification is the process of being set apart by God from the sinful world).
- When we are set apart, God works within us to make us more like Jesus. He does this giving us the Word of God as a guide, the Bible, and helping us to understand it with the help of the Holy Spirit.
- He also uses situations in our life to remind us to seek Him and follow His ways. It is in Sanctification that believers are transformed into the image of Jesus.

Salvation then is God's initiative in His Sovereign Will, it is the way His Grace extends and covers us, which is infinitely greater than our disobedience. The just thing is for everyone to receive eternal condemnation, but in His Mercy, as a gift, He acts and loves the one who He wants.

Hope is then because our Salvation is secure, He dwells in the believer. In other words, His Spirit is in them and it is He who seals us at the moment we are saved, sanctifies us day after day (a process that lasts the rest of our lives), and saves us to live in God's presence for eternity.

Look at it this way, **sanctification is to restore the believer**, who was corrupted by sin, to the image of God. It **transforms** us into the image of Christ because one day we will be Glorified (which is when we will be brought back to life, given a new body, and live in Heaven with Christ). That is why the **suffering in Sanctification reminds us that one day we will be in the presence of God**! What Hope that should give us. Therefore, being Justified is guaranteed that we will be Glorified. It is a package ... God is not going to start something in us, but then just wait for His purpose to simply happen ... No, He makes sure that this will emerge in us by training us, changing us, and living in us. His Love will complete the work He started in us. *Philippians 1:6* says,

"And I am sure of this, that he who began a good work in you will bring it to completion at the day of Jesus Christ."

The Glorification is the end of Sanctification and the end of our sufferings. It is the end of the Christian life in this world, but the beginning of the new eternal life that God promised us. It is when we can completely do what we were created for. In the same way that the believer will then be Holy because God is Holy, the believer is glorified in Christ because God is Glory. This is the foundation of our Hope.

A study of the Bible shows us that we are not alone in this race. We can see biblical figures like Abraham, David, and especially the apostle Paul who had to endure pain, suffering, and restitution; but through it all, they understood and had the Hope in the promises of God. We truly see this in our Lord and Savior who suffered on the Cross as an undeserved gift to humanity, to free us from sin. The irony is that His suffering gives us freedom, security, and Hope. He trusted and depended on His Father who Promised that He would resurrect to life in Glory for eternity. That is the hope and assurance that we need to have, the Promise of God that He saves, Sanctifies and Glorifies the believers and that **even the sufferings are for their good**.

With the understanding of Salvation, my intention in this chapter is to show that when we are of God, we can have Hope even during sickness. More specifically I want to show that suffering is a gift of God and that we can rejoice and have Hope while enduring. Probably at this time, it is difficult to understand that suffering is a gift from God and that He uses it for the ultimate good, but again we have to study the scripture to see it.

Let's examine in the Epistle (Letter) to the Romans, chapter 5. Paul explains here the reason for the sufferings and why God allows them. He shows us in this chapter the guarantee to the believer of his Salvation, but more specifically in the first verses, he teaches us how this security is the Hope that strengthens. We see that Hope is in the Glorification, which begins with our Sanctification in Justification. *Romans 5:1-5* says,

> *Therefore, since we have been justified by faith, we have peace with God through our Lord Jesus Christ. Through him we have also obtained access by faith into this grace in which we stand, and we rejoice in hope of the glory of God. Not only that, but we rejoice in our sufferings, knowing that suffering produces endurance, and endurance produces character, and character produces hope, 5 and hope does not put us to shame, because God's love has been poured into our hearts through the Holy Spirit who has been given to us.*

In the first two verses, we see that the Grace of God is what is necessary for Hope. Here Paul says that by being justified we are now at peace with God. In other words, no more enmity with Him because Jesus Christ paid the debt of His adopted brothers (believers); He is the mediator that brings Peace. Notice that Paul is very emphatic here, that we have been justified by faith in Christ. It is not anything that the believer could have done. The merit for the Justification of the believer is only in Christ; the basis of Salvation and therefore Hope.

What does Paul tell us then? He shows that, without Salvation, without being Justified we are at war with God, separated from Him. ***It is only by the undeserved Sacrifice of Christ that we can again be in communion with God, in peace. This not a "feeling", but more importantly a state of being.*** Why is this peace so important? Let me answer this with another question. Can we depend, feel Hope, and rest in someone we reject and do not respect? Can we have hope in someone with whom we are at war and we do not trust? No! It is also through Jesus Christ that we receive the faith that restores that Divine Relationship with God. Therefore, He is our mediator, our intercessor. Now we can see the truth and understand our evil, but more importantly, we see the need for Justification. It is through Him that we receive, as Paul says, Grace; the undeserved Gift. **That is why we persevere**.

Grace is then given only by Love, which is a gift that we have to understand to really appreciate. It is free for the Church (believers), but it came at a very high cost, a very dear price for Christ; His Humiliation, Suffering, and Death on the Cross. Therefore, God is not going to let this Sacrifice be wasted. This is security in Salvation that causes Hope. If, when we were most disobedient, God called us, saved us, and gave us His Spirit - only by Grace, so how can our hope be lost? It can't! It is assured. That is why Paul said, *"in which we stand"*. What God begins (His plan for our Salvation) He does not abandon, but in Christ God completes it. Paul called it *"... the Hope of the Glory of God"*. This is our guarantee in which we find Hope.

In *vs.3-4* we see then how this Hope is reached and strengthened; it is through the Sanctification, through our sufferings. Paul probably refers here specifically to the persecution of Christians, but we know that sufferings happen in different ways to Christians and even to non-Christians. Paul expands his explanation here by giving us the chain of events of how God strengthens this Hope. He simply tells us that it is in the tribulations, in the suffering that God orchestrates. Yes, God allows suffering, even for His people, because they serve a purpose. I like how Paul starts in *v.3*, he says, *"not only that"*. In other words, there is more ... much more, it's like we see on a television infomercial when they say, "but wait, there is more!" Let us think then of what Paul says that "we *rejoice in our sufferings*". Confusing isn't it? Do we glorify in suffering? Simply put, it is through **suffering** that God **transforms** us for His Glory. Look,

Paul tells us that sufferings produce endurance. The apostle Peter says in *1 Peter 5:10*,

> *"And after you have suffered a little while, the God of all grace, who has called you to his eternal glory in Christ, will himself restore, confirm, strengthen, and establish you."*

Suffering will lead to God's restoral, confirmation, strengthening, and establishing us. Paul says here that *"suffering produces endurance"*.

What is endurance? Endurance is going through a difficult process or situation, over a long distance or time, without giving up. Understand that endurance leads to character formation. Endurance is obtained by trust and dependence on God. Often when we encounter suffering and trials, we want to take control. When we can't, we get desperate. Understand then that endurance is a fruit of the Spirit, and it is through reliance on Him that we can relax during suffering and trials. That's why we have to be saved first; to have God working within us.

Endurance, as Paul tells us, is key to Hope. Notice, when Paul says that *"endurance produces character,"* he is saying that endurance shapes our character, our spiritual maturity. The more we are tested the more we can persevere; it is how God strengthens us and develops our resistance. That's also the way with physical exercise, right? The more we persevere exercising the body, the stronger the muscles, and the respiratory and circulatory system. Therefore, just as Christ suffered and persevered on the Cross to be Glorified, in our suffering we unite ourselves to Christ and in Him, we will be Glorified. Therefore, he who has endurance trusts and depends on Christ, he who has endurance has persevered in Christ. It is the product of faith in God that assures us who we are (Saved), which then gives us hope and peace that we are not alone, that we are loved by God; He is in control and He ensures our eternity.

What this means is that suffering is the biggest part of our sanctification, the method that brings us closer to God and makes us more pious. This forces the believer to look to God for our comfort and for strength. Look at it this way, what is the end of God's Will? The Glorification of His own for His Adoration and Glory. Again, the Hope is when we rejoice in our sufferings; the progressive sanctification that ends when we are in His presence. Each time we persevere, we mature because we see the love and care of God, this strengthens our faith and we believe what God has done and is doing. This then strengthens our confidence in what He will do in the future.

Finally, in *v 5*, we see the result of Hope which the production of encouragement and satisfaction is given by the Love of God. This is one of my favorite verses, I love the word *"poured"*, showing that God does not skimp on His Love for His people. The proof of God pouring out is in the Gift of His beloved Son for our Salvation. We see here that our hope has been secured and for this reason, we can be comforted and calmed as we persevere. Paul says, *"and hope does not put us to shame,"* that is, it does not disappoint us because it is guaranteed by the Faithful Love of God.

Our hope comes from the perfect, agape (unconditional) love of our faithful Father, who hears our cries and rescues us, even pouring out His love on His children, by salvation through His Son. That is the foundation of Hope in our trials and sufferings. Do you see now how the believer goes from being at war with God to a peace in an intimate relationship of Love, sealed and assured by the Holy Spirit?

We have received within us His Holy Spirit, love, infinite and unimaginable. Let us remember then that like endurance, love is also the fruit of the Spirit. I once heard this said (but can't remember where or by whom) *Just as a baby feels safe/secure because of his mother's love, the Christian feels safe/secure because of God's love.* Understand then, the people around us, even those supporting us in our sufferings and trials, will eventually disappoint us, but God will never disappoint us. What better guarantee than this? It was out of love that God created the world and saved us, out of love He sacrificed His son, it is through love that He provides for us, cares for us, sanctifies us, and disciplines us. More importantly, it is because of love that He will Glorify and Bless us forever.

Remember then, we will all suffer. Jesus himself told us in *Luke 9:23,*

> *"...If anyone would come after me, let him deny himself and take up his cross daily and follow me."*

Therefore, it is not whether we will suffer, but when. Here we see that not only must we expect to suffer, but we must accept it and live with it in our walk with God. However, here we see that Paul encourages us to rejoice in our sufferings as they strengthen our relationship with God, and lead us to be more like our Savior, Christ Jesus.

We live in a world full of suffering and being a Christian does not reduce the suffering. Moreover, because of our faith, we will probably be attacked, and we may have more suffering. However, as we have just seen, the promise and hope we have are that we are not alone, that God is in control and even in death He gives us the Security of His Divine Gift. Sufferings for the believers serves as a guide, the way God, like a parent, teaches us the right way. The Psalmist says,

> *"It is good for me that I was afflicted, that I might learn your statutes. The law of your mouth is better to me than thousands of gold and silver pieces."*
> *(Psalm 119:71-72)*

Do not forget that humanity caused suffering but the Love of God frees us, and it is this love that our hope is ensured. It is difficult to think of Glory in suffering, but suffering:

- humbles us,
- purifies us,
- strengthens our faith,
- forces us to seek God,
- makes us more like Christ,
- makes us more sensitive to others and their needs,
- and it cleanses our character, making us more holy.

Don't forget that the Love of God is the foundation of Hope.

Did you know that God speaks to us through suffering and reminds us that we are a work in progress that He will finish? The author C. S. Lewis says,

"Pain insists upon being attended to. God whispers to us in our pleasures, speaks in our consciences, but shouts in our pains. It is his megaphone to rouse a deaf world."

The suffering of the believers is temporary because when we are glorified, God:

...will wipe away every tear from their eyes, and death shall be no more, neither shall there be mourning, nor crying, nor pain anymore, for the former things have passed away." And he who was seated on the throne said, "Behold, I am making all things new." (Revelation 21:4-5a, NLT)

Caregiver, and suffer alike, remember that every gift that God gives us is not only for us but for sharing. Paul said in *2 Corinthians 1:3-4,*

*Blessed be the God and Father of our Lord Jesus
Christ, the Father of mercies and God of all
comfort, who comforts us in all our affliction, so
that we may be able to comfort those who are in any
affliction, with the comfort with which we ourselves
are comforted by God.*

As you can see, we can, and we must comfort and help others. God comforts so we can comfort our brothers. It is a way to love your neighbor and serve their needs by showing them the hope we have in Christ when we are children of God.

The saddest thing is that without God there is no Hope; without God, what we have is an eternity in suffering. Understand, if you are going through suffering it may be because God is calling you, that He wants to humble you so you turn to Him, so you can live in Peace and with Hope. God desires to be reconciled with you. Repent, do not harden your heart. Instead put your trust in the undeserved sacrifice of Christ so that you can be saved. Find a healthy biblical church where you can congregate, grow and mature. God will give you the Hope to get you through your sufferings.

Finally, readers, as we saw the pains and sufferings, even though they are the devil's plan for evil, they are sanctioned by God for His perfect Plan. God uses them to show His great Power and Glory. They draw us to Him, they also develop spiritual gifts, but most of all they lead us to trust and depend on God; they reinforce the hope that Paul showed us. Let us rejoice in the sufferings knowing that God is working on our character and that we are closer to our Glorification. *1 Peter 4:12-13* that says,

*Beloved, do not be surprised at the fiery trial when
it comes upon you to test you, as though something
strange were happening to you. But rejoice insofar*

*as you share Christ's sufferings, that you may also
rejoice and be glad when his glory is revealed.*

Chapter 19 - Epilogue

About 4 years after I sketched out the chapters for this book, I learned more about the hereditary nature of ALS, or FALS (Familial ALS). This part of the book was written after that time and the discovery of what this disease may mean to my family.

When my mom was diagnosed with ALS, I did not know of any other family members with the disease. Most instances of ALS are considered spontaneous (or sporadic) – only a small fraction is familial (called FALS) which means hereditary. In simple terms this means a disease that "runs in the family". After my mom was diagnosed, we began to learn of another branch of the family who also had ALS in their line. These were descendants of my great-grandfather's brother (my great-uncle). Soon after my mother was diagnosed, her first cousin was diagnosed with ALS as well. She had been having symptoms for years, and her ALS was more "standard" in that it didn't progress as quickly and began with her extremities, unlike my mom's Bulbar type of ALS. Then a few years later, another first cousin of my mother's was diagnosed with Bulbar ALS, and later died. Three first cousins all died within a handful of years from the same rare disease.

The third cousin to be diagnosed (my first cousin, once removed) and I communicated via email a lot the last year or so of her life. She told me of a connection between a type of dementia and ALS. She had been researching our family and this disease and believed the issue was wider spread than we realized. She shared this with me, and I continued to follow the internet studies linking dementia and ALS after she died. I was convinced, as she was, that our family had both of these diseases in our family, as some of my mother's family appeared to have a type of (high functioning, slow progressing) dementia, including my mother.

It had been a bit of a family joke (not funny, haha joke, more like, ARGH, give me patience) – how difficult some of our family was to communicate with, especially via the phone. It hadn't been much of a joke for me, as I had begun to really struggle with communicating with my mother while I was in high school. Her inability to focus, especially on the phone, meant that I had spent many hours stuck at school because she didn't remember it was time to pick me up and didn't understand who I was when I called from the payphone. I also learned that walking 3 miles home late at night was preferable sometimes to ineffectually calling over and over again, only to have a confused mother pick up and not recognize the voice of her only daughter, who was repeatably calling her mom. Oh, to have been a high schooler in today's time with cell phones and UBER!

When I was in my mid-40s, they had identified several genes that appeared to be linked to ALS, and one, in particular, that is linked to ALS and dementia. I was very interested in genetic testing, but I was really afraid of the cost, so I had put it off. However, in the mornings I had begun to notice that there was a numb spot on the bottom of my left foot, about the size of a silver dollar. It was most noticeable when I would wake up and stand for the first time. I also noticed some lack of balance at about the same time, mostly in the morning. I didn't ignore it, but I wasn't overly alarmed, as I didn't associate this with ALS. However, a few months later, my toes began to burn. A little burning at first, only in the morning, and only on the left foot, but then the burning began in the toes of my right foot as well, and not just in the morning. Sometimes I would hop up and down, frustrated that while part of my foot was numb, other parts were burning, all at once. I remembered that my mom's cousin, the second one to be diagnosed with the more standard ALS, had suffered for years with strange, hard to diagnose symptoms, and I began to worry.

I had dwelled a lot on death after dad had died, which I wrote about in a previous chapter. I thought I had worked through those concerns; however, they came back. Thoughts began to go through my head. What if I have ALS? My kids are young, younger than I was when I lost my mom. What if my husband can't take care of them or pay for their college because of medical expenses for me and the loss of income? What if I am just the first in my generation to get this disease? What if this just keeps devastating our family, generation after generation? Are there studies that we can take part in? Experimental medicines and trials?

I spoke to my husband and he suggested I see a doctor about my symptoms. He didn't believe that I had ALS or that I should spend time worrying about it, but he did believe I needed to take better care of myself. So, I took myself off to the doctor and was referred to a neurologist. It took a few months (which drove me crazy) to get an appointment. I was able to get an appointment with a genetic counselor as well. When the day arrived, I was all ready to get tested for ALS and get answers!

The day I met the genetic counselor, I was ready. I had done my version of a genetic family tree, to the best of my ability. I had contacted the distant cousin who had ALS in his family and my great aunt, who is our family historian. I had a chart and was ready to show how our family had both ALS and dementia. We sat and interviewed, and she seemed to agree with me. She created a chart and said she would get back to me with a report. A few weeks later, I received her report along with suggestions for types of genetic testing and enough evidence that would more than likely lead an insurance company to pay for my genetic testing. She had a very helpful suggestion, as well. As I didn't have any real signs of either dementia or ALS, she suggested that I ask two relatives – both of whom showed signs of our strange family memory/behavior issues.

How was I going to broach the subject gently with my family members, without hurting or offending two women I loved dearly? I needed help for these tests to be accurate and relevant for our family, but at what expense? I couldn't ask my mom or aunt (both who had dementia) because they had both died.

I called my cousin's husband. I told him what would be needed, and he agreed to discuss it with both my cousin and my aunt. They called back later and said they agreed to go to a neurologist for testing. YAY! We had our best option for testing!

I am writing this, however, with no results or knowledge of my status regarding the ALS gene. I can't tell you if I am going to need the type of care my mother needed. What I can tell you is, that as a caregiver of a family member with a genetically inheritable gene, you might need to look into your future and how you believe.

Here are some things I am still considering as a caregiver and Christian.

Question: Is genetic testing moral/ethical and is it the right thing to do?

In my case, I did not see a moral or ethical reason against it and I even consulted my church denomination's view. The reason for this is the following.

1. I was not going to abort a child if I found I (or the baby) had the genetic trait. We believe abortion is wrong from our Christian standpoint and genetic testing shouldn't be done to end a life.
2. The desire to find cures and treatments for diseases is morally good. To participate in studies towards this goal would be contributing to the health and wellbeing potentially for myself and others.
3. I had no intention of harming myself if I found out I carried the trait.
4. I was not going to wait until I found out I had the trait for a fatal disease and then buy a huge amount of life insurance

without disclosure. This isn't illegal at this point, as the laws protect you from having to disclose genetic predisposition to a disease, and ALS isn't on the life insurance questionnaires. Not being illegal, doesn't mean it is not immoral. To be moral, I had life insurance already, before any testing might take place.

That answers the moral/ethical question. What about, is it the right thing to do?

This is why I am still not tested. My husband is worried about HOW I will react to the news if I carry the ALS gene. How will I react to the knowledge that I will more than likely die young (based on the ALS and FALS averages/data and our family history) of an untreatable disease that is 100% fatal? A disease that I can't prevent by changing my lifestyle, habits, etc. My husband is concerned with my wellbeing. He isn't the only one. The neurologist expressed the same concerns. He said – you have a 50% chance of having it, and 50% of not having it – and no test will change that. Why do you need to know in advance?

I have tried arguing against this logic and reasoning with the following opinions:

1. I am not the "depressed, woe is me", type of person.
2. I am already worried about it, this won't add to my worry, and it may 100% eradicate it.
3. Knowing will allow me to prepare for the future. Items to consider:
   a. Housing considerations (handicap accessibility)
   b. Savings plans
   c. Writing letters and buying gifts for future or my children for events I might miss to include: weddings, graduations, the birth of babies, birthdays, etc.
   d. Preparing a will/trust and Powers of Attorney and Medical Protectorate.
4. We may be able to be part of studies that find a cure or treatment for this devastating disease

5. We will be able to give information to our family that may help them with their choices (some have already considered adoption over biological children). Once again, we would NEVER suggest using this information to harm an unborn child.

I even brought up these arguments with our pastor. He also wanted to hear my husband's concerns and seemed to see both sides.

My husband's response – *you can do most of that already, without knowing*. Preparing for our future is a great idea, even if you don't have a life-threatening genetic trait.

He is right. But. ARGH. I am not going to lie; I dislike that argument and disagreed and was frustrated. However, we did come to a compromise. If my cousin and great-aunt have the trait, I can get tested – but, as of now, I will not find out the results. It will help our family, potentially, be made available for research trials, and the information will be available, when and if I need to know. It will help our family know that there is a gene they can test for, and we can get metrics for our family. For now, I am content.

Why did I include this in the book on caregiving? I believe that being a caregiver raises all kinds of questions and concerns about your own future. I believe it is better to discuss these moral and ethical (and Christian) concerns before you are facing life-threatening decisions. I think you need to know where the Bible stands on matters of health and health decisions. Some Christians might make decisions without knowledge, and those choices may contradict their beliefs (example – using the wrong type of birth control is not preventing fertilization, but implantation and most Christians believe that life begins with fertilization. Thus, birth control that affects the baby after fertilization is aborting a fertilized egg. This isn't necessarily well known, so some Christians might make a choice unknowingly compromising their beliefs).

When mom was sick we discussed different types of treatments and the tests that were underway for cures for various diseases. I know my mom wanted to be sure that she was not using any medicine that hindered her thought process or that used testing practices that she found morally wrong. You might want to research ahead of time and know what it is you are agreeing to from a medical and treatment aspect. I hope that including this in the book helped encourage discussion and agreement between you and your loved ones when it comes to treatment.

Chapter 20 – Interesting Caregiving Facts

Before the book ends, I thought it might be good to discuss some statistics around Caregiving. These statistics will be old before the book is even printed, so I am including where I found the information.

It is common knowledge that the Baby Boomer generation in the United States of America was huge, and they are now aging and reaching retirement and an age frequently in need of caregiving. This has affected the demographics of our nation.

> *"The aging of the baby boom generation could fuel more than a 50 percent increase in the number of Americans ages 65 and older requiring nursing home care, to about 1.9 million in 2030 from 1.2 million in 2017." (Found on https://www.prb.org/aging-unitedstates-fact-sheet/)*

The two generations after the Baby Boomers (BBs) have decreased in size in comparison to the BBs, meaning that there are proportionally smaller numbers to care for the aging generation.

> *"The number of Americans ages 65 and older is projected to nearly double from 52 million in 2018 to 95 million by 2060, and the 65-and-older age group's share of the total population will rise from 16 percent to 23 percent."*

This means that competition for long term care may increase. Nursing homes may be inadequate to care for the aging population, may become extremely expensive (supply and demand and the rising cost of medical care), and they may not be able to staff appropriately (not enough medical staff to meet the need). This may increase the need for people to provide in-home care for their loved ones.

Increased life expectancy has also increased the need for caregiving as people are living longer. Increased instances of diseases typically found in the elderly, such as Alzheimer's disease, also contribute to the need for caregiving.

> *"Demand for elder care will also be driven by a steep rise in the number of Americans living with Alzheimer's disease, which could more than double by 2050 to 13.8 million, from 5.8 million today."*

The good news is that there has been a lot in the press of potentially identifying Alzheimer's disease earlier, and even potential for treatment or a cure. Praise the Lord!

Along with this increased life expectancy, however, comes complex changes in our culture that make providing that caregiving more complicated. Historically, the spouse and female children were the primary caregivers.

> *"Nine out of 10 informal caregivers are family members, mainly spouses or adult children (Spillman et al. 2014)."*
> *(https://www.prb.org/todays-research-aging-caregiving/*

Per the same article *"A variety of trends have contributed to a widening gap between older Americans' need for care and the availability of family members to provide that care, raising the potential for growing unmet needs, a heavier burden on individual caregivers, and increased demand for paid care."*

Some of these trends in our culture include:

Delayed Childbearing - Older parents are raising children, which makes it difficult to also care for an aging parent. Also, this means that adult children are younger when their aging parents need care. They may not be as financially stable themselves.

Divorce – A person may not be able to rely on spousal care, because they are divorced. Children may have not been raised with the parent who needs care, so the bond isn't as strong. A single mom (or dad) might have more difficulty caring for an aging parent while being a single parent. Multiple parents (mom, dad, step-mom, step-dad) increases the impact on the child, as all the parents might be aging and in need of care.

Higher employment numbers for women – traditionally and historically, female children were the primary caregivers after the spouse. More women are in the workforce, and their income is needed. This means they are less available to be caregivers, as it impacts the finances of their nuclear family. These family constraints make it difficult for the traditional in-home caregiving scenario.

"Using the nationally representative Panel Survey of Income Dynamics (PSID), Wiemers and Bianchi (2015) showed a 20 percent increase between 1988 and 2007 in the share of women ages 45 to 64 who had both children and living parents or parents-in-law. One in 10 women in this age group provided significant parental care and either financial assistance or housing (within their homes for one year or more) to both an adult child (age 25 or older) and a parent during the period."

Distance between family members – With a global economy, ease of teleworking, and of transportation, it is not uncommon for family members to not only live in different cities within the same state but also live in different states or even countries. This means that children are not near their aging family.

"Piette and colleagues (2010). Their analysis of HRS data showed that one in three chronically ill older adults had no children nearby but did have adult children living elsewhere."

Another article pointed out that:

- parental expectations on who should be the caregiver,
- frequency of contact between family members,
- parental support and financial assistance, and
- if a child is the beneficiary of a will

all contributed to the culture trend towards family caregiving (An Leopold, Raab, and Engelhart (2014) analysis of HRS data.

There are benefits to caregiving, including financial benefits to "informal" or in-home caregiving. One benefit to caregiving is the high and rising costs of formal, or nursing home, caregiving. Per an article found here:

https://www.seniorlink.com/blog/nursing-home-costs-vs.-the-cost-of-in-home-caregivers

> *"There are three types of in-home care; non-medical, home health care, and skilled care. Non-medical home care assists seniors with day-to-day living, doing things like laundry, assisting with personal hygiene, cooking, cleaning, and transportation. In 2017, the national average for a non-medical in-home aide was $21 an hour."*

> *Home health care is someone who provides medical aide at home, assisting with things like checking pulses, temperature, and helping out with any medical equipment like ventilators. The average hourly rate for a home health care aide in 2017 was also $21 an hour.*

> *Skilled nursing care involves providers who are trained nurses or therapists and can assist with things like injury care, wound care, and*

medications. This can be quite expensive, costing upwards of $220 a day.

As you can see, skilled nursing is much more expensive than typical in-home care. National averages of long-term care facilities put the expense per month between $6-8,000. Even hiring a health aide at the national average ($20.5/hour) for 40 hours a week, is much more affordable.

40 hours, 4, weeks per month = 160 hours per month

160 hours x $20.50 p/h = $3,280

Average costs found: https://longtermcare.acl.gov/costs-how-to-pay/costs-of-care.html

These costs are with a full-time weekday helper. If a family can work together to cover weekends or can split time away or work part-time, these numbers would decrease. Also, some individuals might not need full-time care, but part-time supervisory care around bathing times, meal and medication times, as an example.

The final benefit of being a caregiver in the home is the relationship aspect. By personally caring for someone you love, you not only honor God and His guidance in the Bible, but you also show honor and respect to the person for whom you care.

In interviews, nearly two out of three caregivers rated their caregiving experience as largely positive, pointing to benefits such as feeling closer to the care recipient and assured that the recipient was receiving high-quality care (Spillman et al. 2014).

https://www.prb.org/todays-research-aging-caregiving/

Chapter 21 - Extras

Here are a few examples of documentation that may come in handy if you are a caregiver, or you want to help the person that one day might care for you.

Checklists and Tools

Call Checklist

Have a list of 5 people who will help you form a call tree. These people will, in turn, have their list of people to call. This will be convenient when you

A. Need help (moving, cleaning, food, transportation) or

B. When you need help communicating something medical/health-related (in the hospital, change in condition, and even notification of death).

This list should also have information such as:

- Primary Care Physician
- Specialist Physicians (oncology, neurologist, pain management, etc)
- Hospital of Choice
- Transportation Options (such as MedRide or non-emergency ambulance service)
- Pharmacy of Choice
- Nursing Home
- Lawyer/Trust preparer
- Banking facility

Location Checklist

Where can items of importance be found? This includes:

- Will/Trust/Power of Attorney/Medical Protectorate

- o Both official copy and reference copy
- Keys – house, car, safety deposit box (bank), safe (key or code)
- Specific Valuables (jewelry, guns, family heirlooms)
- Paperwork (such as past taxes, deeds, identifications, military discharge paperwork)

Codes Checklist

In today's age of technology, sometimes it isn't a key you need, but a code. It would be good to make sure that you have access to passwords and codes for someone you are caring for (depending on the level of caregiving you are giving. I don't advocate forcing someone to give you code access, this is a trust matter between the caregiver and care receiver).

- Online Accounts (mortgage, investments, banking, credit cards, insurance)
- Social Media Accounts
- Door/Safe Codes
- Bank Call in Codes
- Phone call-in codes (such as "secret" words set up at banks or other financial institutions)
- Computers
- Online Subscriptions
- Email
- Account Validation questions

Medical Checklist (Journal)

Medical Checklists may include the following:

- List of physicians (and their specialty)
- List of Medications (name (generic and name brand), dosage, frequency)

- "Problem List" (list of diagnoses)
- List of Tests conducted (when, where and by whom ordered) such as MRI, CT, lab/blood work, etc.
- List of Surgeries (when, where and by whom performed)
- Appointments
- Insurance Contacts/Card information
- Copies of Do Not Resuscitate (DNR) or Health Protectorate Designation paperwork
- Multiple copies of Death Certificates (10-20)

Financial Consideration Checklist(s)

I suggest that you do not conduct any Will/Trust/Estate related business via phone call or text (only) but have some sort of material copy/record of discussions and decisions, be it paper or email.

Institutions that may need a copy of a Will/Trust and/or POA

- Bank
- Insurance Companies (house, car, life, possibly medical)
- Mortgage Company
- Investment Companies
- Rental companies (if you lease/rent an apartment)
- Long Term Care facilities
- Hospitals
- Social Security
- Employer (care receiver) or caregiver
- Disability Program
- Legal representative
- State "lost/found" money program

These might need the document to allow the designated trustee/executor to be able to discuss concerns of the caregiver or make decisions and take actions on behalf of the person you care for.

When Enacting a Will/Trust Considerations

- Distribution Outline – this will outline who and what and what portion of resources have been left according to a Will or Trust.
- Distribution Log – anytime anything is distributed by the Estate, log it. This can be goods (furniture, clothing, dishes), financial (death benefits, IRA, petty cash) or even if someone decides to take the family dog.
- Distribution To-Do List – includes such items as appraising the house, transferring the title on a car, quick claim deed for a timeshare transfer, etc.
- Communication Log – track all calls and communication (including mail sent, email sent) regarding Trust/Will activities. I would do this in an excel spreadsheet, but that might be too nerdy and unnecessary for you. This will help you know who you called, when, who you spoke with, what was discussed, any action items you have to follow up on, etc. Example of log entries:
  - Called XYZ IRA Company, phone number 888-888-8888 – Date: 12/1/2008. Spoke with: Cathy in distributions. She can not speak to me about funds on the account unless she has a copy of 1. The Trust and 2. My driver's license. Email these to cathy@xyzira.com, or mail them to XXX, or fax them to XXXXXXXX.
    - Action Item: Sent copies required via email 12/3/2008.
  - Called XYZ IRA Company back. Date: 12/08/2008. Spoke to Cathy again. She verified she has received the information that they require to speak to me regarding the IRA. She walked me through setting up access to the account online so that I can distribute the

IRA to the Trust. Account information is recorded in the Accounts List.

- Email Repository – Save every email you send and receive regarding your role as caregiver and if you are a trustee or manager of the estate.
- Expense Report – as a trustee and caregiver you may or may not pay yourself (and the Trust may or may not allow you to), but it is a good thing to keep a log of your time and monies spent while enacting a Trust or Will. It can take days, weeks, months to administer an Estate. If you are setting up an estate (Trust), you may wish to consider the time and expenses involved. Often, a trustee must take days off of work to properly carry out the activities.
  - o Example: If you have to drive to another town/county to file paperwork, log the trip, mileage, if you had to take off from work, the filing fee, time, meals purchased, etc.
  - o If you have to take ½ off of work in order to sit in the Social Security Office and review benefits with the government, log it.

Tax Check List

You will need to do taxes, or have taxes done as part of the caregiver role and/or as part of the trustee role.

- Where paperwork is stored
- Who filed taxes (suggest at least the first year post-death to pay someone to do the taxes. This protects you and helps with the most complicated year.)
  - o Tax Official, Office Location, Phone Number
- File for an Estate ID
- Cost of filing taxes
- Estimated Tax payment or return
- Any distribution based on the Tax return

- Information needed by beneficiaries (forms for their taxes)
- Certified Mailed Paperwork to beneficiaries

Institution Notification Log – after someone you are caring for passes, you will need to contact these institutions and file a death certificate.

- Name of Financial Institution, with contact information.
    - What you provided for them.
    - When you provided it
    - Who you spoke with
    - Action Items (theirs and yours)

Income– after you notify companies, you may be expecting income. You will need to track this.

- Institution Name
- Expected Distribution/Income
- When received
- How was it handled (put in bank account XXX, distributed to XYZ, used to pay account PDQ, etc.)?
- Action Items

Funeral Arrangements
- Where the funeral will be held (contact information)
- Who will perform/conduct the funeral
- Burial Preferences
- Burial Arrangements
    - Pre-Purchased Plan
    - Plot location
    - Cremation Considerations
    - Marker Arrangements
- Funeral preparation
    - Pall Bearers
    - Photo Tribute

- Worship Songs/Leadership
- Flowers vs Donations
- Military Honors Arrangements (if applicable) – What branch of the armed forces, the discharge paperwork ID. Phone number to contact. Funeral Homes frequently assist with this.

Lessons Learned Compiled:

Below, in the approximate order found in the book, is an abbreviated list of the Lessons Learned. I have taken out some of the "story aspects" to focus on the actual lesson. This was my husband's idea. His comment – sometimes people just need the "meat" from a book - particularly busy or stressed people (like caregivers). Why don't you include the Lessons just in case they need to get the facts, then have time to read the context later. Clever husband.

Lesson Learned: I quickly learned that when I was working with Alzheimer's patients, to them I was mother, sister, daughter, friend, care team member. Most of them could not remember me specifically from day-to-day but it seemed as if they came to recognize my face and my presence, so I became familiar even if they didn't know who I was.

Lesson Learned: If you don't know the history of the person you are caring for, try and learn it. This will help you be a better caregiver.

Lesson Learned: There are various stages in Alzheimer's and other dementia-related disorders. Sometimes you can interact as if there is nothing wrong, have lengthy, in-depth conversations. Other times you may see someone gazing off and not saying a word.

Lesson Learned: Sundowners is when someone tries to go home when the sun goes down. This is something to be aware of, as you don't want to have to issue a Silver Alert because your care receiver is out looking for home.

Lesson Learned: Benefits your family may reap when you are a caregiver and they actively participate in the care of your loved one:

- Patience – caregiving can take time and specific care that builds patience.
- Service – they can learn to think of others before themselves and to sacrifice.
- Wisdom – particularly if you are caring for someone who is elderly, you can receive such amazing wisdom by interacting with them and learning from them.
- Self-Sacrifice – giving up to give to someone else is a beautiful lesson to be learned in caregiving.
- Trust – the ability to put your faith in God to get you through every activity
- Bravery – facing illness, injury, and even death strengthens you and allows you to learn to look up to God for strength.
- Time – being a caregiver allows you to fully understand the meaning of time. See Patience

Lesson Learned: If you aren't the caregiver, but have an opportunity to help, be respite care. Give someone who is giving care a few hours, an overnight, a day or two, respite.

Lesson Learned: Take pictures of your care receiver.

Lesson learned: Many people diagnosed with terminal illnesses develop difficulty swallowing. They may need specifically sized or textured food, thickened liquids, special cups, straws (or no straws), and constant observation to prevent aspiration (when food or liquid goes down your trachea instead of your esophagus) which can lead to infection and choking. Learning to recognize signs of difficulty swallowing and taking measures to help with food consistency and fluid density, can save the life of someone in your care.

Lesson Learned: Making note of symptoms and when they appear can be valuable when visiting multiple doctors over long periods of time. In this day, electronic medical records (EHRs) help document and transmit records, but keeping a small notebook with symptoms, doctors' names, diagnosis, medications, medical history, etc. can speed up the process of filling out paperwork and also help make sure you don't inadvertently "miss something" that might be vital to treatment and care.

Lesson Learned: If you have family members, particularly young children, who are unused to seeing people post-surgery, complete with catheters, monitors, IVs, intubated, you might consider prepping them before they visit.

Lesson Learned: I strongly advocate caregivers continuing to fulfill the caregiver role, even if the person they are caring for is in a hospital or nursing home setting.

Lesson Learned: If you have someone you love or are caring for in ICU or critical care, I highly suggest you have someone with them.

Lesson Learned: Familiarize yourself with the equipment and monitors in the room. Make sure that the area is kept tidy. This means cables, cords, tables, sheets, blankets, etc. Know what is beeping, and how critical that device is.

Lesson Learned: Alcohol has many side effects. Check with a medical provider before your care receiver consumes alcohol.

Lesson Learned: If people do not visit your care receiver, do not cover for those people. I highly suggest praying for those people, honestly but kindly answering inquiries about them from the person you are caring for and find other ways to bolster the spirits of your loved one. Lying (by deceit) to make someone feel better is still a lie and lies have a habit of trapping you.

Lesson Learned: Listen to advice. It doesn't obligate you to follow that advice if it is not in the best interest of the person in which you care. Be humble enough to quiet the objections and listen, and then, pray and do what is right in the eyes of the Lord.

Lesson Learned: If you can create a break for yourself, do it. It will take a lot of planning.

Lesson Learned: It is good to establish limits in relationships.

Lesson Learned: If you are caring for someone who has difficulty being transported, make arrangements beforehand. I have noticed most of those who are having to be cared for can become embarrassed enough by the "hassle" they BELIEVE they cause others, to decide to forgo attending services or events. Take away their excuse by being very organized and thoughtfully remove barriers.

Lesson Learned: Ill people aren't always rational or reasonable. Some of this may be caused by actual physical results of their illness and some may be manifestations of the emotional anguish that comes with their physical state. You can spend your time being frustrated and arguing with them, or you can just choose to love and abide together (Romans 12:10 and Ephesians 4:32). It doesn't mean you can't try to reason with them, just don't try and grind in a point to the extent where animosity is maintained, and bitterness has a chance to flourish and grow. Heed Proverbs 15:1 and let soft words turn away anger.

Lesson Learned: Sometimes people seem to know when they are dying or getting close to death. If we do not listen to them, respect them, we might pressure them into a level of care they don't want. If the person you love is a believer, and they are ready to die, consider asking their wishes, respecting those wishes, enjoying time with them, and comforting them as they make a dignified exit from their mortal life, into their eternal one.

Lesson Learned: Consolidated Omnibus Budget Reconciliation Act of 1985 (COBRA). Per the Department of Labor website: "The Consolidated Omnibus Budget Reconciliation Act (COBRA) gives workers and their families who lose their health benefits the right to choose to continue group health benefits provided by their group health plan for limited periods of time under certain circumstances such as voluntary or involuntary job loss, reduction in the hours worked, transition between jobs, death, divorce, and other life events. Qualified individuals may be required to pay the entire premium for coverage up to 102% of the cost to the plan."

Lesson Learned: Doctors do not have all the right answers, all the time. There may be periods of no diagnosis, misdiagnosis, partial diagnosis. I highly recommend that you educate yourself on every potential as they are presented. That you learn what the diagnostic tests can determine, or not determine. That you begin to understand the use of specific blood tests, diagnostic tests, diagnostic equipment, and other tests such as lab tests and results. This will help you understand when it seems like the doctors and nurses and technicians are speaking a foreign language. It is my observation that being able to speak the same language brings respect and a better chance of them being forthright with you. This might take writing everything down that they say, asking questions, taking home and reading the paperwork, and hours of googling.

Lesson Learned: Technology. There is an ever-growing reservoir of technology available that can help caregivers and patients. Learn what technology is available to meet your needs.

Lesson Learned: They will probably tell you not to put regular food into a feeding tube. Sometimes you don't always have to follow the rules.

Lesson Learned: You might have options you are not aware of. Advocated for these options directly with both his primary doctor, specialists, and the insurance company.

Lesson Learned: Governance of controlled substances. States have different laws around controlled substances, such as narcotics. Know the laws in your state and the rules of your physician, so that you are prepared for what it takes to help your loved one who takes pain medication.

Lesson Learned: Keep a health journal. It should contain the following type of information:

• Medication List

- Pharmacy contact information
- Insurance Contact information
- Physician List
- Hospital Visits (date, reason)
- Allergies
- Diagnosis Lists
- Changes in Condition

Lesson Learned: Find out what your insurance covers and doesn't cover. Some need very specific wording or diagnosis to qualify for services. Some services are only available to someone on hospice, some services are not available to someone on hospice. You must become an insurance detective (or find someone to help you) to track down what you can get for your loved one. In this ever-changing world of insurance, you can't be too diligent.

Lesson Learned: Poop. Get used to it. Being bed-bound contributes to constipation. Narcotics/pain medications contribute to constipation. Dehydration (frequent for people who don't feel like drinking because they aren't exerting themselves physically) leads to constipation. Learn how to track bowel and bladder output.

Lesson Learned: Be honest with your pastor.

Lesson Learned: I have mentioned FMLA before. Last time I checked, FMLA allowed an employee to leave their position for up to 12 weeks per year to care for a qualified person (parent, spouse, child) with the proper paperwork and supporting medical qualifications. This is unpaid leave, but it holds your position (or a like one) while you are gone. This might not benefit everyone, as many can't afford to go unpaid for that long. This is good to know if you are afraid of losing your job if you do the right thing for your loved one.

Lessons Learned: As a caregiver, there are certain skills and knowledge that will benefit you to learn. These include, but are not limited it: CPR and Basic First Aid, Transferring patients, Making a Bed with someone in it, How to clean someone bed-ridden, Proper mouth and foot care, Bathing techniques, How to check skin integrity, Ways to adjust someone so as to decrease likelihood of bedsores, More than one way to take temperature, How to Crush Medication, Nutritional Supplements. I learned this information by taking classes, asking medical professionals, and observation.

Lesson Learned: If you can make doorways at least 32-36 inches in width, this increases ease of movement. This isn't a "hard number" however, as some wheelchairs have larger wheels, they are deeper or wider than others, depending on the size of the patient and the type of support needed. Electronic wheelchairs or mobility units are also much larger and have different turning radiuses. All of these should be considered when making accommodations. I have known people to move their loved ones into the formal dining room, putting up temporary walls, simply because this was the only room in the house they could make accessible.

Lesson Learned: Here are two things that might make transportation better (besides, of course, having no or low-profile transitions). First, get a wheelchair with bigger wheels, if you can. Second, if the large wheel is on the back of the wheelchair, back into doorways with high transitions, instead of going forward.

Lesson Learned: We found that walking backward, locking our arms with theirs, was a safer way to help someone walk across floor changes and transitions. If you are standing beside the person, holding only one arm, you cannot stop them well if they pitch forward or fall backward. They also could wrench your arm (or visa versa). The two-arm clasp seemed to be better. This would not be a solution for a lengthy walk, but navigating within a house or building it works well. One person on each side, if there is space, also helps.

Lesson Learned: I believe that there is often pressure for caregivers to move into the house of the one they are caring for so that this person has continuity and feels at home. In the caregiving support group, I was in, I heard arguments for this arrangement, but also the stress and pressure it put on the caregiver. I think you should evaluate seriously the condition of the person you are caring for (for instance, how long will they need your care), the condition of the home they are living in, and your own condition. If that person has dementia, moving them might cause extreme emotional trauma, or if they have a sight impairment, they might not be able to learn to navigate a new home. These should be taken into consideration. However, if you can openly and honestly communicate with your loved one, be honest. I think that denying yourself or not communicating your own needs is not the way to find the best solution.

Lesson Learned: If someone is shut in an interior room all of the time, they may lose track of time. Not knowing day and night, much less what day or season it is. If you can help with this, that is advisable. Open the curtains, talk about the outdoors (especially if you can't take them outside). Show them pictures you take on your phone that show the passing of the season.

Lesson Learned: This is based on my understanding and experience – but I am not clinical, please remember that fact. Constipation can lead to UTIs. Constipation can be caused by dehydration, slow digestion, poor fiber consumption, lack of movement, drug interactions. When your body is constipated, it tries to move fluid into the bowel, to help move waste along. This also takes fluid out of your digestive system. Your body also tries to start pushing more to rid itself of the waste. If the bowel has become impacted, the squeezing can cause the mucus around the bowel (there to grease the works) out of your body. This mucus has bacteria and waste in it, and it can get caught in your clothing (underwear) or bedding, close to your urethra. This bacterium can cause infection. Also, someone who is severely impacted, that is a lot of pressure in the abdomen, putting pressure on other organs and systems, causing issues as well. This was explained to me by various doctors. I learned that even some children's bodies remove too much fluid from their intestinal system, causing chronic constipation. Urinary infections can cause sepsis, which is very dangerous.

Lesson Learned: For people who spend a lot of time in bed or a chair, it is vital to prevent bedsores (pressure sores). Use pillows, rolled towels, sheets or blankets, to prop them into different positions. In the hospital, nurses have a routine schedule to change their patient's position, and this is a good routine to set as a caregiver. Often, the patient resists, but be persistent. Some mattresses help with this as well, and frequently your provider can help you acquire one if you qualify. I also found on medical supply catalogs and websites, affordable mattress toppers that would accomplish nearly the same effect as hospital air beds, using air to distribute the patient's weight and move them into different positions.

Lesson Learned: Ambulance transportation for emergencies. Insurance might dictate where you go and what is covered from the ride standpoint. You should know which facilities and circumstances your insurance covers. Ambulances may have zones in which they have to transport you to a specific facility within that zone. Coordinators may direct their drivers to specific locations depending on the type of injury. If you have a burn, for example, it doesn't make sense to take you to a hospital that doesn't have a specific burn department if it is available to you. One hospital might be better and dealing with different levels of trauma, is another example of why you might be transported to a specific location.

Lesson Learned: FIND OUT HOW TO TAKE CARE OF YOUR BACK. Find a nurse or nurse aide. Ask them how to do transfers. Ask them how to safely lift patients.

Lesson Learned: Even if you hate wearing gloves, consider using them. Your hands will become cracked and dry from frequent washing. Cracked and dry hands aren't only painful, they can be dangerous for you and the person you are caring for. Infection can set in, and if you are cleaning someone, that infection can spread to the person you are caring for.

Lesson Learned: Advocate strongly for your patient. Speak up if you have preferences.

Lesson Learned: As a caregiver, you might be judged and persecuted. Your caregiving, my Christian brother or sister, is a service "to the least of these" and it comes from the love of Christ. Be encouraged!

Lesson Learned: Not every care facility is equal. Do your research. Voice your preferences.

Lesson Learned: Illness or treatment causing a change in taste. Don't be afraid or ashamed to sneak in healthy food whenever and however you can. It is for their benefit.

Lesson Learned: Balance. Let some things slide. I will say you can't make the "sliding" be the majority of the time because that is dangerous for the long-term health and care of your patient. However, the occasional give in I think is okay. This person isn't just a "client", this person is your loved one who you are caring for from a holistic standpoint. Their heart, mind, body, soul.

Lesson Learned: It is important to read about the medications, ask questions of the physicians and pharmacists, document changes that might occur when new medications are started. A medication journal/list with the date of prescription start, any interactions observed, side effects, dosages, etc. will help track. Without the journal, it is hard to remember what changed and when.

Lesson Learned: Here is my limited knowledge and opinion on when to decide to engage hospice:

1. Is the condition terminal, with little treatment or cure options? If yes, then hospice can help with end of life palliative treatment and care.

2.   Does the care receiver have any mental, emotional, or spiritual conflict with the philosophy of hospice?

3.   Does going on hospice prevent the patient from receiving something that is seen as vital to comfort, either emotionally or physically?   This includes counseling, particular medications, benefits, etc. The caregiver may want to check with the insurance.

4.   Does utilizing hospice GAIN the care receiver or the caregiver something valuable?   This includes in-home assistance, equipment, respite care, etc.

Lesson Learned: Have the hard discussions. What form or level of life assistance does the person you are caring for want? Do they want to sign a DNR (Do Not Resuscitate) form? Do they have a Living Will and a Medical Protectorate? What do they think about blood transfusions, experimental treatments, palliative care, and hospice? These conversations don't get easier if you put them off.

Lesson Learned: Medical professionals are not perfect.   When you are advocating for the person you are a caregiver for, do it with confidence and strength. Be an advocate!

Lesson Learned: Learn to be thankful and celebrate no matter where you are, when you are, and your circumstances.

Lesson Learned: Encourage relationships. If you are caring for someone, help them to keep and maintain relationships. Life is so much more fulfilling shared, and you might grow to have a deep friendship with their friends.

Lesson Learned: The person struggling with illness frequently will try and hide or minimize the illness to protect their loved ones. This is bad for them, as they suffer alone, and for the caregiver, who can't help as efficiently and thoroughly, if you don't have the big picture!

Lesson Learned: GO. If you can, GO. Don't contemplate – should I wait until the person really needs me. I know it isn't always practical, but PRAY, talk to your spouse if you have one, and if at all possible, GO.

Lesson Learned: Get multiple copies of Medical Directives, Medical Protectorate Designations, and DNRs that states the patient's desire in case of extreme situations. Make sure that the doctor has a copy, the hospitals have copies, the nursing homes, etc. This is the only way the wishes of your patient can be carried out.

Lesson Learned: When dealing with having to make decisions about end-of-life it's very important to know your role in those decisions, and how you can support each other depending on those roles.

Tribute: Pastor Bill

As mentioned in the chapter on Legacy, Pastor Bill was my pastor when I was in high school, in Merrimack, New Hampshire. He and his wife were wonderful examples of a pastor and pastor's wife! Grace Baptist Church was a fairly small church, and the body of believers knew and supported one another well. We enjoyed our time as a family at this church, and we enjoyed getting to know the Balson family. They lived just around the corner from us, so it was only about 3 minutes from our house to theirs. Once or twice I house sat (and pet sat) while they were on vacation, and I graduated with their eldest daughter.

My family moved away from Merrimack and I lost contact with this wonderful family, until many years later. Thanks to social media, we were able to reunite as "friends" on Facebook. I was glad to "virtually" catch up with their family and enjoyed seeing their posts.

When I found out that Pastor Bill was ill, I mourned with them from afar. Having lost both of my parents, I knew what their family was preparing to go through. However, I was so blessed by the uplifting postings of my former pastor. In typical Pastor Bill fashion, he wasn't going to let life-threatening disease and illness take away his joy in the Lord. I was in the process of writing this book, and it occurred to me to get a pastor's perspective. A pastor, who for most of his life was the caregiver to a flock, the church body, was now the care-receiver. I wanted to know what this wise man of God could share with caregivers. Pastor Bill agreed and sent me the chapter "The Care Receiver".

I am so grateful that he shared his perspective, words of wisdom, and the need for the Gospel, with us caregivers. I wanted to share a little more of Pastor Bill in this book, as well. I think you will be encouraged as was I, by his posts and poems. I did screen grabs from his Facebook page and captured a few of the posts that I think show his wonderful, God-given, perspective on life. I hope you appreciate them as much as I do. I also included some of his poetry. Thank you, Pastor Bill, and Nancy Jean, for modeling how to be a caregiver and a care-receiver, who still has so much to offer your brothers and sisters in Christ.

Thank you for your Testimony

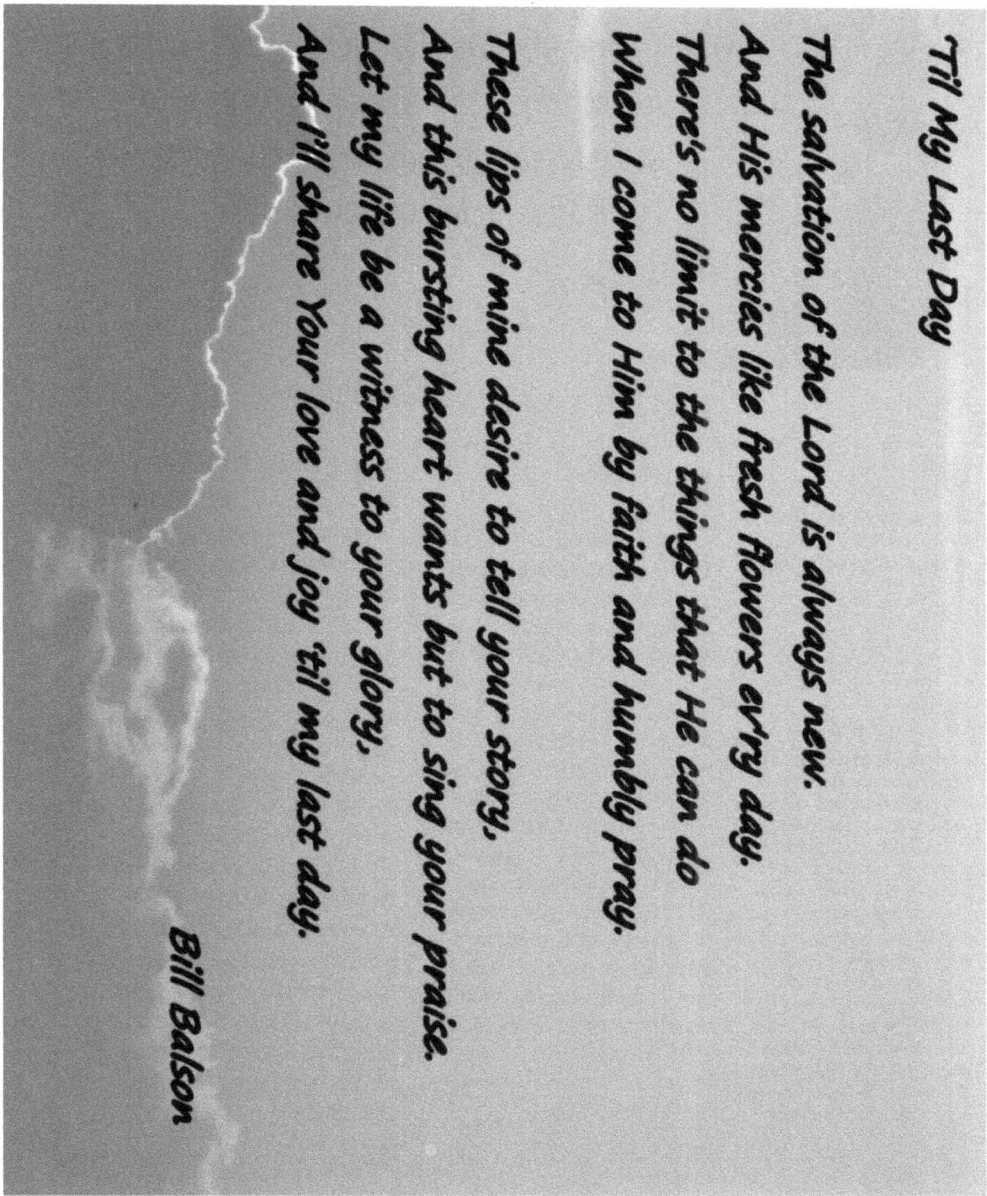

"Til My Last Day

The salvation of the Lord is always new:
And His mercies like fresh flowers ev'ry day.
There's no limit to the things that He can do
When I come to Him by faith and humbly pray.

These lips of mine desire to tell your story,
And this bursting heart wants but to sing your praise.
Let my life be a witness to your glory,
And I'll share Your love and joy 'til my last day.

Bill Balson

Bill Balson
July 9 ·

Finally got my new ride. It cost more than a new car when we first got married. I just thank God that He provided this at no cost to us. Appreciate your prayers as I go in tomorrow morning for my 11th heart cath. God bless.

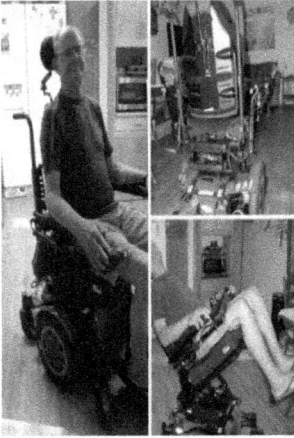

OO♥ 49   30 Comments

Bill Balson
January 11 ·

My heart doctor says to be very careful about gaining any weight. If I gain more than a few pounds he wants to know. My MD doctor says that my BMI is too low and that he would like for me to gain some weight so that I have some reserve to fight the muscular dystrophy. I think I like my MD doctor. :-)

O😆O 26   12 Comments 1 Share

😆 Haha   💬 Comment   ↪ Share

Bill Balson
November 22, 2018 ·

My wife, family, friends, home, food, my salvation, a life of adventure, ministry, joy and purpose; ...so many things to be thankful to God for!!

OO 40   7 Comments 1 Share

👍 Like   💬 Comment   ↪ Share

Bill Balson
December 5, 2018 ·

Agreement vs. Acceptance : Sadly, it has become all too common for people to hate whoever disagrees with them. This is not only Biblically wrong, but it's immature. It's like a child saying if you don't like my clothes, then you don't like me and I hate you. Before we can truly love someone we have to accept them for the person that they are. We can't reject them simply because they are not like us. That, however, does not mean that we have to agree on anything. Families and friends regularly disagree on many things, yet they still love one another. Who completely agrees with their enemies, yet Christ tells us to love them. It's OK to disagree with each other and still love one another. This would cure a lot of the animosity in our country today.

OO 30   2 Shares

👍 Like   💬 Comment   ↪ Share

Bill Balson
November 4, 2018 ·

"You have left your first love..." (Rev.2:4) How can we rekindle a love that seems to be lost? 1.) By remembering why we loved them at the very first, when we were alone or felt some need, when they filled us and brought us some joy; when we saw their beauty or goodness. 2.) By looking past what we may perceive as their shortcomings or supposed failures, (because we all have them), and seeing their value and respecting them. 3.) By knowing that they likely still love you, (or want to), even though you are imperfect. 4.) By making the choice to want to love them and the effort to do so. 5.) By remembering the history of your love, the joy that it brought and the fact that you can learn to love them again. 6.) By confessing that you have been blessed by that person, that anybody's love is a gift we do not deserve. 7.) By asking God to help us. ...It is much the same when we have lost our 1st love with Christ.

OO 19   7 Comments

👍 Like   💬 Comment   ↪ Share

Bill Balson updated his status.
January 17 ·

Double by-pass, cancer, MD, heart failure ... and yesterday my eye doctor told us that I have glaucoma in both eyes. It's the type that the ducts are narrow and partly blocked. When one becomes fully blocked I will have to race to the nearest hospital for emergency eye surgery to relieve the pressure. The longer it takes the more likely to become partially or totally blind. My first response was to shake my head in amused unbelief; then I began to think of what bad could happen, (blind in a power wheelchair), and finally I settled my heart on Christ, prayed and remembered how faithful He has been for my whole life. I am rich, have my wife and God near me, and when this is all over I go to a better home. The peace of God settled over me like a warm blanket and I knew that all is well with my soul. If I start to worry again I just rinse and repeat.

OO 45   27 Comments 6 Shares

❤ Love   💬 Comment   ↪ Share

Bill Balson
February 26 · 🌐

Today my doctors decided to put me into the palliative care program. This will be a great opportunity as I will be able to meet and build relationships with people who are nearing the end of their life. I can only pray that God will give me some open doors to be a testimony for Him. "When Jesus heard that, he said, This sickness is not unto death, but for the glory of God, that the Son of God might be glorified thereby." John 11:4

👍😊 32   25 Comments 7 Shares

👍 Like   💬 Comment   ↪ Share

Bill Balson
June 24 · 🌐

I failed another cardiac stress test. Dr. just called and is going to schedule me for my 11th catheterization, A portion of my heart is not getting enough blood. I live only by people's prayers and the grace of God.

👍😊😢 26   27 Comments

👍 Like   💬 Comment   ↪ Share

Bill Balson
July 22 · 👥

NJ and I would I would like to thank God for the love that so many people have shown to us in so many different ways. Every day is a blessing when you trust God.

👍😊 42   8 Comments

💙 Love   💬 Comment

8:13 ⌁   ⏳ LTE 🔋

‹   🔍 Bill Balson

Bill Balson
Sunday at 5:48 PM · 👥

Thank you to all of you who prayed for and contributed to the go-fund-me page for the wheelchair van. Its 21 years old, 57,000 miles and in great shape. Thank you especially to Mike Rutter. Now I have a lot more freedom. God always provides.

‹   🔍 Bill Balson

👍😊 40   7 Comments

👍 Like   💬 Comment   ↪ Share

Bill Balson
July 9 · 👥

Our neighbors here in the trailer park have gotten together on their own and have secured a wheelchair lift for me and are installing it The estimate that we had gotten for it was $11,500. I never cease to marvel at how God answers prayers.

👍😊😢 57   10 Comments

💙 Love   💬 Comment

Bill Balson
October 1, 2018 ·

Spent the last few days in the hospital. It wasn't a big problem,...I just couldn't breathe. Turns out that my body was filling up with fluid from the congestive heart failure. From now on I am married to an oxygen tank. I just thank God for each new day and look forward to what He has for me.

OO 33   22 Comments 1 Share

Love   Comment   Share

Bill Balson
May 18, 2018 ·

I think that I'm in that movie; "The Curious Case of Benjamin Button". I'm finishing my life by coming down with a childhood disease that will cause my muscles to atrophy and waste away. Inside, however, NJ and I have never felt so close to God and so blessed in so many ways. WE talked this week about doing one last big thing before I can't do anything. We realized that we had already done all that we wanted to do and wanted nothing more than to be together. Now, that's a gift from God!

OO 52   9 Comments

Like   Comment   Share

Bill Balson
June 1, 2018 ·

I have been in a bit of a struggle today that I think all of us face from time to time; and that is letting go of some of the things of this world. We are having to down-size about 80%. Part of that means all of the hard copies of my sermons and studies that I have saved over 40 years. (thousands of files) A lot of it has been copied and saved onto my computer, but these are the originals, going back to my first sermon in 1975. They would have been useless to me if somebody had just given them to me. It was the study, the labor, the prayers and the lessons that God taught me through each one that was their true value. The rest is just paper. I thank God when He forces my eyes open and allows me to see what true spiritual treasures are.

OO 39   11 Comments 1 Share

Love   Comment   Share

Bill Balson
October 17, 2018 · 🌐

The MD is starting to effect my brain. After 40 years of ministry; over 10,000 sermons and lessons and reading through the Bible numerous times...as I sit here I can't remember but a few verses. But, when I open the Bible to a passage He brings it all back like a flood. None of our relationship is lost. I don't really know what's happening, but its all in God's loving hands...and I trust Him. He is my hope and joy.

👍❤️😢 45   26 Comments 2 Shares

🤍 Love   💬 Comment   ↪ Share

Bill Balson
November 10, 2018 · 🌐

I have a "spiritual service dog". A few years ago I started to give her a treat every morning when I had devotions. Now, as soon as I'm dressed, she sits in front of me and looks at the big black book, then back at me, until I have devotions and give her another treat.

Bill Balson
October 26, 2018 · 🌐

Some people have a misconception about eternal life. He said, "I am come that they might have life, and that they might have it more abundantly." (Jn.10:10) Just as a lamp has light because it is plugged into an electrical outlet, so we have life because we are connected to God in Christ. God did not give us life as we would give a gift to another person. The gift was Himself. It has never been about religiousness or denominations. Without Him I die and in Him I have new life, abundant life and eternal life. I have life because He, by His loving grace, has plugged me into the Source of life. Eternal life is just a hard-wired connection.

👍❤️ 29   8 Comments 4 Shares

🤍 Love   💬 Comment   ↪ Share

Bill Balson
October 30, 2018 · 🌐

A lot of people in our society are calling for tolerance. Tolerance is neither biblical, nor even good. The definition is to endure: ("To put up with someone who has a different opinion or practice.") Ambivalence is a superior attitude; "Having both positive and negative feelings toward the same person, including their beliefs or actions, at the same time without inward conflict. (" I don't agree with your beliefs or actions, but I do still love you.") It is even far better for people to have a godly love for one another. Godly love is the ability to love people as God empowers us; a love that is evidenced through actions; willing to put another person before our self; to give to them sacrificially. The Bible tells us to love our family, our neighbor and even our enemy. Would anyone prefer to be tolerated rather than be loved? While we were still His enemies God loved us enough to give us life through the sacrifice of His Son.". (Mathew 5:43-48; Romans 5:10) Do not be tolerant of others, love them.

👍❤️ 23   6 Comments 1 Share

👍 Like   💬 Comment   ↪ Share

Poems

While going through dad's paperwork a year after he died, I found a poem my mom had written for him, tucked into a card he had saved. It appears to have been written in their first year of marriage, so about 1981 or '82. I couldn't resist including this beautiful poem of love in the book, dedicated to my loving parents.

Following her poem are a few poems I wrote dedicated to my parents (and grandmother).

Poem for My Husband

By: Nancy Carol Toms

I love you for your hand of kindness,
Because you unveil my worldly blindness.
So I can see the glories of God (and one of them is you),
The seas and skies of blue.

When shadows haunt from night 'til day,
Then I kneel down to pray.
So that my Lord will keep you strong,
From all evil and wrong.

I love you for the things you do,
For the good, you bring out in me too.
I love you for your strong belief,
That keeps and gives me relief.

And most of all, I love you for being yourself,
A man with strong determination,
One who is so proud of his nation.

One who will keep me safe and sound,
So I can kneel before you on the ground.
To love and cherish you from now 'til death,
With every simple little breath.

For God gave you for me to love,
Now I give praise to the One above.

I miss you, mom

I miss you mom,
When I'm not strong
On days like this when I want your kiss.
I miss you mom
When I do wrong
Craving guidance and comfort from you.
I miss you mom
When my kids are great
Thinking how amazed and proud of them you would be.
I miss you mom,
When my kids are terrible
Knowing you would be sympathetic and a guide for me.
I miss you mom when I am mad
This too I figure with me you could relate
You must have felt that way at least once or twice,
After all, you were married to dad, and to be fair, I am the daughter
that you had.
I miss you mom when I feel unloved, unappreciated, sad and alone.
I wish I could hear words from you.
The words I would hear, they ring in my ear,
Would be 'God and will I always love you'.
You would tell me to stop feeling sorry and sad,
You would tell me that very little comes from mad,
You would tell me that kids will be bad,
But still having kids is a great joy to be had.
You would tell me I am blessed with this family of mine.
You would tell me that you didn't want to leave me behind.
I miss you mom, I still have to say. I miss you mom, especially on
this day!

Step (Above) Dad

He didn't have to be the dad he was to me.
He didn't have to marry a mother of three.
He didn't have to hand me water when I was sick.
Or give me a hug when I was overcome by tears.
He didn't have to pay out of state tuition.
Or help me get my very first home.
He had to be a man who walked with God, at which he excelled.
A man who lovingly cared for his dying wife, my mom.
A man who suffered silently,
Yet shared his words of wisdom with me.
He was a step ABOVE dad.

No More Sorrows

When sorrows crowd into your mind
And all your joy seems far behind
Just close your eyes and say a prayer
And let The Comforter your burdens bear.
His angels come with wings to sweep
Your concerns and fears beneath His feet
He lifts you up in arms of love
For your sorrows, concerns, cares, and fears
To Him belong
At His feet, worries be trampled there
Joy, He restores - taking your cares
And reminds you of blessings from above.

Tribute

She gave me life,
She gives me song,
She gives me hope,
to carry on.
Thank you for my Mother.
She gives me love,
She soothes my fear,
She lets me know,
she's always here.
Thank you for my Mother.
You gave her life,
Sang her that song,
So one day,
she might pass it on.
Thank you, Grandmother.

About the Author

Kimberly Cordoves lives with her husband, Tony, and their three children in Oklahoma City, OK. She began writing children's stories only after she became a mom. She has worked in the Information Technology field since before the turn of the 21st century, and some might consider her a geek. She loves animals, having been surrounded by dogs and cats her entire life. She is passionate about digital photography. She is also an active member of a church, Iglesia Bautista Central (Central Baptist Church), a Spanish speaking congregation.

Christian Children Books by Kimberly Cordoves
Can be found on Amazon.com

Journey to Christmas (bilingual English/Spanish)
Tails from the Bible
Baby Mouse Learns to Pray (bilingual English/Spanish)
Rich Man, Poor Man
You OTTER
The Legend of Noah's Doves
A Not So Silent Night

www.ingramcontent.com/pod-product-compliance
Lightning Source LLC
Chambersburg PA
CBHW080322070426
42446CB00017BC/3412